GUIDE TO
SAVING AND INVESTMENT

'Extremely superior sample of the genre . . . the style is crisp, the examples clear, and the advice on tactics both incisive and shrewd. If any book can turn you into a successful investor, this is it.' – *The Sunday Times*

'Very little knowledge of investment matters is assumed . . . but the authors proceed to a level of sophistication where even professionals may find the odd addition to their knowledge.' – *The Investment Analyst. The Journal of the Society of Investment Analysts*

'Includes clear and assimilable lessons on investment arithmetic, and a valuable section on taxes.' – *The Economist*

'A lively, comprehensive survey of the whole field of saving and investment.' – *The Weekly Scotsman*

'The merits of this book are that it offers practical facts and figures to illustrate its arguments. It is crisply written . . . covers a number of fields which not all experts will be familiar with.' – *The Investors Chronicle*

GUIDE TO
SAVING AND INVESTMENT

JAMES ROWLATT
and
DAVID DAVENPORT

A PAN ORIGINAL

Revised and brought up to date

PAN BOOKS LTD · LONDON

First published 1965 by
PAN BOOKS LTD
33 Tothill Street, London, S.W.1

330   33092   6

2nd Printing (revised) 1966
3rd Printing (revised and reset) 1970

Printed in Great Britain by Richard Clay (The Chaucer Press), Ltd.,
Bungay, Suffolk

CONTENTS

PART III UNQUOTED INVESTMENTS

PART IV TAX

AUTHOR'S NOTE

Every effort has been made to ensure that the factual information contained in this book is accurate at the time of writing, but it cannot be guaranteed.

INTRODUCTION

The Investment Revolution

REVOLUTIONS MAY be two a penny these days, but among the more significant of them is the revolution in investment. What, before the war, was the privilege of a rich and limited circle has become a matter of day-to-day concern for many millions of people. Takeovers are news; the BBC has a late-night round-up of Stock Exchange movements; and dividends are a talking-point among people whose fathers thought only of unemployment.

Investment, in short, has become mass business, or mass entertainment, if you prefer. One out of every fifteen of us in Britain is a shareholder, and many more besides if you count in people whose interest comes from their pensions, insurance policies or union funds. But the novelty does not just lie in the sheer numbers involved in the gradual trend towards popular capitalism. No less intriguing has been the decisive shift away from the old, revered holdings of government stock towards companies, or rather their ordinary shares.

To get this second revolution into perspective, let us go back a good many years, to 1848. That was a crucial year for world capitalism, in view of the publication of Karl Marx's *Communist Manifesto*. But it saw another occasion, also pretty pervasive in its consequences. For in that year, just two days before Christmas, a modest insurance venture was started on a capital of £5,839. It was given the name Prudential.

If you had had free capital of £5,839 in 1848 you would probably not have been bothering with new-fangled notions like insurance. With a sum like that invested in the irreproachable, top-quality investment of the day, 2½% Consols, you could have been a personage of consequence without taking risks at all. The income, £146 a year and no tax, could have put you in the carriage-and-pair bracket.

But suppose you had swept aside the conventional wisdom

of the times and subscribed £58 7s. 10d. for a 1% interest in the Pru. Suppose also that you (and your descendants) had held on to those two investments ever since, taking bonus issues when they were offered, but never putting up another penny for new capital. How would things be today?

Well, the Consols holding would be looking a little blue. The price, always hovering around 100 in Victorian days, is in the mid twenties as we write. The total value is down to around £1,500. The income, still £146 a year, is worth only £86 after tax at 8s. 3d. in the £. That is about 33s. a week – not enough for the HP payments on a Mini. In short, your days of consequence would be over, but for your little nest-egg in the Pru. That £58 worth would have grown, even if you had simply ignored your rights to subscribe for new shares, to a holding of 800,000 'A' shares in Britain's biggest insurance group, worth about £2,100,000.

Of course there are a good many reservations about that story. What about death duties? What if you had put the money in some other insurance company which had fizzled out into bankruptcy? This is not the sort of game where you just sit back for a century or so and let it happen.

But the hard core of truth remains. Over the last three generations the wealth of companies has flourished, boosted by the immense expansion of business and industry. At the same time the worth of the Government's bond has sadly declined under the impact of wars and inflation.

As we write the introduction to this edition, there are signs, at long last, of a turn in the tide. The economic order of the Western world, established in the aftermath of Hitler's war, is creaking audibly. New ground rules and new guide posts may soon become necessary. In our attempts to interpret the investment revolution of the past twenty years we are not unaware that it will not be the last revolution ever.

Whatever new investment developments there may be, the Stock Exchange will be deeply involved in them, so that is where we start. We explain what the Stock Exchange is and what people do there. We show you how to assess the securities quoted on the Exchange. Afterwards, in the third part of the book, we go back to the beginning and trace the steps from the opening of a Post Office Savings Account to the consideration of a suitable insurance plan.

Ultimately that brings us back to the Stock Exchange, the outlet for modern thrift. Directly or indirectly, that is the place where most of your savings will end up being invested. It is also the place where a sensible investment policy is most likely to meet with success. That is why it is so important for all savers, even if they have never seen a stockbroker in their lives, to appreciate what is going on there.

Making money on the Stock Exchange is not child's play. Ignorance, stupidity and greed are rapidly rewarded with losses. The crucial thing is to work out the most suitable investment policy for someone in your own circumstances. After that you should deploy your resources accordingly, as a matter of conscious choice.

In a book of this kind, it does not take long to pick up the basic knowledge and go through the common-sense ways of applying it. Quite quickly you come up against the fringes of investment theory. We have not attempted a thoroughgoing exposition, but we have tried to say enough to let you know what you would be letting yourself in for if you should want to take the matter any further.

Again, investment borders on the law, particularly tax law, which is both tricky and boring. Wherever tax considerations have a bearing on investment policy we have taken them into account. But for the sake of completeness we have added a special section on tax at the end of the book, including a full discussion of capital gains tax.

PART I

INTRODUCING INVESTMENT

Chapter One

Throgmorton Street

IF YOU walk past the columns of the Royal Exchange, and turn east past the Bank of England, you will see a thick tower sprouting up above a huddle of nondescript buildings. The members of the London Stock Exchange, ignoring Professor Parkinson's law that institutions only achieve a perfection of planned layout when they are on the point of collapse, have determined to have a new home for themselves. From 1970 onwards, this skyscraper is it.

Although the trappings of the latest Exchange make concessions to the electronic age, the human arrangements remain as persistently British as beefeaters. If you try and go in, to mingle democratically with the brokers on their trading floor, you will be instantly thrown out again. The Stock Exchange is constituted like a club, and only members and their representative clerks are allowed inside. Nevertheless, you can look down on them from a public gallery, and wonder at the activity below.

Superficially, this market is much like any other market; it might almost be Billingsgate, except the working clothes are dark suits instead of white overalls. There are a lot of bored-looking men standing about at their trading pitches, talking. Between them, other men rush to and fro, and in the background, lights flash without anyone seeming to pay much attention. But this is deceptive. The London Exchange is not only unlike other markets, it is not even like other stock exchanges.

This is because the trading system is unique. Everywhere else there are stockbrokers who buy and sell shares from one another in a perfectly straightforward way. But in London such simple arrangements are actually forbidden. According to the rules, brokers have to work through a special class of dealers, known as jobbers. These men, who are the ones stationed at the pitches, make the market in securities. They buy and sell on their own account and with their own money. Brokers, on the other hand, merely represent the public who are not allowed to bargain with jobbers direct. In technical language, jobbers are principals, just as you are when you buy or sell shares, but brokers are agents carrying out clients' instructions.

What happens in a typical deal is a copybook example of how a free market works, in theory at any rate. The broker comes into the Stock Exchange armed with an order from you to buy, say, 200 shares in Woolworths. He threads his way to the jobbers' pitch close where he knows they specialize in stores and asks a price. The jobber answers something like 'twenty-one-and-six-ten-and-a-half', by which he means he will buy from the broker at 21s. 6d., and sell to him at 21s. 10½d. a share. As yet, he does not know which the broker wants to do.

Your broker, if he is doing his job properly, will then slip off to the other jobbers who deal in Woolworths and go through the same procedure again. This time the jobber may say 'one-four-and-a-half-nine' (they usually drop the big figure). Still further on the answer may be 'one-seven-and-a-half-two-bob'. In this way the broker has cut down the difference between the prices at which he can buy and sell from 4½d. to 1½d. Sometimes he can even make it disappear altogether.

Coming back to Woolworths, your broker will now fasten on the jobber who quoted 21s. 9d. and bargain some more. With luck, he may manage to beat him down further to 21s. 8¼d. or 21s. 7½d. In that case he would have saved you 3d. a share, or 50s. all told, by going round the market. Such a small amount may seem scarcely worth all the palaver, but over the years the savings of conscientiousness add up. Compare it, anyway, with the broker's commission on this bargain – £2 14s. 0d.

The ritual, once the broker is satisfied he is buying as cheaply as possible, is for him to say 'Buy 200 Woolworths at 21s. 7½d.' and for the jobber to repeat it back again. Both sides then note the bargain in a little book (to be verified by their clerks next morning), and from that moment the shares are yours.

Actual transactions can be made only by members or their

special representatives. Other people on the floor, named after the oblong blue buttons they wear, are there to fetch prices and run errands. The flashing lights are also part of the communication system. Each broker has his own number, which is lit up when his partners, back in the office, want to speak to him. The whole apparatus is run by special attendants who (with the incorrigible British taste for flaunting antiquities) are dressed up in red-and-blue uniforms and called waiters as a left-over from the days when share dealings were done in coffee houses.

From your look-out in the gallery you can hardly expect to learn much of the nuances of life in the Stock Exchange. For that, you must turn back some little way to the recorded evidence which jobbers and brokers gave to the Bank Rate Tribunal in 1957.

One Wednesday afternoon in mid-September 1957 the jobbers who specialize in Government securities became aware, with the instinct which all market men develop, that sentiment had taken a turn for the worse. So far that week, prices had been gently rising – as they would put it, the market was firm – and most of them had been adding to their holdings of securities in the expectation that prices would go better still.

In the event they were wrong, so they reacted as jobbers will in such circumstances. They lowered their selling prices a little to try to attract people to take some stock off their hands. That was the note on which the Stock Exchange closed, as usual, at 3.30 p.m.

The point of the early closing is to allow members time to clear up their routine work in the office before going home, but as a matter of courtesy most jobbers will go on arranging deals over the telephone up till about five o'clock. Not that they like doing so. Away from their competitors, they lose touch with the feel of the market place. They become claustrophobically uneasy that, elsewhere, prices are changing rapidly and they will not know anything about it until after concluding a catastrophic deal.

On that particular afternoon one jobbing firm was rung up in quick succession by a couple of brokers. In each case the reluctant jobber tried to fob them off with an unattractive quote. In each case, to his surprise, they accepted a low price without haggling or arguing at all. From then on the jobber and his partners were anxious enough to decide to call off deals for the rest of the day. The prices they quoted were only rough ones. Contrary to the popular myth that jobbers will always deal, they simply said they were not interested.

The following day was Thursday, which has a special significance in the rhythm of the Stock Exchange week. On Thursdays, at quarter to twelve in the morning, word comes from the Bank of England of any change in the rate which it will charge on its loans. This is not the place for a discussion of the significance of Bank rate. It should just be accepted here that Government manipulation of Bank rate is one way of pepping up the economy or slowing it down.

On that Thursday, September 19th, Bank rate was given the biggest upward jerk since the war – from 5 to 7%. One of the things most closely related to Government changes in Bank rate is the return which you can expect on the Government's own securities. It is conceivable, possibly, that the Government could decide to pay more interest on its issued loans when it increases Bank rate. In practice, it does nothing of the kind. The one way in which existing securities can reflect higher interest rates is by a fall in prices. That Thursday prices did not just fall, they collapsed.

To understand what this could mean to jobbers who had more securities on their books than they could pay for, you must take a closer look at the way they do their business. On Wednesday, September 18th, jobbers bought £16½ million of Government securities and sold £14 million back to the public. No one would regard that, or even the £62 million turnover of the following Wednesday, as more than a routine amount of business. But jobbers do not, themselves, have anything like that sort of money. They operate by depositing their capital with their bank, and borrowing on day-to-day overdrafts to finance their deals.

One of the crucial functions a jobber has to perform (in fact, it is the only way he can hope to make much money) is to take a view on whether the market is going to go up or down. If he refuses to buy stock until he knows where he is going to sell it he might just as well not be there. He must back his judgement on the trend of the market – buying in stock on borrowed money when he thinks prices will rise and selling stock he does not own on the contrary tack.

For that reason there was nothing extraordinary in the fact that the jobbers bought £2½ million more stock than they sold that Wednesday. Neither would it be in any way abnormal if the banks had lent them all but a few thousands out of that £2½ million. From the banks' point of view, their security was the Government stock the jobbers had been buying that day. In any case, they knew the position would be evened out again before very long. Last but not least, they knew it was the jobbers who were taking the risk on any change in the prices of Government stock.

Next morning, to their horror, the jobbers had to shoulder Wednesday's risks in full measure. It could well be (details were not divulged) that over 90 per cent of a jobber's holdings could have been bank-financed that day. In that case, when the value of his book sagged in response to the Bank-rate change, the entire weight of the fall would have borne down on his personal 10%. After that brief Bank-rate announcement about £75,000 would have been wiped off the value of that £2½ million of stock. No wonder one jobber complained he had 'caught a cold'.

It is not relevant here that, in the anger of the moment, some people were accused of being in the know, of shovelling heavy losses on to the jobbers by inspired selling of Government securities before the bombshell burst. In any event, the Bank Rate Tribunal acquitted everyone concerned of improper behaviour. What the Bank-rate incident threw into such fascinating perspective was the intimate nature of Stock Exchange operations. For the first time members were forced to repeat in public the rapid, jargon-ridden patter in which even huge deals are settled; to formalize the instinctive shrewdness which prompts jobbers to shift their quotes; and to explain the chivalry of Stock Exchange honour, which in some ways scrupulously forbids, and in others almost seems to encourage, the most ruthless exploitation of the main chance.

From the Bank-rate proceedings a clearer picture also emerges of the sort of people stockbrokers are. They turn out not to be as privileged and remote as their top-hat-and-striped-trousers image suggests. True, there is a smattering of the nobility among the 3,400 members of the Stock Exchange, but they are outnumbered by the peers within the much smaller coterie of the merchant banks. True, Etonians and their friends dominate one sector of the market – the specialized dealings in short-dated Government securities – which is why people say gentlemen prefer bonds. Part of the explanation is that really large-scale operations in Government stock, including official transactions controlled from the Bank of England, are handled by firms that have been established long enough for wealth to have exerted its mollifying effects over several generations. Besides, some firms take on partners with illustrious family backgrounds for the sake of prestige.

For all that, the majority of brokers are as indistinguishably middle-class as the general run of accountants or solicitors, and predominantly, but by no means universally, Conservatives. Now, as a hundred years ago, they like to live in comfortable villas outside London. Surrey, the popular idea of the stockbroker's stamping ground, is in fact their favourite county, but they can be found wherever there is a fast train service into town. Broadly speaking, they are not particularly rich, and violent fluctuations in the amount of business available from one year to the next are faithfully recorded in their incomes. On the other hand, anyone with good connections in a large, prosperous firm can make a bigger salary, while still in his early thirties, than most people of the same age outside the City could hope for.

Nowadays everyone who wants to be a member of the Stock Exchange has to serve as a so-called clerk for at least two years, and the number of people for whom this is simply an initiation ceremony, like the brief dipping of would-be army officers into the realities of barrack-room life, is steadily diminishing. You could, at a pinch, contend that stockbroking has been more democratic than the professions because there is no qualifying exam for membership, although no one will be able to get in without sitting one after August 1971. Nominations for membership have to be bought, but compared with the huge sums needed for a seat on the New York Stock Exchange, they are cheap. Since the war they have varied between almost nothing when Labour has been riding high, and about £2,000 when its influence has been on the wane. Even at its peak, however, this sum is not a serious deterrent; neither are the entrance fee of 1,000 guineas and the annual subscription of 250.

Stock Exchange publicists like to picture brokers as serious men, seldom buying for less than a three-year view, and trying earnestly to steer their clients away from in-and-out operations for a quick profit. Certainly some members are as strait-laced as civil servants; and surprisingly, there are plenty of able dealers about who live on a never-touch-the-stuff-myself principle, and do not own a single share. Nevertheless, it is silly to pretend that the Stock Exchange does not present an attractive way of life for born gamblers. Dickens' Wilkins Flasher, who was overheard betting with another broker whether an expelled member would commit suicide, and if so how, is still alive in spirit. Brokers like to while away a dull afternoon betting on cricket results or majorities at elections (although such speculation is not allowed on the floor of the Exchange), as well as the more obvious dabbling in shares.

Alongside this gaming element there has grown up a sober, professional approach to the problems of investment analysis. The high priests of the scientific movement are the actuaries, dedicated mathematicians who have drudged their way through a six-year course in the intricacies of life assurance. About half of the select body of Fellows of the Institute of Actuaries – perhaps 800 strong in Britain – are still employed by the big insurance groups. But broking firms have also equipped themselves with actuaries to help cater for the enormous, but specialized, investment appetites of the Pru, the Pearl and the rest. As a result, no other professional caste can expect to be so highly paid at the zenith of their careers.

Following in the wake of actuaries, other new recruits have started turning up in brokers' offices, or usually in their back-rooms: graduates, more often than not from Oxbridge. As a rule they are economists, or arts men. Scientists are still City rarities. But between them they are enough to keep the in-tellectual quality of City life moving ahead – witness the thoroughness and sophistication of the best of the circulars which brokers send round to their institutional clients. Collec-tively broker-boffins are grouped, together with their opposite numbers in the institutions, in the 1,000-strong Society of In-vestment Analysts, whose fortnightly meetings, addressed by company chairmen, provide some link between the slide rules of the City and the flesh-and-blood realities they are trying to measure. More importantly, the Society's European conferences have cut preliminary clearways through the thickets of international accountancy methods. Already British investment on the Continent is that much more soundly conceived.

So, like many other institutions in this country, the Stock Exchange is gradually inching up to date, adopting new machinery, new methods and even new men. Nevertheless, the Stock Exchange remains apart from the main current of national life, inhabiting a close-knit, gossiping village of its own and clinging defensively to traditions and taboos (e.g. the exclusion of women). Changes will continue, of course. But as it is the Stock Exchange is a product of coherent develop-ment, of historical necessity if you prefer. To understand that, you must consider what purpose it is supposed to serve and how it has set about doing so.

CHAPTER TWO

Why a Stock Exchange?

IT IS natural to want to buy security; saving is not just a matter of cash leftovers. People put money on one side of their own free will, and though they talk of thrift as a virtue, they often find it a pleasure. To take an example near at hand: the share of Britain's national income devoted to saving has risen in most years since the 1950s. This cannot be simply explained away as a natural outcome of increasing prosperity, because the proportion has gone on rising in years when prosperity has ebbed away. The reason is that savings include items which people choose to buy, like pensions and insurance policies.

In primitive circumstances, which can exist in present-day India or France no less than in the Middle Ages, savers prefer to hoard, usually gold. The trouble is, thieves can overturn mattresses and unearth treasure chests. It is worth depositing one's money somewhere where it will be safely looked after, and yet be freely available whenever one wants it.

The original purpose of banks was to meet this need. But it was quickly discovered that much of the money entrusted to them lay idle in the vaults, while only a comparatively small proportion of it was needed to repay depositors on demand. Of course adequate safety margins had to be worked out in case of emergencies. In fact, banks now keep 8 per cent of their assets in cash and about 21 per cent in securities which can be turned into cash at short notice. But the balance of the funds over and above that could be made available to lend to other people. Skilful bankers earn enough in the process to be able to afford to pay interest on money deposited with them.

Banks, if properly run, are ideally placed to provide the basic requirements of investors – security, an adequate return on their money and the ability to cash it when they want to. Other institutions, every bit as hungry to borrow, can be equally scrupulous about providing security and paying interest, and probably at a higher rate because banks work on small margins. It may not suit them, however, to pay back capital on demand (suppose it had been used to build something permanent like a steelworks). The difficulty is, enterprises often want to borrow money for longer periods than investors are prepared to go without it.

One solution to this problem is for borrowers to pay rates of interest sufficiently high to compensate investors for sacrificing the right to cash on demand. But that would be expensive. Besides, events can move swiftly, so that investors who thought they could afford to lock up their money for two or three years suddenly discover they need it tomorrow. The solution is for there to be a market where loans can be sold. That is what a stock exchange is.

It is not only in the interest of stockholders to have a market place. For anyone who wants to borrow money on a large scale it is the obvious place to turn to. Governments in particular, who can finance only a part of their expenditure out of taxes, are in urgent need of somewhere to borrow. In Britain the State has been calling on the City of London for funds since Queen Elizabeth started the idea in the 1570s. On top of that, the capital requirements of modern industry are enormous. Companies with extensive and complicated plants, such as oil groups, chemical firms or motor manufacturers, have to think in terms of millions of pounds. In 1968 alone British firms raised £864 million on the Stock Exchange, and they would have been hard put to find money like that anywhere else.

Besides, once a stock exchange has become established, it is an invaluable guide to the cost of money. When companies are planning additions to their productive capacity the interest they will have to pay on the money locked up in a new factory and equipment is a significant part of the cost. By looking at the yields on existing securities, finance directors can see how great this expense will be, and so calculate whether their own plans are worth while.

Even if everyone agrees that a stock market has its uses, there is still considerable difficulty about how it should be organized. Compare it with a vegetable market like Covent Garden. That is essentially somewhere for growers or wholesalers to sell their produce. Everyone there knows more or less who is selling or who is buying, and some sort of limit on the scope of dealings is set by the certainty that in due course the vegetables will go bad.

With a stock exchange, on the other hand, the situation is completely different. Everyone is potentially either a buyer or a seller – there is no means of knowing which – and the same shares can change hands over and over again. It is not immediate satisfaction, like having a cauliflower for dinner, which is being bought and sold, but the future expectation of income or of capital gain.

The prices of securities depend, in the long run, on the interest which they will yield. In the short run, however, they depend on what people think is going to happen next. A return of 8% on one's money may seem generous. So it is, if prices are going to rise, reducing the return to 7%. But if prices are going to fall, making the return 9%, it would obviously be wise to wait till they have.

Since there are always people open to suggestion, a market based on expectations is easy to rig. A group of rogues can get a share moving up by what the Americans call boiler-room tactics – spreading rumours of easy pickings and selling each other shares at rising prices. At the right moment they dump all their shares on a gullible public and make off with the proceeds. Not unnaturally, this game is illegal – but that is not to say it has not been tried over and over again, along with countless other techniques for nudging the market in the required direction. Human nature being what it is, behaviour in a stock exchange quickly becomes as tender-hearted as the Amazon jungle, unless there are rules to prevent it.

For this reason records of attempts to control market practices are almost as old as organized dealing itself. Many of the things dealt with in the Act to Restrain the Number and Ill Practice of Brokers and Stockjobbers – passed in 1697, after a hectic sequence of boom, slump and Parliamentary inquiry – have a distinctly modern ring. Since then, occasional moves have been made, usually after a crisis, like the bursting of the

South Sea Bubble in 1720, to inject some measure of public control into share dealings. Brokers have responded by adapting their own procedures – partly, it is true, to increase efficiency but also to protect their collective good name and to forestall active government intervention.

Although the development of an organized market would naturally work to the advantage of full-time specialists, there was no particular intention, at the outset, of keeping the public away. Actually, the Bank of England, which was in a strong position because it kept the register of most Government securities, did as a matter of principle maintain a public market on its own premises till nearly halfway through the nineteenth century. (Eventually it was given up during rebuilding and never started again afterwards.) While the arrangement lasted, anyone could come into the Exchange, agree a price with a broker for his stock and then go straight to the Bank's clerks to record the change of ownership. But according to people who were there, it was a scene of pandemonium and uproar – not the best circumstances for newcomers to outsmart professionals, as amateurs betting at a crowded race meeting nowadays can discover. In any case some of the more substantial brokers, who disliked the inconvenience of dealing in the Bank's Rotunda, or in the coffee houses near the Royal Exchange, decided to hire more comfortable premises of their own. It was they who laid the foundations for the present club-like arrangements, which have proved the most viable over time.

Apart from convenience, there were other more important reasons why brokers came more and more to deal only with each other. From about the middle of the eighteenth century bargains were increasingly struck for settlement not in cash, but on some future day. This not only saved business time. It also meant that settlement could eventually be made between the original seller and the final buyer, with adjustments in cash for the intervening deals. But in such circumstances it is obviously vital to deal only with people whom one knows can be relied on to pay – the more so after 1734 when, by Sir John Barnard's Act, brokers were forbidden to claim against clients who had speculated, lost and refused to pay. Without legal redress against outsiders, brokers naturally came to regard each other as responsible for honouring bargains made in good faith, and to turn to their own committee if things went wrong. Although strictly speaking brokers are agents, buying and selling on other people's instructions, they do in fact regard each other as principals. To this day, moreover, they cannot take fellow-brokers to law. Under the rules of the Stock Exchange they must refer grievances to the Council instead. But nowadays they can at least sue defaulting clients as a last resort.

In the circumstances it is not surprising that brokers have done their best to ensure that their colleagues are honest. Early in the nineteenth century, when the idea of an exchange with its own members was under heavy attack, they could be heard grumbling that all they wanted to do was to keep out 'notorious cheats'. Nowadays, broking firms have to have net assets of not less than £5,000 for each partner, which means in effect a minimum of £10,000 per firm, because partnerships must have two members. (For jobbers the minimum is even higher at £15,000.) Furthermore, prospective entrants get a moral screening because they have to be vouched for by two existing members not in the same firm as themselves, and approved by three-quarters of the Stock Exchange Council.

All this is part and parcel of the determination of the exchange to keep a healthy reputation for itself. It is carried to the point of a compensation fund which is available for making good the losses of the public if a broker should fail. At present the fund is kept at a level of £200 per member, a total of some £700,000. This fund is, of course, just the liquid and visible reserve, and more could be forthcoming in an emergency. Ultimately, so the Council likes to claim, the Stock Exchange would pay up to the hilt of what it has.

The development of a stock exchange, in short, is the product of economic forces, softened by convenience and influenced by the law. Differences between the exchanges in one country and the next are nearly always a matter of the law. So far as anyone knows, London seems to have acquired a separate jobbing system because at one stage, a long time ago, it was illegal for brokers to deal on their own account. (Even now broking firms are not allowed to deal for themselves, although members, as individuals, can.) In the same way London has so far avoided a regulatory body like the Securities & Exchange Commission in America which, as an arm of the federal government, enforces an extremely rigorous control over security dealings, particularly offerings to the public. The London atmosphere is relaxed by comparison and control is exercised largely through the Stock Exchange Council backed upon occasions by the legislative power, actual or potential, of the government. In this way the authorities have managed to provide a fairly flexible framework capable of restraining some of the more dubious tendencies that can arise in share dealings while ensuring that the free operation of the market does not become stifled by clumsy-fingered bureaucracy.

However, hard-fought bid battles do not bring out the best in people, and it has been found necessary to introduce a code of conduct for company takeovers. The object of the exercise, in broadest terms, is to ensure fair and equal treatment for all shareholders, without any of them being exceptionally favoured or unwittingly penalised. The first, tentative efforts at regulation were honoured almost as much in the breach as the observance, and a tougher approach has become called for. To its credit, the government has resisted the urge to do this by the erection of elaborate legal processes. No doubt this was partly a matter of prudence; such processes would be time-consuming and difficult to put into practice. As it stands, the system is a voluntary one, though with the shadow of sanctions in the background. It is too early to say how effectively the Panel will cope with the City's more predatory members. But now that there is a well-respected merchant banker at its head, and a full-time staff at its disposal, temperate optimism is not out of place.

CHAPTER THREE

The Goods Catalogue

ALTOGETHER BETWEEN nine and ten thousand securities are quoted on the London Stock Exchange and a few hundred more (not counting duplicates) on other British stock exchanges. These securities are divided up into a number of broad categories, but perhaps the most important distinction depends on who takes the responsibility for paying interest or dividends on them.

In Britain there are innumerable public authorities, from the central government itself to the smallest local council, which pay for part of their activities from borrowings, over and above what they get from taxation. The more important of them borrow by raising money on the Stock Exchange, the security for the loans they offer being provided by their tax revenues. These are the main categories:

1. *British Government and Guaranteed Securities* – the so-called gilt-edged stocks. British Government securities are what is known as the National Debt. They represent the State's borrowings from the public, abroad as well as at home. They are grouped under a number of broad headings, like Treasury, Funding, Exchequer and Conversion stocks. Most of the amounts outstanding were originally raised to pay for wars. The well-known War Loan can trace its roots back to an enormous Government issue during the Kaiser's war.

Sometimes the Government has felt obliged to pay compensation for something which it has done on social grounds. In 1833, for instance, it paid up £20 million to former owners of emancipated slaves. In terms of money, however, the most important compensation payments were made to the former owners of nationalized industries; altogether they totted up to £2,300 million. In addition, another £1,400 million worth of stock was issued by the nationalized industries to pay for their capital development (that is, up to 1955, after which they have borrowed direct from the Exchequer).

These securities (called British Gas, British Electricity and so on) are effectively on the same footing as the National Debt, because their capital and interest are guaranteed by the Government. Mercifully, perhaps, their payments have nothing to do with the year-by-year results of public bodies like BOAC or British Railways.

In addition, of course, the Government borrows large sums of money through unquoted securities like National Savings Certificates, British Savings Bonds and Premium Bonds.

2. *British Corporation and County Stocks*. Dublin was the first corporation to raise money on the Stock Exchange, as long ago as 1819. Now it is commonplace for cities and counties alike. They generally have to offer a slightly higher rate of interest to investors than the Government does, because their credit standing, however excellent, can obviously never be quite so good. Here again, a considerable slice of local-authority borrowings are met by unquoted mortgage loans and short bonds.

3. *Dominion, Provincial and Colonial Government Securities*. Members of the Commonwealth have for a long time enjoyed the right of borrowing in London. Australia has twenty loans quoted here and New Zealand fifteen, with nominal values of £277 million and £141 million respectively.

The old-established Dominions have all the advantages of high creditworthiness in a much richer financial centre than they have access to at home. How effective these privileges are for more recently independent territories is open to doubt. Nowadays British investors do not particularly relish lending to the governments of African countries (regardless of their colour), and most of the loans already in existence stand at a discount.

Other countries, as well as Britain, have their own national debts, and it is possible to buy them in London. The most popular are US Federal Bonds, but in addition, there are a number of foreign stocks left over from before the war, when overseas governments, cities, railways and so on used to come to London for funds. Political upheavals have occasionally meant interruptions in interest payments; this is a sector of the market where risk-bearing can be experienced in the raw. But by this time most international lending at top level is channelled through international agencies like the World Bank, which do their own borrowing in financial centres, including London. One feature of World Bank policy is that it will not lend to any country which is in default on past debt, so there has been considerable incentive to tidy up old loans almost everywhere outside the Communist bloc.

Since the early sixties the supremacy of the international agencies has been modified in two ways. As a part of the EFTA agreement the Outer Seven countries of Europe are permitted access to the London market. In consequence, their municipalities have become more active in seeking funds over here. There is also a growing demand for loan finance for large investment projects, particularly in Scandinavia and Portugal. Distinct from these EFTA arrangements, enterprising merchant banks have been exploiting the market facilities of London. With the positive encouragement of the Bank of England, they have been floating foreign loans which are denominated in non-sterling currencies. British capital is not directly involved in these operations; the loans are held by foreigners, and it is merely the convenience of a quotation which is being supplied in London. The point is to keep the City in the forefront of international capital markets, pending further developments in the political future of Europe.

There is one technical point about buying foreign, or rather non-sterling, securities which ought to be noted. You have first of all to buy the necessary currency – dollars, francs or whatever it is – and because the supply of foreign exchange available for this purpose is limited by the Bank of England it is not always possible to get it at the fixed rate of exchange. In fact, during recent years there has been a premium to pay on foreign currency, sometimes amounting to more than 50%. The net result is, of course, that you end up paying that much more for your securities.

There is one other unpleasant snag about the currency premium when you sell foreign securities. Since the 1965 Budget, you lose one-quarter of the premium on foreign currency whenever you make a sale. For example, if the premium were 40%, you would in fact receive only 30%, or three-quarters of 40%. This applies even if you immediately reinvest in some other foreign stock.

4. *The Private Sector*. Nationalization notwithstanding, most of industry and commerce is in private hands and financed by capital which is quoted on the Stock Exchange. In that case the borrower who takes responsibility for the capital, and the interest payments on it, is a limited company.

That word 'limited', which all British public companies have to have after their names, refers to the fact that the liability of the shareholders is limited to the capital of the company.

It dates back to legislation in the middle of the nineteenth century, before which most business enterprises were not incorporated into companies, and the owners were liable to the full extent of everything they had if their businesses got into difficulties.

The effect of this was to restrict the ownership of businesses to individuals, or at most small groups of people who knew each other. At the time it did not matter much, because industrial processes were simpler than they are now, and not much money was needed to finance them. But modern industry needs enormous resources, far more than individuals can command. The adoption of limited liability, which means in effect that people can be shareholders in a company without risking anything beyond the amount which they have paid for their stake in it, was an essential feature of the development of modern finance.

For an understanding of company financing, the best place to start is with the balance sheet. This is the statement of its affairs which every company has to publish each year. It shows the firm's assets, conventionally on the right-hand side, and also the claims against those assets, known as liabilities. Let us see how this works out in practice.

Let us assume that a group of businessmen are starting up a grocery store chain. They reckon that a quarter of a million pounds is what they need to get it going with a bang. With £120,000 of the money, they acquire premises – freeholds or leaseholds of land and buildings. Another £60,000 goes towards plant, like shelving, lights, frozen-food cabinets and so on. Stocking the shop with goods absorbs, say, another £60,000 which leaves them with a cash float of £10,000.

Maybe a quarter of a million pounds is rather more than they had really hoped to have to find, but fortunately the chairman has a family trust which needs a high income on its investments, and he feels able to put up £50,000 of its money on preferential terms. The terms agreed are the usual ones for what is known as preference capital. There is a fixed return on the money at 9% a year, which must be paid before there can be any dividend on the rest of the capital. If for some reason the firm cannot pay up one year its responsibility to do so remains. Technically, the interest is cumulative, and past arrears of preference interest must also be paid before there can be any dividend on the rest of the capital. If the worst comes to the worst and the company goes broke and has to be sold up, the first £50,000 (after commercial debts have been met) must be applied to paying off the preference capital before a penny is repaid to the other shareholders.

The remaining £200,000 needed for this grocery business is to take the form of ordinary share capital, issued, say, in the form of 800,000 5s. shares. (It could have been 200,000 £1 shares, 2,000,000 2s. shares or anything else convenient, provided only each share has some value, known as a par value.) These shares are the bedrock finance of the company. They carry the most risk, but they also stand to gain most. For the preference capital, in exchange for its rights, sacrifices any further participation in the profits or assets of the company on top of what has been agreed. The ordinary capital has the equity of a business, which is the legal term for what is left over after all other claims have been met. (That, incidentally, is why ordinary shares are often called equities.) As a rule, it also commands all the voting power of a company, except when something affecting the rights of preference holders occurs, in which case they can usually vote too. Directly, or through an appointed board, ordinary shareholders run a company and decide what to do with its profits.

In balance-sheet terms, assuming that a balance sheet were to be drawn up at this stage of the company's life, the position would look like this:

Liabilities

	£	£
Share Capital		
9% £1 cumulative preference shares	50,000	
800,000 5s. ordinary shares	200,000	
		250,000

Assets

	£	
Fixed Assets		
Freehold premises	120,000	
Plant, fixtures and fittings	60,000	
	180,000	
Current Assets		
Stocks	60,000	
Cash in hand	10,000	
	70,000	
		250,000

Let us assume now that the chain does an excellent trade for several years, paying out dividends and ploughing back profits. Then, just when its directors are thinking of branching out in another district, they hear of a bargain offer of new premises, exactly where they would like them. The trouble is, the sellers want £100,000, which is more than our board can spare in cash. It decides to raise the money by issuing loan capital.

Loan capital is a somewhat different type of being from issued share capital, which is what we were considering when the company was started. It is part of the debt of a business; there is a legal obligation for the company to pay the interest. In default of this, loan-capital holders can appoint a receiver who, as a last resort, can wind up the company and, if possible, pay them back their money. Frequently some of the company's assets are charged specifically against loan capital, and they can be sold to repay the amount of the loan. In this respect it is like a mortgage on a house. In other ways, the rights of loan capital are superficially similar to those of preference capital – there is a fixed rate of interest without further participation and prior rights to capital if the company is wound up. From this you will realize that it ranks before preference capital; indeed, the grocery chain board would probably have to secure the consent of the preference holders before it could raise loan capital that would relegate them to second place.

As it is, all shareholders consent to the operation, so the board issues £100,000 of 8% mortgage debenture. It might have decided to offer unsecured loan stock, but in that case it would have proved necessary to fix the interest rate higher, say $8\frac{1}{4}\%$, because the loan would not have been charged specifically against the company's assets. Either way, the superior position of the loan capital means that the interest coupon would at least be lower than the 9% of the preference.

Now we can turn back to the balance sheet – and see an up-to-date version of it this time:

Liabilities

	£	£
Share Capital and Reserve		
9% £1 cumulative preference shares	50,000	
800,000 5s. ordinary shares	200,000	
	250,000	
General revenue reserve	75,000	
Total, share capital and reserve		325,000
Loan Capital		
8% mortgage debenture stock		100,000
Future Taxation		40,000
Current Liabilities		
Creditors	55,000	
Current taxation	25,000	
Proposed dividends	5,000	
		85,000
		550,000

Assets

Fixed Assets

	At cost	Less depreciation	Net
Freehold premises	220,000	40,000	180,000
Plant, fixtures and fittings	200,000	60,000	140,000
	420,000	100,000	320,000

Current Assets

Stocks	175,000	
Debtors	25,000	
Cash in hand	30,000	
		230,000
		550,000

This balance sheet is quite a bit longer than the previous one, because it takes into account not only the new debenture, and the additional premises which it has financed, but also the realities of trading. For example, all companies are for ever in the process of paying debts and having debts paid to them. Creditors are naturally part of the liabilities, because before long their bills will have to be paid. In the same way, debtors will presumably come up with their payments in due course, so they come under assets.

One of the most important creditors of any business, in a category apart, is the Inland Revenue. Tax must be paid – some of it right away and some in future. As it is only prudent to make some provision this year for the inevitable demand next year, tax comes in two sections, part of it being a current liability (£25,000 in our example) and the other part (£40,000) a future commitment. Finally, the shareholders themselves are, in a way, creditors, as their dividend must be paid after the balance sheet has been presented to them in general meeting.

It will also be noticed that the sums involved are now substantially larger than they were when the company was started – £550,000 all told against £250,000. Of course, £100,000 of this is new money, raised by the debenture issue. Another £125,000, made up of creditors, tax and dividends due, is in a sense being borrowed until the time comes for them to be paid out. The company's resources have also been supplemented by depreciation charges. This is because it is allowed to set aside a certain amount of profits each year against the gradual consumption of capital, as plant wears out. It need not be spent, right away, on capital replacements. Even though it will eventually be needed for that purpose, it is effectively a source of cash in the short run. Not, of course, that depreciation increases total assets. The flow of cash represented by depreciation is offset, in balance-sheet terms, by deductions from premises and plant.

The last £75,000 of the increase is what the company has earned, but not paid out in dividends. It has, in this case, been transferred to general reserve. If the board had wished it could have been transferred to a reserve for some specific purpose or it could have been left as the amount in the profit and loss account carried forward. Either way, it is effectively a reserve. From the point of view of the debenture and preference holders it adds an extra margin of safety for their capital. From the point of view of ordinary shareholders it is an addition to the value of the assets which belong to them.

Every company security quoted on the Stock Exchange represents a claim on the assets of that company. It is necessarily a public concern in the sense that anyone can look at its balance sheet. (In the other sense public companies are like public schools – private in fact.) It is possible to find out very quickly what the rights of any security are, and to assess whether they are firmly based on assets.

The division of capital into loan and share capital is a loose one. There can be many securities within those broad classifications, each with varying rights. Let us take as an example a brewery company which has been in existence a long time and has grown by merging with other old-established businesses. Watney Mann has ten debentures, with different rates of interest depending on their original dates of issue; three unsecured loan stocks; four preference issues; and some ordinnary shares. There could have been more besides, such as secured loan stocks or loan notes (these are loan capital), or preferred ordinary, deferred ordinary or even non-voting ordinary among the share capital. In some cases there are securities where the rights of the different classes overlap. Some loan capital is convertible into ordinary shares. Rather more rarely, the same privileges are extended to preference shares. A few companies have participating preference issues, which are entitled to a fixed annual dividend plus a proportion of the surplus profits which would otherwise belong to the equity. The combinations are endless.

5. *Foreign Securities.* In addition to British shares you can also buy any quoted foreign security through the London market. This operation may be slightly expensive, however. In the first place there may be a currency premium to pay on non-sterling securities which can make a significant difference to the cost. Secondly, the jobbers will often have to buy the securities in an overseas market, and will therefore pay commission to the brokers there just like any other client. Not unnaturally they will allow for their expenses in the price which they quote to you.

In spite of these drawbacks, numerous investors have been attracted to foreign shares. During the Common Market negotiations several enterprising broking firms established links on the Continent in order to help satisfy British demand for European stocks. Owing to the excellent growth records of many leading Continental companies, this interest has outlasted the breakdown of the Common Market talks. More recently the biggest Japanese security houses have set up London offices.

Even so, American and Canadian shares are still perhaps the most popular with British investors. It is worth noting therefore that they are often quoted in terms of London dollars. This is a relic of exchange controls set up at the beginning of the war, when an arbitrary exchange rate of $5 to £1 was adopted. This convention has now outlived any usefulness it may once have had; but as a source of confusion it still lingers on. You can find out what the London equivalent of an American price is by dividing by 2·40 (the current rate of exchange), multiplying by 5 and allowing for the currency premium. For example, when the premium is 50% the London equivalent of Standard Oil of New Jersey at US$80 is L$250. Properly speaking, British quotations should be marked L$ (London dollars) or D$ (dummy dollars) to try to keep misunderstandings to a minimum.

CHAPTER FOUR

Inevitable Sums

FUNDAMENTALLY, THE reason for buying securities is to get a return on your investment. This return is an amalgam of interest or dividend payments and changes in capital value. And it depends, of course, on the price which you pay. It is now time to see how to calculate what your return is going to be.

Let us start by working out the interest return on a gilt-edged stock – say Conversion 5% 1971. The 5% represents the rate of interest payable on the stock (usually, as in this case, in two half-yearly instalments). Technically it is known as the coupon. Suppose, now, the price is 100 – in other words you are paying par, or £100, for every nominal £100 of stock. The annual return on your investment, which is known as the yield, would be 5%.

But the prices of quoted securities fluctuate. It may be that the price of Conversion 5% has fallen to 95. In that case £100 nominal of stock would cost only £95, or in other words you would be paying less in order to get your £5 of annual interest. Now a yield is expressed as a percentage; it is the return you would get each year for £100. Therefore when you can buy £5 a year for £95 you would obviously get more for £100. You can work out exactly how much more by the following formula for calculating yields:

$$\frac{\text{Par value}}{\text{Price}} \times \text{Coupon}$$

In our example

$$\frac{100 \ (\text{par value})}{95 \ (\text{price})} \times 5\% \ (\text{Coupon})$$

$$= \frac{500}{95} = 5 \cdot 26\% \text{ or in money terms } £5 \ 5s. \ 3d.\%$$

Now suppose the price rose to £105. The yield would move in exactly the same way, only in the opposite direction:

$$\frac{100 \text{ (par value)}}{105 \text{ (price)}} \times 5\% \text{ (Coupon)}$$

$$= \frac{500}{105} = 4 \cdot 76\% \text{ or } \pounds 4 \text{ } 15s. \text{ } 3d.\%$$

You can go through exactly the same process for working out the yield on ordinary shares. This time let us take Woolworths as our example. This company pays 20% on its 5s. ordinary shares, and their price is (say) 21s. By applying the usual formula you can calculate what the yield is:

$$\frac{5 \text{ (par value)}}{21 \text{ (price)}} \times 20 \text{ (dividend)} = \frac{100}{21} = 4 \cdot 76\% \text{ or } \pounds 4 \text{ } 15s. \text{ } 3d.\%$$

So far we have been dealing with yields without any mention of tax – in other words gross yields. It is usual to quote yields gross because tax rates vary for individuals, depending on their income. Nevertheless, tax has to be paid. Here is an example of how to calculate a net yield, taking tax at the current rate of 41·25%.

Gross yield on Woolworths 4·76%
Less tax at 41·25% of gross dividend

Therefore divide the gross yield by 100 and multiply the result by the difference between 100 and 41·25%.

$$4 \cdot 76 \times \frac{(100 - 41 \cdot 25)}{100} = 4 \cdot 76 \times \frac{58 \cdot 75}{100} = 2 \cdot 80\%$$

$$= \pounds 2 \text{ } 16s. \text{ } 0d.\%$$

There is more to yields than the simple annual income produced by your investment. The return can be affected by changes in capital values. To go back to Conversion 5% 1971, the date at the end of its title represents the year in which the capital is due to be repaid. And since this repayment has been promised by the Government, it is safe to assume the promise will be kept. You can therefore take account of it in your calculation of the return on your investment.

Suppose Conversion 5% 1971 were standing, some time in 1969, at 98. You would know that two years later in 1971 the stock was going to be repaid at par, or £2 more than it then was. Roughly you could say that it would rise at the rate of £1 a year, or about 1% a year. So on top of the usual income yield of £5 2s. 1d.% (calculated as before as $\frac{100}{98} \times 5$) you can add another £1% which is the expected annual increase in capital. The result is known as a redemption yield, and it works out at £6 2s. 1d.%. One can, of course, do a similar sum with a stock standing above par. If Conversion 5% 1971 were quoted at 102 you would know you would lose about £1 each year over the following two years. You would have to subtract £1% from the flat yield of £4 18s. 0d.% to leave a redemption yield of only £3 18s. 0d.%.

This is no more than a rough-and-ready way of doing a sum which can in fact be worked out completely accurately allowing for compound interest. The point to note here is that changes in capital values are as much a part of the return on your investment as annual income payments. As long as your money is invested in a dated security, and you hold it until its redemption date is reached, you can know in advance exactly what the overall return on your investment will be.

Redemption yields can also be adapted to take account of the tax which is payable on income and on capital gains. However, long-term capital-gains tax is not payable on gilt-edged stocks, so we must alter our example accordingly. Assuming we had been working with an industrial debenture with the same coupon and redemption date, the income part of the yield can be netted down by taking out 41·25% and then adjustments made for changes in capital. For the purposes of this exercise we have taken a 30% rate for capital-gains tax although, as we shall see later, it may often be lower.

	£	s.	d.	£	s.	d.	£	s.	d.	£	s.	d.
Gross yields	5	2	1				4	18	0			
Net at 58·75%				3	0	0				2	17	7
Capital changes	+1	0	0				−1	0	0			
Net at 30% capital-gains tax				+14	0					−14	0	
Net redemption yield				£3	14	0				£2	3	7

In the case of a gilt-edged stock, the sum would be exactly the same except that capital changes are taken gross, and the yield figures are, therefore, £4% and £1 17s. 7d.% respectively.

When it comes to equities the concept of a yield becomes much more complex, because it is a curious mixture of past, present and future. As we have already seen, you can work out a yield on the basis of last year's dividend. But this is only an historical calculation. If it turns out that next year's dividend is increased, or reduced, your answer will have been wrong. It may be more realistic to make assumptions about future dividends – upwards or downwards – than to work on the basis that things will stay the same as they are.

Much the most helpful guide to the future is the amount of earnings which are *available* for dividends, even if they are not actually paid out. To go back to Woolworths, for 1968 the group made £22·2 million, after allowing for corporation tax. This sum was available to pay the dividend of 20%, which, on an ordinary share capital of £94·5 million, would cost £18·9 million before income tax.

From this point on, you can proceed in two ways. Either you can divide the available earnings by the cost of the dividend $\left(\dfrac{22·2}{18·9}\right)$ and say that the payment was covered 1·17 times. Alternatively you can express the earnings as a percentage of the ordinary share capital $\left(\dfrac{22·2 \times 100}{94·5}\right)$ and say that earnings were 23·5%.

The next step is to work out what earnings are in relation to the price of the shares. Here again there are two possibilities. The one which has gained most favour since the introduction of corporation tax is the price/earning ratio, or P/E ratio for short. For this you simply express earnings in terms of shillings and divide this into the price. Thus, for Woolworth

$$23.5 \text{ (earnings)} \times 5 \text{ (par value)} = 1·175s. \quad \frac{21}{1·175} = 17·9$$

This method has long been in use in the States, but its arrival over here is comparatively recent. Previously, the usual practice was to apply the yield formula to earnings, $\frac{5 \text{ (par value)}}{21 \text{ (price)}} \times 23 \cdot 5 \text{ (earnings)} = 5 \cdot 59\%$, to get the earnings yield. Since the introduction of corporation tax, the use of P/E ratios has been gaining ground at the expense of earnings yields, which in one way is a pity. An earnings yield has a much simpler relationship with dividend yield and times cover. To use P/E ratios effectively you have to be agile at working out reciprocals in your head.

Ordinary shares do not have redemption dates, so it is impossible to work out in advance an accurate yield taking account of their capital element. But that is no reason for thinking that the capital element does not exist. On the contrary, progressive increases in dividend almost certainly result in higher market prices, as other investors, attracted by the record, decide to buy the shares. Suppose, for example, that you bought a 5s. share standing at 20s. and paying a dividend of 16%. You would have invested your money on a 4% yield basis $\left(\frac{5}{20} \times 16 \right)$. Now suppose a year later the company pays 20%, and investment demand forces up the price so the shares once more stand on a 4% yield basis. Their price would then be 25s. $\left(\frac{5}{25} \times 20 = 4 \right)$, and in effect you would have made a capital profit of 5s. a share, or 25 per cent. If you then sold the shares you could say that the gross yield to your redemption date was 5% (remember that you bought at 20s. and received a 20% dividend a year later) plus 25% capital appreciation – a total redemption yield of 30%.

The point perhaps comes home more forcefully if we take a less successful example. Suppose the company had merely maintained its 16% dividend and disappointed investors allowed the price to fall to 18s., at which point you decided it was prudent to cut your loss. Your gross yield to redemption would therefore have been 4% less 10% (or 2s. a share) capital loss. In other words, your yield to redemption would have been negative, -6%.

Here again we can adjust for taxes:

	£	s.	d.	£	s.	d.	£	s.	d.	£	s.	d.
Gross yields, %	5	0	0				4	0	0			
Net at 58·75				2	18	9				2	7	0
Capital changes	+25	0	0				−10	0	0			
Net at 30% capital gains tax				17	10	0				−7	0	0
Net yields to your redemption date, %				20	8	9				−4	13	0

We can sum up all these calculations by saying that there is an essential unity of capital and income. However sacred you may feel their historic separation to be, you can in fact allow for both factors at the same time. As we shall see later, this should have a vital bearing on your investment policy.

So much for yields. The other most important sums which you will be called upon to do are those which arise from changes in a company's capital structure. Take, for example, the procedure by which firms increase their issued capital. It often happens that under the twin pressures of growth and inflation a company's resources expand so greatly that the original equity subscribed by the shareholders bears very little relation to the funds actually employed in the business. The board may then decide to correct the anomaly by increasing the share capital, which usually takes the form of issuing more shares without payment. In the City this is generally known as a scrip issue (although punctiliously it ought to be known as a free scrip issue, because scrip is just an old-fashioned word for stocks or shares).

The important thing to bear in mind about a scrip issue is that it is simply a book-keeping transaction. It does not, of itself, involve any change in the realities of the situation. If a company with an issued equity capital of £1 million has, in the course of its operations, built up reserves of another £1 million it can capitalize, say, half of that sum by a scrip issue of one new share for every two held, without altering anything except the balance between these two items. All that will have happened after the issue is that the capital will be £1½ million and the reserves £500,000.

Now it follows that if there has been no change in the underlying situation there ought not to be any change in the total value of the shares either. What happens in fact is that the share price is adjusted in exact mathematical proportion to the size of the issue. Take, for example, the one for two scrip issue effected by Beecham, the penicillin and soft drinks firm, in 1968. Before the issue the shares were standing at about 51s., after it they were 34s.

The simplest way to understand the mechanics of this operation is to think of the number of shares you had before the issue and the number of shares you will have after it, and adjust the price accordingly. For example, with a one for two scrip issue, for every two shares you had you will shortly have three. So you can say with Beecham, that every two 51s. will soon be split into three, in other words $\frac{51s. \times 2}{3} = 34s.$

Had the terms of the issue been two for three, you could have said that for every three shares you would soon have five, i.e.

$$\frac{51s. \times 3}{5} = 30s.\ 6d.$$

and so on.

To take the calculation a stage further, a company sometimes splits the units of denomination, or par value, of its shares in order to make for easier dealings. Here is an example from 1969. Bolton Textiles, makers of paper panties and other disposables, split its 2s. shares into 1s. shares. At the same time it announced a one for three scrip issue. This involves a two-tier calculation. First you must reckon that for every three shares you will soon have four, on account of the scrip issue, and then you must go on to say you will have twice as many as that (eight) because of the share split. In other words (taking the original Bolton price at 52s. a share)

$$\frac{52 \times 3}{2 \times 4} = 19s.\ 6d.$$

We can now move on to another slightly more complicated set of calculations. Sometimes a company wishing to raise fresh funds to finance expansion decides that the best way to do so is to offer more shares to the public. By tradition, existing share-holders are given the first refusal in an operation of this kind – they are offered the right to subscribe for new shares in direct proportion to the number they already hold. This is known as a rights issue.

For example, imagine that Beecham, instead of having its one for two issue for free, had decided to offer the shares at 30s. each. The sum we did before would have to be adapted to take account of this new factor, as follows:

Two shares at 51s. = 102s.
Add 30s. subscription price = 132s.
Divide by three (two old shares and one new one) = 44s.

This is known as the ex-rights price.

So far, so good. The calculation is exactly the same as for scrip issues, except that you have to add in the price of the new share you are being offered. But at this point the terminology becomes confusing unless you watch it very carefully.

When a company has a rights issue it sends a special letter to each of its shareholders showing how many shares they have been provisionally allotted, and how much it will cost to take them up. A short interval is left for shareholders to make up their minds what to do, and during that time there is a market in the unpaid letters of allotment. The price is the difference between the ex-rights price and the subscription price. In our example it is 44s. (ex-rights price) minus 30s. (subscription price) or 14s. premium – premium because it is additional to the 30s.

Now the point to remember about this premium is that it is not the same thing as the so-called value of the rights per share. The easiest way to check this value is to think what you would lose if you simply allowed your rights to lapse. As we have seen in our example, Beecham were 51s. when the issue was announced. Other things being equal, they will be 44s. ex-rights. If you do nothing about your rights you will lose the difference between these two figures – 7s. Another way of doing this sum, which some people prefer, is to divide the premium by the terms of the issue, i.e. 14s. divided by one for two $= \dfrac{14s. \times 1}{2}$ or 7s.

Scrip issues carry implications about dividends, no less than prices. They must be adjusted in exactly the same way, short of a forecast to the contrary from the board. In the Beecham example the final dividend before the issue was announced was 10%, and strictly you should have expected to be paid in future two-thirds of that amount, or $6\frac{2}{3}\%$. The board, however, foreshadowed a $7\frac{1}{4}\%$ payment. In the Bolton example the dividend must be scaled down to take account of the one for three scrip issue only. As dividends are expressed as a percentage of par values, the share split makes no difference.

Unlike scrip issues, rights issues do not, of themselves, involve any change in the dividend. That is not to deny that they are often accompanied by dividend changes; but when they are it really means a scrip element has been slipped into the package as well. This is frequently misunderstood, so it is worth going into in detail.

Suppose Company A's £1 shares are standing at 100s. and paying 20%. It offers one new share for two at 40s. and forecasts a 15% dividend.

Here is the calculation

	s.
For every 2 shares at 100s.	= 200
Add one at 40s.	40
	240

Divide by 3 for an ex-rights price of 80s.

From this you might expect a quote of 40s. premium, and a rights value of 20s. a share. You might even argue that as you were going to buy a new share for 40s. and receive a 15% dividend on it, you were being offered a snip with a yield of $7\frac{1}{2}\%$.

In fact, this would be very naïve. If you think about it you were getting an overall yield of 4% before this issue was mentioned. By our usual formula:

$$\frac{\text{Par } (\pounds 1 \text{ or } 20s.)}{\text{Price } (100s.)} \times \text{Dividend } (20) = \frac{400}{100} = 4$$

Ex-rights the position is this:

$$\frac{\text{Par } (20s.)}{\text{Price } (80s.)} \times \text{Dividend } (15) = \frac{300}{80} = 3\frac{3}{4}$$

So far from being a snip, you would be worse off!

The explanation is that this issue is not a simple rights operation. There is a scrip element as well. Split into its constituent parts, the issue is really a one for three scrip issue combined with a one for six rights issue at 120s. a share.

This is how the sum works out:

	s.
For every six shares at 100s. =	600
Add one at 120s. =	120
Add *two* free shares (1 for 3) =	Nil
Total, nine shares	720

Divide by nine to give an ex-rights price of 80s.

Raising money at 120s. a share when the existing price is only 100s. is scarcely calculated to appeal to the investing public. In fact, rights issues always have to better shareholders' immediate position. Why else should they bother to put up more money? And the measure of this betterment is the difference between the yields before and after the issue.

CHAPTER FIVE

Becoming an Investor

IF YOU are to become an investor you must first of all find someone through whom you can deal on the Stock Exchange. Ideally, if you want to take an active interest in looking after your own investments, that means you ought to get in touch with a stockbroker direct. But unfortunately it is not always as simple as it sounds. You cannot just bounce into a stock-broker's office in the way that you can (if the advertisements are to be believed) into a bank manager's parlour. Dealing for strangers is against Stock Exchange rules.

The official attitude of the Stock Exchange is not very encouraging either. In an open letter to the Would-be Investor, the Council writes: 'As the relationship between Stockbroker and Client is one of mutual trust and confidence, the Council of the Stock Exchange consider that the best way for a member of the public to get in touch with a Broker is by personal introduction.'

The trouble is many people do not have friends in the City, so special arrangements have had to be made to overcome this problem. Each month a list of about twenty member firms is prepared, from which you can choose. You should write to the Secretary of the Stock Exchange for a copy. If asked, he will tell you who a firm's partners are. But you will not get any other help than that.

Another possibility, certainly, is to consult your bank manager, but he will very likely advise you to make use of the bank's own investment machinery. Again if you turn to professional men, like accountants or solicitors, they may offer to help you themselves. They are recognized Stock Exchange agents, who can represent private individuals in their dealings with brokers. Indeed, many do so with competence and discretion. But unless you have reason to believe they are organized to manage investments, instead of merely acting as buffers between the brokers and yourself, you can try asking for a personal introduction instead. There is no doubt that if you want to concern yourself closely with your investment policy you should be in direct contact with a broker yourself.

Before you start dealing with your stockbroker it is as well to remember what his function is. First and foremost he is a negotiator, who is there to bring buyers and sellers together. His economic interest is in arranging a deal, for he lives solely by commissions on orders actually completed. Naturally he needs to know a good deal about his markets, and to be able to offer information and advice about individual shares. Still he is an agent, and his natural impulse is to generate orders for buying and selling, on which his income depends. So, though there is nothing in the rules to stop you giving him *carte blanche* to buy and sell whatever he thinks best, it would be inappropriate to do so. You should be prepared to play your part in vetting his suggestions and making the final decisions, or else engage an investment manager to do it for you.

What, then, can you expect from your stockbroker? Apart from dealing for you he should, first of all, be able to help you to work out an investment policy which dovetails in with your requirements. Then, within the framework of that policy, he will recommend some individual investments for you to buy. Ideally he will suggest more than you really need, so that you can pick and choose. In any case you must always feel free to reject his ideas if you don't like them. It is your money, not his, that is being invested, and you must not be overawed. Your broker should be able to tell you a good deal about any share he recommends; if you feel he has left some gaps, question him. Should he not know the answer himself, he may be able to find out by asking in the market. This generally means sounding out the jobbers, or perhaps passing on an inquiry to the brokers to the company, generally known as 'the shop'.

Having accepted at least some of your broker's suggestions, you buy some shares. It is now that the quality of your broker can make all the difference. A good broker will make a note of your purchases and get in touch with you if ever he thinks one of them should be sold. You should also feel free to ring him up occasionally and ask for a progress report. Of course, if your purchases were your own idea and not your broker's you cannot expect the same after-sales service. He probably never claimed to know much about the shares in the first place, and that is one reason for not going against your broker's advice unless you feel very sure of your ground.

This is not to say you are allowed no ideas of your own. Brokers are sometimes too close to the market, and an outsider may spot an opportunity in an unfashionable sector that his broker might miss. But it is wise to ask him for his assessment before going ahead, and if it is adverse you should normally accept it. For example, suppose you get a good tip from a friend you can trust (and remember anyone who gives you a tip has always got a reason for doing so). You can hardly ask your broker for confirmation. But you can ask him to give an expert assessment of the shares and see if they seem worth their price, even if your information turns out to be wrong. If they look high on normal grounds you may be sure that someone else knows your story and has got in first. Suppose you really have been told the truth, it may still not make much difference to the share price when it is published. Either way, if you decide to act on a tip the responsibility can only be yours, not your broker's.

How much information and advice can you expect from your broker without your asking for it? The answer, in all probability, is very little. Most brokers make out a valuation of their clients' portfolios once, perhaps twice, a year. They may also send out some advice on one or two share exchanges at the same time. This may seem pretty inadequate, but a good deal depends on how active you really intend to be, and how prompt you are in dealing with their suggestions. If one had to select the commonest single cause for deteriorating relations between stockbrokers and their clients one would say that it was clients' inattention to letters or telephone messages. Carefully worked-out schemes for switching investments inevitably depend on current market prices, and if you wait for several days before making up your mind what to do prices will as likely as not have moved out of line.

Some brokers circulate their clients with a regular monthly letter, discussing the market outlook and perhaps suggesting a few favourite shares. The larger firms, which can support elaborate research staffs, often publish closely reasoned arguments for buying or selling a particular share. Inevitably this type of circular is angled at the big institutions, like investment trusts and insurance companies. But unlike the general practice on Wall Street, where brokers are usually happy to show their work to anyone who asks for it, most firms over here are reluctant to let their publications go outside a fairly small circle. Private individuals, unless they know their brokers well, are unlikely to catch a glimpse of these recommendations. Your best sources for more sophisticated treatment of investment matters are likely to be the specialist weeklies, like the *Investors' Chronicle*, and increasingly the quality Press. If you read one or other of them regularly you should soon be well enough informed to keep your end up in a discussion with your broker. And that is the way to get the best out of him.

One last thing to remember about your broker is that sooner or later he will give you some bad advice. You cannot expect a winner every time. Generally the fairest thing to do would be to give him another chance, and in that case it is most important to let bygones be bygones. Any broker who is constantly being reminded of past mistakes will soon become so unnerved that he will give up advising you altogether. For beneath the Stock Exchange Council's clichés about mutual trust and confidence there is this nugget of truth; once you get on poor terms with your broker the chief sufferer is you.

The Mechanism of Dealing

Whatever your relations with your stockbroker, it will undoubtedly be helpful if you understand the processes of dealing. So let us assume that you have just given him an order – say you want to buy 100 Unilever. We can now go through the mechanics of a stock-exchange bargain and see how it affects you.

In most brokers' offices the work is divided between the partners, some of them negotiating with the public and some of them transacting business in the Stock Exchange itself. After speaking to you your broker will therefore probably put in another call, this time to his dealing partner. The instructions he gives should be detailed; if you are wise you will make sure they are. You do this by setting limits at which you are prepared to do business. Let us say you are anxious not to pay more than the price at the previous evening's close, when the quote was 62s. 6d. (to sell) to 63s. (to buy). Your broker therefore relays your order to his dealer accordingly: buy 100 Unilever at 63s. a share.

The importance of setting a price limit is worth going into in some detail. Unknown to you, or even to your broker, because he cannot keep track of several thousand prices at once, a rumour may have got about that frozen peas are to be supplied to NATO in unprecedented quantities. On the strength of its control of Bird's Eye, Unilever may have shot up to 67s. to 67s. 6d. If at this point you sent your broker into the market to buy your 100 shares without a limit he would probably do as he was told, even if by a quirk of fortune he had to pay 68s. a share. Later that day, perhaps, a War Office spokesman might deny the whole story, and Unilever would come tumbling back to 62s. 6d. to 63s. again. You would then have paid 5s. a share too much for your 100 shares – a total of £25.

Of course, if you do set a limit your broker may soon ring up to say he cannot buy at your price, adding that 63s. 6d. is the best he can manage. In that case, and assuming that your limit was sensibly chosen in the first place, do not meekly give in and pay the extra. Ask your broker to keep the limit on for a specified time – for the rest of the day, for instance. Shares fluctuate up and down, and by careful timing you can make considerable savings.

Clumsy limit setting, on the other hand, can simply be a waste of time. When markets are soaring day after day, for instance, there is no point in naming a price a few pence below reality. In any case a limit should be what you are really prepared to pay, not an incentive to keep your broker on his toes. A good dealer will automatically go for the best price he can get, even if it is inside your limit. As a general rule, moreover, it is not a good plan to change your limit. If it is proving impossible to meet you should probably resign yourself to not doing your bargain, and keep in touch with developments by watching the newspapers.

However, let us assume that he eventually gets your 100 Unilever for 63s. That evening he will send you a contract note. This is a fairly imposing document, as indeed it should be, because it is the legal evidence that you have done the bargain. In this case it would read like this:

> *Bought* 100 Unilever Ltd.
> 5s. ordinary shares

Then comes a list of figures. The first is the *price* you paid per share: 63s. The *consideration*, which follows, is the price multiplied by the number of shares 63s. × 100 = £315.

Next come a couple of government duties – *transfer stamp*, at 1 per cent of the consideration, and the *contract stamp*, which has to go on the contract note, rather like the stamp one puts on receipts. They are £3 3s. and 2s. respectively in this case.

Next comes the *registration fee* of 2s. 6d. Some companies (let us say Unilever is among them) make this nominal charge for putting your name on the shareholders' register.

Next there is the stockbrokers' *commission*. There is no bargaining about that. It is fixed by the rules of the Stock Exchange (decorously they call it a minimum rate of commission) at $1\frac{1}{4}$% or 3d. in the £. On £315 that is £3 18s. 9d.

Add all these items together and the *total* is £322 6s. 3d., which is what you owe your broker.

One final detail on the contract note is the date of settlement. That is the day on which you must put the broker in funds – for example, if you pay by cheque it should arrive in time for it to be cleared by settlement day.

For simplicity this description covers a straightforward purchase of shares, but there can be a number of variations in the contract note depending on the transaction.

Suppose you had sold 100 shares at 63s. There is no transfer duty on sales and, of course, no registration. Contract stamp and commission would be the same, but they would be deducted from the consideration to show in the final column the amount that the broker will pay you on settlement day – £315 minus £3 18s. 9d. and 2s. = £310 19s. 3d.

Other variations can also occur on a contract note. For clarity's sake they are listed below under the main headings.

Contract Stamp. The amount varies with the size of the consideration. Under £100 it is 1s., from £100 to £500 2s., from £500 to £1,000 4s., and so on.

Transfer Duty. The 1% very often does not work out exactly. It is charged on the nearest £50 above. With some purchases it does not have to be paid at all, notably with bearer securities, foreign securities and gilt-edged. The Government, being anxious to promote dealings in its own stocks, makes the cost of buying them cheaper. Most important of all, there is a special concession on new issues of securities. Transfer duty is not charged for a limited period after a new issue of securities comes to the market. All such issues are included – whether they come from companies never dealt in before or whether they are new types of stock issued by well-known firms, free issues of shares and issues for cash.

Commission. Commission rates vary according to the type of stock you are dealing in, and the amount of it. Commission on gilt-edged bargains, for instance, is only $\frac{3}{8}$%, and with bargains worth over £5,000 there are reductions on the excess. At the other end of the scale, there is a special rule about minimum commissions. Except where a broker is entitled to charge commission at his discretion – such as on very small bargains of under £10 – there is a minimum of £1 commission on bargains up to £100 and £2 above that. It looks likely that the rules about commission will shortly be changed, but the effect of this will probably be confined to the institutional investor with larger bargains attracting lower rates. Full details about commission rates can be seen in Appendix B.

Settlement Date. To save time and trouble, the Stock Exchange settles up its bargains at set intervals instead of day by day. The arrangement is that the year is divided up into periods, known as accounts, which usually last a fortnight. There are a few three-week accounts covering the major public holidays. (For some reason a long account is thought to have some mystic influence on the habits of speculators, and few press commentators can resist the temptation to mention this influence from time to time.) Accounts run from Monday to Friday week, and most of the bargains falling within that period are for settlement eleven days after the end of the account (that is, on Tuesday week). In the normal way the settlement date shown on your contract note will be the date of that Tuesday. For example, an account opening on Monday, May 1st, will close on Friday, May 12th, and settlement day will be Tuesday, May 23rd.

But sometimes you will see the word 'cash' written in on your contract note, which means you must put the wheels of settlement in motion immediately. The transactions which are normally for cash are the same as those for which there is no transfer duty: bearer securities, foreign securities, gilt-edged and new issues.

If you want to *sell* a stock for settlement in the usual way, and *buy* one for cash settlement, you should not automatically assume that your broker will finance you during the gap between one settlement day and the other. You should check with him first.

There is one other detail on which your contract note may say something special: the price. Sooner or later the time comes round when dividends are about to be paid. To avoid arguments, a day is chosen (usually the first of a new account) on which all future deals will be transacted as though the dividend had already been paid. Technically the shares are then said to be quoted ex-dividend. At that time the company closes its register of shareholders for about a fortnight and gets down to the business of preparing its dividend warrants.

If you deal after the shares have gone ex-dividend the price shown on your contract note will be followed by the letters 'xd'. It is the same with scrip issues, rights issues, capital repayments and so on. If you deal after the entitlement to such benefits has lapsed the contract notes will say 'xc' (ex scrip – the 'c' standing for capitalization) 'xr' (ex rights) or in more complicated cases 'xa' (ex all). If you are still entitled to dividends, scrip, rights, etc., you may see 'cd' or 'cum div', 'cum scrip' and so on after the price on your contract note.

If you are in any doubt about some detail on your contract note do not hesitate to get in touch with your broker right away. Mistakes or misunderstandings can usually be put right very readily at the time – rather more painfully, if at all, later on.

There is one final detail to remember about contract notes. They may be called in evidence in any assessment for capital gains tax, so obviously they ought to be kept very carefully.

After your bargain has been transacted the machinery for changing the ownership of the shares comes into action. If you are the buyer the processes go silently forward; you will hear nothing more about the deal until you, or your bank, receive the certificate issued by the company whose shares you have bought. If you are the seller, however, you will usually receive a stock transfer form attached to your contract note.

This stock transfer form will give the number and details of the shares you have sold, together with your name and address. You should sign this form right away in the place indicated and return it, undated, to your broker. At the same time you should arrange for the certificate covering the shares to be sent to his office. Even if you intend to buy the shares back in the same account you should still complete the stock transfer form. Your broker will return it to you, cancelled, if you do in fact buy them back within the account. Otherwise you can expect your cheque on settlement day, provided, of course, that all the documents (transfer form and certificate) are in your broker's hands by then.

All this means life is extremely simple for investors, thanks to the Stock Transfer Act of 1963. Still it is worth quickly following through the handling of a stock transfer form, after it has been signed by the seller, because it brings out several points which ought to be borne in mind. If the holding you have sold has to be split among several buyers – as it probably will – your broker will cancel the buyer's part of the form; fill in, on the back, the numbers into which the holding is to be split; and send it off with the certificate to the company's registrar. At the same time he will fill in the numbers on a broker's transfer form for each buyer, have the forms stamped by the Inland Revenue and send them on to the buying brokers, who will fill in the buyer's name and send the form on to the registrar. The important point here is that details of the buyer's name are now the responsibility of the buying broker. Obviously, when you are buying it is vital that your broker should have your address right, because nobody else will be in a position to check it at this stage. It is also worth noting that brokers handling these forms stamp their own name and address on them at each stage, so everybody knows who to turn to if the machinery breaks down.

At this stage a buying broker will also make the necessary arrangement for the payment of dividends. Many investors choose to have dividends paid direct to their bank. This is, in fact, the procedure which most companies prefer, because it is cheaper and easier for them. If you want your dividends paid in this way, or more accurately if you want them paid to any other address than the one you have given for registration, your broker will send a dividend mandate form for you to sign which will give the appropriate instructions to the company.

The streamlining of settlements resulting from the Stock Transfer Act has in most cases cut down the delay before shareholders receive their certificates. Even so, the gap still tends to be far longer than would be tolerated in America, where settlements have to be complete in four days from the date of sale or purchase, and certificates are habitually ready very soon afterwards. But this is something which the City, ever ambitious to assert its supremacy as the financial capital of Europe, is watching with the greatest care.

Some investors, even among those most interested in what their holdings are, dislike having to bother with the paperwork which is an inevitable part of investment. This difficulty can be got round by giving your bank, or some such body, a power of attorney to sign on your behalf. Perhaps the neatest arrangement, however, is to arrange for your securities to be registered in the name of your bank's nominee company, which will then handle all documents on your behalf. Bank services of this kind are usually excellent, but from time to time there have been complaints in the correspondence columns of the financial papers about the high charges some banks make for handling securities. Before embarking on an arrangement of this kind you should carefully check its cost to see whether you think it worth while.

One final detail about correspondence with your broker concerns dividend claims. Sometimes you will find yourself buying or selling just about the time when dividends are due. It may then happen, if you are a buyer, that you will not be on the register in time for the warrant to be made out to you. Alternatively, as a seller, you may be sent a dividend you are no longer entitled to. In that case your broker will make the appropriate claim. If the claim is being made on your behalf the broker will also send you a voucher certificate, saying that tax has been deducted and that you have received only the net amount of the dividend. This can be sent to your tax inspector along with any other vouchers.

PART II

CHOOSING YOUR INVESTMENTS

CHAPTER SIX

Some First Principles

THE FIRST thing for potential investors to get clear is the fundamental distinction between fixed-interest stocks and equities. With fixed-interest stocks, particularly government stocks, the accent is heavily on certainty. You know pretty precisely where you are, both as far as income and capital are concerned – but in money terms, not allowing for inflation. With equities, the potential risks and rewards are both much greater. What you are getting is a stake in the economy, for better or for worse. Overall, no doubt, the economy will grow, and if you have picked your share in it correctly you should prosper. But it is only too easy to choose wrongly – or, if your choice is right, to buy at the wrong time. Once you start buying equities you are in altogether deeper water.

Granted the existence of important differences between these two investment categories, what is their significance for you? The thing to do first is to examine the recent records of fixed-interest stocks and equities, to see if any worthwhile principles emerge. What we are interested in is the real return on one's investment, after allowing for tax and changes in the value of money. Furthermore, we must as far as possible eliminate chance by averaging out the return over sustained periods of time.

In the following table every attempt has been made to iron out the quirks of fortune and make the test as fair as possible. A cross-section of well-known equities has been pitched against a representative fixed-interest stock – $2\frac{1}{2}$% Consols, the irredeemable government security which was the darling of respectable Victorians. It has been assumed that on each January 1st for a period of over forty years an equal sum of money in real terms (that is, of constant purchasing power) was invested in these securities. Credit was taken for interest and dividends, after deducting tax at the standard rate ruling at the time. Then, since the return on one's investment involves changes in capital values as well as income, the securities were in due course sold. Actually the test was run over a whole series of eleven-year periods (1919–30, 1920–31 and so on) and the results averaged out. It is as foolproof and realistic as anything you are likely to see. And here are the results:

Real Rates of Return

	2½% Consols %	Equities %
Average between the wars (1919–38)	8·7	10·9
Average since the war (1945–63)	−5·3	7·6
Average over the whole period, including the war (1919–63)	−1·4	5·8

Note: The data for equities is based on the *Financial Times* Industrial Ordinary Share Index.

Source: 'Return on Equities and Fixed Interest securities 1919–63', A. J. Merrett and Allen Sykes, *The District Bank Review*, No. 148, December 1963. The authors, in *Capital Budgeting & Company Finance* (Longmans, 1966) subsequently updated the equity calculation to 1966, and found the average over the whole period 1919–66 unchanged at 5·8%. The comparable figure for Consols, if it were available, would be worse than −1·4%.

Now there are several interesting features about this table. In the first place 2½% Consols were a perfectly satisfactory investment in the period between the wars, because the value of money was rising and interest rates were tending to decline. In consequence, the average annual return was a fat 8·7%. Since the war, however, exactly the opposite has been happening. Inflation has eaten away at the value of money, and interest rates have moved upwards, thus causing long-term gilts to fall. After allowing for these factors – not to mention the substantial increase in personal tax – the real return on Consols has been a minus quantity. Indeed, if you include the war the setback since 1939 has been enough to wipe out all the earlier gains. If you had had your money in Consols ever since 1919 its value would have declined, on average, by 1·4% a year – and that even after allowing for the interest on your investment.

Not so equities. Notwithstanding the slump, the war and

several years of austerity and dividend restraint, the average return on equities for the whole period has been nearly 6% a year. Even in the pre-war period, which was a good time for gilt-edged investment, equities put up a better performance. And even if you had sold out the previous eleven years' equity investments at the depths of the depression, your real return would still have been a hair's breadth better than the Consols return at 9·1%.

At first sight these figures may not seem very startling. We live, after all, in an age of economic growth. Besides, companies regularly plough back a proportion of their profits to help boost their expansion. In the circumstances one might expect equity returns to be higher, and indeed by international standards they are on the modest side. Still, what is impressive is their consistency. In spite of higher wages and higher taxes, companies have managed to pass on such major increases in costs by raising selling prices. To that extent they can opt out of inflation. And, interestingly, the same pattern of overall consistency has occurred in the United States.

On this evidence, equities have made resoundingly better investments than the classic nineteenth-century choice, an irredeemable gilt-edged stock. You can get another slant on the comparison from the chart appearing on page 55, which shows the downward drift in Consols since the war alongside the upward progress of Moodies' Equity Index. Since devaluation in 1967, a fresh body blow to the purchasing power of fixed money incomes, the position of Consols has deteriorated more sharply than ever.

Of course, all this is history, and it is fair to ask whether it will continue. The arguments in favour of equities certainly remain impressive. The major political parties are committed to policies of economic growth and full employment, which more or less inevitably involve some inflation. Even if the agonized defence of the sterling exchange rate keeps the overall growth of the economy in continued check, new demands, and the new technologies required to service them, will expand far faster than average.

Another highly significant consideration is the public esteem in which equities are now held. Since the Keynesian revolution people have come to believe that the days of acute economic depression are over. Pension and insurance moneys have been ploughed heavily into ordinary shares on the strength of the investment lessons of the past thirty years. In consequence, equities have become more institutionalized – tamer, if you prefer. In recent years even trustees operating under the provisions of the Trustee Investment Act have been permitted to put half their funds into ordinary shares.

With this three-pronged argument in favour of equities as long-term investments – growth, inflation and public confidence – it seems almost foolhardy to speak up for fixed-interest stocks. But it is not the purpose of this book to predict the immediate course of markets. It is more a matter of our reminding you that there must be a point when the prolonged bear market in gilts, which has been going on for over twenty years, comes to an end.

Look at it from the point of view of an institutional fund manager – say a man who is responsible for investing some hundreds of thousands of pounds' worth of pension-fund money each week. He has to think in terms of the return required on his funds. According to a survey in 1968, he will be satisfied with a bit under 9%, if his expectations are as modest as those of the managers polled on that occasion. If so, by 1969, 10% on good-quality blue-chip debentures was by no means out of the way. Even if he remembers that the average gross return on ordinary share investments made between 1919 and 1966 has been calculated, by Merrett and Sykes in the study quoted above, at over 10% (in money terms), is he really justified in playing the equity market on a large scale for so little extra?

That must depend to some extent on his expectations about ordinary share prices. And it is surprising, in a way, how seldom the market's implicit assumptions are spelt out. This is no place to go into the mathematics underlying long-term projections; it can simply be taken as a rule-of-thumb measure that the long-term rate of return is the current dividend yield plus the annual rate of growth in dividends. To be precise, this only holds good if the shares are held for ever, but, if you ignore the possibility of a change in price/earnings ratios between buying and selling, and work with the compound growth rate of earnings per share, you get roughly the same effect.

With the aid of this formula we can consider what the market was going for in spring 1969, after nearly 2½ years of bull market. Well, the average yield was about 3½%, so the implied growth factor was 5½%, to achieve an overall return of 9%, and 6–6½% to keep up with blue-chip debentures. So what, you may say, the underlying growth rate, in real terms, of the country's gross national product is somewhere between 3 and 3½%. Add on roughly the same for retail-price inflation, and we should be home and dry. Unfortunately, profits do not keep completely in step with growth-plus-inflation. The actual rise in profits since the mid-fifties has been a bit under 5% a year, and the return on companies' equity assets has been edging downwards. Implicitly, the market seemed to be relying either on a further upward move in the status of equities or an acceleration of inflation, or both. But with an average price/earnings multiple of nearly 20, and official dividend restraint, how much further could an uncritical cult of the equity go?

Even if we are right, and gilts do recover in the foreseeable future, that will simply be a correcting swing of the pendulum, not a signal to abandon equities for ever more. It will still be possible to make rational calculations about the comparative advantages of different forms of investment. And before very long we would expect the pattern of the past fifty years to re-assert itself, leaving equities decisively more attractive than fixed-interest stocks.

Given such circumstances, the general rule is, the longer the time span you are considering, the greater the chance that the long-term rising trend in equities will prevail over shorter-term fluctuations. In practice, therefore, if you can take a fairly relaxed view of your capital over five years, with no particular financial ambitions except that you want it to work for you as hard as possible, you should be on the look-out for equities.

Against this backdrop of general considerations, we are now ready to approach the detailed business of choosing individual investments. We begin with fixed-interest stocks, discussing how to test their quality, their suitability for different investment requirements and the proper price to pay for them. We then move on to the more complex processes of balance-sheet analysis, and the art of portfolio planning.

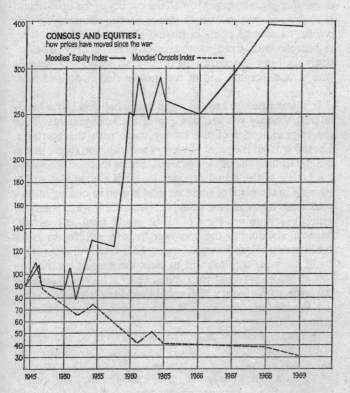

CONSOLS AND EQUITIES:
how prices have moved since the war

Moodies' Equity Index ——— Moodies' Consols Index – – – –

CHAPTER SEVEN

How to Assess Fixed-interest Stocks

FOR ANY investor who wants to buy fixed-interest securities the proper place to begin is with the quality of the investment. If it fails to measure up to minimum requirements in this respect there is no point in fussing about other details. This is because with fixed-interest investments quality is effectively the same as security. And the first, vital thing is to be sure of one's capital and of the income that is derived from it.

It is important to bear in mind that when you buy a fixed-interest security you are taking over the arrangements which the original lender of the money made with the borrower. Looked at from the point of view of security, you might just as well be lending the money yourself, except that you are spared the bother of the actual negotiations. It is a good idea to put yourself in the place of someone who is used to making loans – your bank manager, for example – and think what points he would check up on. First of all he would want to know the financial standing of the borrower, usually referred to as his credit rating. Next he would assess how readily the borrower could carry his commitment to meet the interest on the loan and, if necessary, repay the capital. Finally, he would consider the terms of the loan, which should include provisions to protect the lender's position. Let us take each of these points in order.

In Britain there are three main categories of borrower. Top of the bill, in terms of credit rating, comes the Government, including nationalized undertakings whose loans are guaranteed by it. On a somewhat junior plane come the local authorities, whose loans are secured against rates, followed by public bodies with public revenues, like water boards, docks and harbours. Finally comes private enterprise, and the loans issued by companies. Here, as we shall see, it is possible to make pretty realistic assessments of credit worthiness on the evidence of balance sheets, backed by general business knowledge.

How readily can these borrowers meet their commitments in income and capital terms? To the officials of the International Monetary Fund, the question of the Government's capabilities in this respect must seem grave indeed. But however much you may feel the country has become, internationally, a bum drinking the HP money on the way home from work, in practice the internal credit of the Government is copper-bottomed (at least in sterling terms). In the same way, it is not actually necessary to calculate from the available statistics how generously the income from rates or dues covers the interest requirement of local authority loans, and such like. Default is not only very unlikely, if past records mean anything; it is also a fair assumption that the Government would step in during a real emergency to salvage public confidence in local authority finance. For companies, the testing ground is the balance sheet. In fact, since the 1967 Companies Act required disclosure of reasonably up-to-date values of fixed assets, the evidence of simple arithmetic has become that much more worthwhile.

The terms of a loan, put shortly, cover the rate of annual interest payable on it, and provisions for the repayment of capital, whether the life originally allotted to the loan is completed or not. This may sound straightforward, but in reality one cannot be completely certain what is involved. This is because real returns, both income yields and variations in capital value, are affected by tax, and the amount of tax payable varies according to which sort of security one holds (to say nothing of the status of the holder). So although the principles involved in the assessment of fixed-interest stocks are the same whatever the issue, in practice there no longer is one big fixed-interest market, but a whole lot of mini-markets, increasingly independent of one another. So rather than discuss a unified set-up, we must take you on a conducted tour, the amount of time worth spending in each place depending on your circumstances.

Not counting subdivisions, there are five main sections of the market – unquoted stocks, gilts, the bonds of other public authorities, company loan capital and company preference shares. The first category is set apart from the other four, because unquoted stocks do not, by their nature, fluctuate in value. The others do. The by-ways of this first market are so extensive that we have devoted a whole section to exploring them later on in this book. There you will find a discussion of all the main types of unquoted security, from bank deposits to premium bonds, with some ideas on which are most suitable for different classes of taxpayer.

There are really only three reasons why these holdings should be appropriate as investments – first because you cannot afford even the possibility of loss inherent in price fluctuations; secondly, because you want to have at least some money earning a decent return but available, intact, in an emergency; and thirdly, because you think other forms of investment are going to go down. At this stage we would merely ask you to be particularly clear about your motives and objectives. For instance, some people who claim they can afford no risk whatever forget that also implies they must give up all prospect of increasing their capital. Over the last inflation-ridden generation this has proved an extremely expensive attitude. In the same way people tend to make far greater provision for emergencies than they really need. With some gentle probing, it often turns out they are insuring against three major cataclysms happening before the next Stock Exchange account day. It is as well to remember that it is the poor who are usually most over-liquid, and to wonder which is cause and which effect.

We can take the second and third markets together. These are the markets for gilt-edged stock, the forty-four securities issued or guaranteed by the British Government, and for all other fixed-interest securities issued by public bodies. Logically, of course, there is no real distinction here. As we have seen, there is no effective loss of security in local authority loans, compared with government ones. Marketability considerations and dealing expenses favour gilts, but all told there is nothing in what has been said so far that cannot be allowed for in a slightly higher yield.

All this was changed by the 1969 Finance Act, which exempted capital gains on government stocks from tax (provided they are held for more than a year). The effect of this can be seen from comparing net redemption yields on two stocks whose terms are exactly the same, except that one is subject to gains tax and the other is not. The gilt we have taken is Savings 3% 1965/75 at 75, and we have assumed it has exactly five years' life left to run. To refresh your memory, we break the calculation down into its constituent parts, taking tax, where appropriate, at the standard rates of 30% and 41·25% respectively.

	Gilt						Other stock					
	%			%			%			%		
	£	s.	d.	£	s.	d.	£	s.	d.	£	s.	d.
Capital part of yield	5	7	7				5	7	7			
Less Capital-gains tax at 30%	Nil			5	7	7	1	6	11	4	0	8
Income part of yield	4	0	0				4	0	0			
Less Income tax at 41·25%	1	13	0	2	7	0	1	13	0	2	7	0
Net redemption yield				£7	14	7				£6	7	8

You may argue that this, too, could be allowed for in terms of extra yield. Once the new differential, taking account of tax, has been established, markets would move more or less in step as before. We are writing too soon after the 1969 Finance Act to say anything definite about the gap in yields on gilts and debentures, but for the time being we think that tax-conscious private investors can virtually ignore this third market, and concentrate instead on the potential in gilts.

If this potential is to be exploited you must define as clearly as possible what you are going for. The first consideration is time span. Obviously anyone who pays any tax at all will expect to be in for at least a year. At the upper end we doubt whether the post-war industrial cycle, lasting four years, will be so decisively broken that you should move all your capital out of equities for as long as that. It seems to us more likely that, when the prolonged bear market in gilts ends, there will be a worthwhile upward adjustment in prices, and after that things will jog along pretty uneventfully. What would really surprise us would be if you beat a good equity portfolio by locking your money away in a twenty-year stock like, say, Treasury 5% 1986/9 until redemption date, however succulent the gross redemption yield of 9⅜% may look today.

In short, the semi-tax-free status of gilts is like oil on a rusted-up rifle. It does not answer all problems, but at least it helps to get gilts back into the investor's armoury. The classic device of putting money away for known commitments will continue to attract devotees, though we doubt whether this should be taken beyond a time horizon of three to four years. For other investors with less precise requirements gilts are worth considering, for the first time in years, as defensive stocks in bear markets. The fact that big bear markets since the war have lasted between about 50 and 150 weeks, with an average of 92, may be of some guidance as to the time span for which you should hold them.

When it comes to choosing an actual stock much will depend on your opinion of market circumstances. If you think interest rates are going to fall you should remember you will undoubtedly make more money buying undated stocks, such as War Loan. But then, if you are wrong, you will not have had any redemption provisions to help you. The advantage of having a dated stock is that the prospect of eventual repayment acts like a magnet for the price. Even if interest rates rise, stocks which are sufficiently short-dated will still keep creeping gradually towards par. As a rule, therefore, conservative investors should keep their choices in the short- and medium-term brackets, say in maturities of ten years or less.

Another important factor in gilt-edged assessment is personal tax. Although a net redemption yield is what investors really need to know, because it shows their real return, it is in fact conventional to show these yields gross. This is because net yields depend on tax rates, which vary from person to person. Gross redemption yields are of general application; individuals can then make allowance for their own tax. A common practice is to work out not only one's own net redemption yield but also its gross equivalent. In effect, this treats the capital part of the yield as thought it were taxed income, and then shows what the equivalent would be before tax. The following examples show the net redemption yield on Savings 3% 1965/75 grossed up at the standard rate and at a high rate of surtax:

	Tax at 41·25%	Tax at 68·75%
Capital part of yield	£5 7s. 7d.	£5 7s. 7d.
Gross up × $\frac{100}{100 - 41·25}$ = £9 3s. 7d.	× $\frac{100}{100 - 68·75}$ = £17 5s. 1d.
Add gross income	£4 0s. 0d.	£4 0s. 0d.
Gross redemption yield	£13 3s. 7d.	£21 5s. 1d.

What this shows up vividly is the importance of a relatively large capital element in the yield if you pay surtax. In other words, surtax payers should usually be interested in low-coupon stocks at a deep relative discount. For standard or substandard taxpayers a different balance between running yield (which is certain) and capital return (which is not, unless you hold the stock to redemption) may well be appropriate.

We are now ready to visit our fourth and fifth mini-markets, one of which concerns company loan capital – that is, debentures and loan stocks – and the other, company preference shares. For the time being we can treat them together, because we must first of all think about assessing their security, and the same techniques apply to both. Later on, when we come to the customers who are likely to be interested, important differences between loan and preference capital will emerge.

You may remember we pointed out at the beginning that anyone buying a fixed-interest stock was, in effect, taking over the original lender's commitments. For a government or other public loan this is only a formality, but with companies you can check – and indeed recheck year by year as fresh balance sheets appear – on the current standing of any investment.

This is the point where you should imagine yourself in your bank manager's chair. You should assess a company's credit rating, as he would, partly by its size, partly by its profit record and partly by the business in which it operates. Size, though it can involve a certain lack of flexibility in a company's operations, is a logical enough guide to security and power of survival. But the other two measures of credit rating are of greater significance still. With profits what one is looking for is a stable record. Growth, in the context of fixed-interest securities, is not particularly important, although in a period of general expansion, such as we have enjoyed since the war, one should expect some advance in profits. The easiest way to ensure confidence in the profit record for the future is to select a business which is naturally consistent. Brewing or flour milling are excellent examples – one should concentrate on day-to-day consumption companies. It is better to avoid industries, however buoyant, which experience acute fluctuations, like motors, metals or papermaking. Another point to remember is to check the kind of assets which a company has, because they, after all, are the security for your investment in the last resort. Freehold properties, cash and marketable securities all make encouraging backing for a fixed-interest investment. Of these considerations, size is by far the least important. In fact, one can often find superior value in the stocks of smaller companies which measure up well to the other standards of safety.

Having assessed credit rating in general terms, you can then get down to the detailed calculation of a company's ability to carry its debt. For this you need to study the balance sheet or, if not you, somebody else must. In fact, it is all worked out by the statistical services, and it is not too much to ask your broker to look up the figures on your behalf. Still, the best way to understand what they mean is to go through the exercise yourself.

You will remember from our earlier discussion of balance sheets that a company's capital, whether it has been subscribed by investors or built up by the accumulation of reserves, is put to use in the assets of the business. These assets belong, of course, to the stockholders, but in order of priority. That is to say, the rights of each class of stockholder will be decided in advance. Generally speaking, debenture or loan stockholders rank first. After them come preference stockholders and finally ordinary stockholders bringing up the rear. Their respective entitlements, to capital and income, can be accurately calculated from the balance sheet.

The way to begin is to take a cold, hard look at the company's assets, to see how far they are available for stockholders. As our example, let us take Fortes, the well-known caterers and hoteliers, whose interests range from airport hotels to the Café Royal. Looking down the 1968 balance sheet one can see the main fixed assets – land and buildings, plant, fittings and vehicles. These all look real enough. So do the current assets (stock, debtors and cash) but of course current liabilities (creditors, tax, dividends due and overdrafts) must be deducted from them. One suspicious item, and a fairly substantial one at £4½ million, is the excess cost of shares in subsidiaries acquired since 1962 over the net asset value at the time they were bought. However justified the price may have been in trading terms, the excess over net asset value was just Fortes' estimate of what it was worth their while to pay. If anything goes wrong, and the company has to go into liquidation, there is no guarantee that anyone else would pay over the odds. In this exercise the realistic thing is to be gloomy, so out this must go.

In addition to current liabilities, which we have already subtracted, there are always some deferred liabilities which have to be taken into account, notably future tax and minority interests. Minority interests appear in the Fortes' balance sheet, so they must come off too. After this we are left with what is known as net tangible assets, and they are represented by stockholders' funds. Here are the actual 1968 figures, in thousands of pounds:

	£000	£000
Current Assets	10,598	
Less Current Liabilities	8,403	
Net Current Assets		2,195
Fixed Assets Investments and Intangibles	31,827	
Less Goodwill	4,563	
		27,264
		29,459
Less Deferred liabilities		6,978
Net tangible Assets		22,481

Represented by	£000	%
5¾% Debenture	4,000	17·8
7¼% Debenture	2,000	8·9
7% Preference	1,500	6·7
7% Second Preference	2,817	12·5
4½% Preference	401	1·8
Ordinary	1,000 ⎫	
A Ordinary	1,971 ⎬	52·3
B Ordinary	1,000 ⎭	
Share Premium A/c and Special Reserve	7,792	
	22,481	100·0

Alongside the figures for stockholders' funds we have shown the percentage which each one represents in the total. Thus the first 17·8% is attributable to the 5¾% Debenture, the next 8·9% to the 7¼% Debenture and so on. Investment experts like to use this information in one of two ways. Either they quote these figures as priority percentages or else they like to talk of overall cover. Priority percentages are the same figures expressed cumulatively, and usually rounded up to the nearest whole number above. Overall cover is calculated by dividing the cumulative amount ranking at each level by the amount available. In other words, capital cover for the 5¾% Debenture is 22,481 (the total available) divided by 4,000 or rather over five times. To calculate overall cover for the 7¼% Debenture you must divide 22,481 by 4,000 + 2,000, which gives you a bit more than 3½ times cover. With the 7% Second Preference and the 4½% issue, the same calculation is done with them both added together because they rank equally (*pari passu* is the technical City term in a rare burst of affection for Latin). The final figures, both for priority percentages and overall cover, are shown in the next table:

	Priority % for capital	Overall cover
5¾% Debenture	0–18	Over 5 times
7¼% Debenture	18–27	Over 3½ times
7% Preference	27–33	3 times
7% Second Preference 4½% Preference }	33–48	Over 2 times

If you are interested in mathematics you will have noticed that the overall cover is simply the reciprocal of the priority percentage (e.g. for the 7¼% Debenture $\frac{100}{27} = 3\frac{1}{2}$ plus). The only practical difference is a matter of usage. The statistical services use the slightly neater priority percentage formula, while merchant bankers or stockbrokers tend to talk of cover.

There is one small, but important, qualification to this discussion of priority percentages. Some fixed-interest issues carry a right to a little bit of extra capital in the event of a winding up of the company. For example, Fortes' preference shares are redeemable either at par in the case of the 7% Preference and at 1s. premium for the 7% Second Preference and 4½% or, if their market prices are higher than that, the average premium during the six months before the winding up. If you allow for this in the priority percentages it would only make a fractional difference to the figures quoted above. But if you are a potential investor in company fixed-interest stocks it can have a significant effect on your position.

Having worked out the capital cover in this way, one can then proceed to do the same for income. The total sum available for interest (net of tax) and dividends in 1968 was £1·694 million. The priority percentages therefore look like this:

	Net Amount required to service capital		Overall
	£000	Priority %	Cover
5¾% Debenture	132	0–8	Nearly 13 times
7¼% Debenture	83	8–13	Nearly 8 times
7% Preference	105	13–19	Over 5 times
7% Second Preference 4½% Preference	} 199	19–31	Over 3 times
Ordinary A Ordinary B Ordinary	} 625	31–68	
Undistributed	550	68–100	

Note: Debenture interest is serviced out of pre-tax profits, but net equivalents are given in the table.

So much for the mechanics of calculation; what do the resulting figures mean? As always with fixed-interest stocks, much depends on the industry in which the company operates. On the capital side you should be wary when fixed-interest stocks contribute much over 25%, that is, if they are covered much less than four times. But in the case of a stores group or a big brewery this rule can be relaxed. For example, the £32 million worth of debentures and loan stock in Watney's 1964 balance sheet totted up to the first 37% of net tangible assets, but when the revaluation of the group's pubs and other properties was incorporated in the 1965 figures, loan capital came down to only 23% of net tangibles. The point is, these are the sort of properties which have a real market value, and one should think in terms of the quality of the assets as well as their balance sheet value.

On the income side a rather lower priority percentage is desirable – say 0–20, or five times' cover. Even Watneys, which we saw just now has a high priority percentage on the capital side, has an income priority percentage only two-thirds as high – 0–14. This is, after all, the vulnerable aspect of fixed-interest investment. A company is far more likely to go through a temporary bad patch, which might mean getting behind on interest payments for a year or two, than to have to be wound up altogether. So the income cover is the more important feature to watch.

Having been through these careful calculations, can you

now feel ready to plunge into the market? Apologetically, (though the concept of priority percentages will be helpful later on) we feel obliged to advise against. All the objections that we raised against local authority loans, as compared with gilts, apply, and with somewhat enhanced force, against company loan capital. Dealing costs are higher again, with brokers' commission $1\frac{1}{4}\%$, and marketability is often outrageously thin. As before, the exemption of gilts from long-term gains tax looks like being a powerful factor attracting private investors away from the corporate bond market, and leaving it to the so-called gross funds, pension funds and charities, who pay no tax.

In these circumstances institutional investors have the whiphand, and this time there is something constructive they can do with the whip. After all, companies, unlike local authorities, have something else to bargain with as well as high interest rates and worthwhile security. They can offer their fixed-interest investors some participation in their equity, whether by a conversion option, by warrants or by rights to subscribe for shares at an attractively pitched price. We expect to see an increasing proportion of company fixed-interest borrowings to have some such equity sweetening from now on. And unless or until there is a substantial widening of yields, as between gilts and conventional company prior charges, we advise you to concentrate exclusively on gilts and convertibles for the fixed-interest sectors of your portfolios. It is premature to analyse convertibles before discussing ordinary shares, but we shall come back to them in Chapter Ten.

We can give the fifth sector – the preference market – even shorter shrift. What separates a preference share from other fixed-interest securities is that they are usually irredeemable and the dividend on them is paid from profits which have already borne corporation tax. Technically, the income from them is franked. In the hands of other companies franked income has a certain value, because it is free of corporation tax. But for private individuals there is no such significance.

For some time after the introduction of corporation tax in 1965 preference shares were in some demand, often from companies anxious to cover their own preference dividends. Such dispositions having been largely made, demand has since died down. Even so, yields are nothing to write home about. At the time of writing the return on the *Financial Times'* index of twenty commercial and industrial preferences is £9 6s. 6d.%. As most preferences are irredeemable, the appropriate comparison is with an irredeemable gilt. Even War Loan has a higher comparable yield (9 guineas %), and an allowance for expenses would flatter the comparison still more. Unless you want franked income, or unless there is an equity interest via a participating preference, preferences are not for you.

To conclude, here is one extra point of practice which is worth knowing. With all fixed-interest stocks there is accrued interest to think of. As everyone knows when the interest on a stock is due, it is possible to adjust the dealing price to take account of the wait until payment is made. For example, a half-year's interest on Savings 3% 1965/75 is payable on August 15th. In mid-June, therefore, it has four months' interest in hand; in mid-September only one month's. It is a matter of moments for your broker to check this detail and work out its significance for you. But a word of warning: gilt-edged stocks go ex-dividend about six weeks before the payment is due, debentures and preferences rather later. If you tried to buy for the August dividend at the end of July you would be too late.

CHAPTER EIGHT

Ordinary Shares: The Growth of Assets

ASSESSING ORDINARY SHARES is a much more subtle and complicated business then anything we have considered in our discussion of fixed-interest stocks. This is because an extra dimension – growth – has been added to the basic investment requirements of security of income and capital. As a result, the potential rewards are richer, the game more fascinating – and the decisions more difficult.

An ordinary share must, above all, offer the possibility of growth. That is the most important single consideration. Security should be borne in mind, obviously, but with ordinary shares you can never make doubly sure (in money terms) the way you can with gilt-edged. All you can aim for is to weigh the possibility of gain against the possibility of loss, and buy when the balance seems to be in your favour.

There are two main strands to company growth. Predominantly growth depends on the overall progress of the industry in which a firm is. Companies are more likely to make money when general expansion is so fast that there is room for everybody. But the skill of individual managements operating within the same industry also has profound effects on the performance of shares. From the point of view of investors it is wise to concentrate first of all on growth industries, because it is much easier to keep track of them rather than individual companies. Very often you can spot a growth situation by simply keeping your eyes and ears open – pop records, Continental holidays and an ever-increasing taste for wine have all made minor fortunes on the Stock Exchange before now. Besides, most industries publish figures of production and exports which appear from time to time in the newspapers. Few firms, on the other hand, produce figures more than once or twice a year (though an improvement is taking place in the information available in interim statements). Besides, fresh developments can blow up unexpectedly quickly inside a company, which outside shareholders will not hear about till long after they have happened. In stressing the importance of looking for suitable industries we are not, in any case, crying down the significance of management. It is more a matter of limiting the area of search.

Different industries have their own characteristic pattern of growth or decline, depending on the needs they cater for. There is the familiar distinction of consumer industries, which tend to advance fairly smoothly, and capital goods industries, which depend on demand from businesses, and whose fortunes therefore fluctuate more sharply. But within these categories one can subdivide industries into essential or non-essential, stable or volatile. Breweries, food, stores, tobacco, fuel and banking are typically solid; metals, machine tools, cars, aircraft and furniture are more flighty. Paper, chemicals and insurance zigzag around a strongly rising trend.

At various times each of these growth patterns can offer the makings of a successful investment, but it is of crucial importance to buy shares in the right companies in each industry. Just how important can be gauged from the history of two broadly competitive companies in the toy industry during the 1960s.

To get the record straight we must go back to September 21st, 1960, when the public was offered 400,000 shares at 20s. each, in Lesney, manufacturers of *Matchbox* die-cast toys. In those days the acknowledged blue chip of the toy world was Lines Brothers, a £10 million enterprise of forty years' standing, which had spearheaded the post-war renaissance of British toys abroad as well as at home. As you can see from the table below, it was about fifteen times the size of Lesney in terms of net assets, and four to five times its size in terms of profits.

Now look at the situation as it was 9 years later, on September 21st, 1969. The picture is totally transformed. Lesney shareholders (including its brilliant managing directors, Leslie Smith and Bill Odell) have multiplied their capital nearly 25 times. Lines shareholders (assuming they did not put up any more for the couple of rights issues they have been offered) have seen their investment nearly halved. The market value of Lines' equity, a solid enough £7½ million, looks peripheral beside Lesney's £57 million.

	Capital employed £000		Earnings per share, %		Dividend, %		Share prices	
	Lines	Lesney	Lines	Lesney	Lines	Lesney	Lines	Lesney
1960/61	9,975	681	49·3	13·3	24·9	7·4	26s. 6d.	1s. 6d.
1964/65	13,180	1,834	31·7	38·4	21·6	14·6	20s. 3d.	10s. 2d.
1967/68	21,677	6,449	32·5	132·2	26·7	17·4	15s. 0d.	38s. 0d.
1967/68 as % of 1960/61	217	947	66	999	107	236	57	2,479

Note: Earnings, dividends and share prices have been adjusted for scrip issues where appropriate. A small preference issue by Lesney and the Lines rights issue have been ignored. Earnings for 1960/61 allow for corporation tax. Prices are for September 21st, 1960, 1964, and 1969.

It is part of the moral of this story that Lines was not noticeably badly managed during this period. Admittedly there was a costly venture into France that had to be written off, but, against that, the ailing Meccano, acquired in 1964, was put right more quickly than anticipated. But the important thing to emphasize is the positive achievements of Lesney: the successful identification of the right specialized product, backed by outstanding engineering and salesmanship. In fact, if one had to put one's finger on the qualities that go into good management, one might say that a company should be this sort of all-rounder – equally at home in product design, manufacturing techniques, merchandising and financial control.

Now this story may suggest to you that the key to investment is to know the right people – to be, as they say in the States, on the inside track. A word in your ear from Mr Smith or Mr Odell would seem to be all that was necessary in this case. Yet the market is a contrary place. It is not just the latest profits that affect the share's rating but a curious blend of sentiment and expectations as well. For example, when Lesney finally came out with their 1969 results, showing a 50% increase, coming on top of 67% increases in each of the two years before that, the shares fell sharply. These results were a disappointment simply because they were what had been forecast. The market was wound up to expecting forecasts being beaten.

So it is not just enough to listen to good stories. One must be able to assess a story's worth, to appreciate what it means in an investment context. For this one must have an awareness of what is possible. And there is no better way of defining the limits of the possible than by a detailed study of company accounts.

Company Accounts

There are two main sets of figures in a company's accounts: the balance sheet and the income statement, often known as the profit and loss account. Before looking at them in detail, it is important to remember what a balance sheet is: an historical record. It is simply intended to show, in accordance with legal requirements, where a company's funds are derived from and how they are being used. It is not – and never should be – the directors' estimate of what the company is worth on the open market. It can fairly be argued that any items in a balance sheet which are misleading ought to be commented on in the directors' report. But otherwise any interpretation of current worth which you may care to put on the figures is a matter for yourself alone.

After this warning the next step, logically, is to consider an actual balance sheet and income statements. However, we have already discussed the main items in a balance sheet in an earlier chapter (see page 20). So rather than interrupt the argument on the analysis of company accounts, we have separated out the raw data into two tables, given on the following pages, together with the relevant notes and explanations. The balance sheet is deliberately printed in the conventional style, with assets and liabilities facing one another, and each item in order of liquidity. This approach is not just old fashioned. It tells you something about the solvency, and therefore the strength, of a business. The regrouping of the figures for dynamic analysis is another phase, not a substitute.

For analytical purposes a single year's figures are not, in themselves, very significant. What is interesting is the interaction of the income statement and the balance sheet over time, the two concepts of particular importance being, first, the

Tesco Stores:
Consolidated Profit and Loss Account, 1968

Trading Account	£000	£000	Notes
Group sales		136,323	(1)
Cost of goods sold	Not Stated		
Wages and salaries	9,781		
Rents and other occupancy costs	Not Stated		
Other expenses	Not Stated	126,211	(2)

Profit and Loss Account			
Trading profit		10,112	
Interest and dividends received		113	
		10,225	
Directors' emoluments	90		
Auditors' remuneration	8		
Supplementary contribution to staff pension	50		(3)
Depreciation	1,757		(4)
Interest paid	7	1,912	(5)
Net profit before tax		8,313	
Corporation tax at current rates	3,457		
Equalisation less overprovisions	259	3,716	(6)
Net profit after tax		4,597	

Appropriation Account			
Minority interests	Nil		
Preference dividend (gross)	Nil	Nil	
Earned for ordinary		4,597	(7)
Interim dividend (gross)	1,117		
Proposed final dividend (gross)	894	2,011	(8)
		2,586	
Transfer to reserves	Nil		
Carried forward	2,586	2,586	(9)

Notes to Profit and Loss Account

The figures shown are the real ones in Tesco's 1968 report and accounts, but the method of presentation, including some items for which figures are not available, has been adapted from the model accounts for stores companies prepared by the Society of Investment Analysts.

(1) Group sales exclude inter-company sales. Exports would be shown, but Tesco's 1968 sales were all UK.

(2) There is no statutory obligation to publish a detailed trading account; Tesco gave sales and wages figures as notes. We list the main items for which information would be welcome. The total expenses (£126 million) are derived by subtraction.

(3) A supplementary contribution to the staff pension scheme is not a regular item in a company's profit and loss account.

(4) Depreciation consists of amounts written off fixed assets and amortization of leaseholds. The figure shown is a provision by the directors, and bears no necessary relationship to the initial and annual writing-down allowances permitted by the Inland Revenue in computing tax liability.

(5) Tesco paid only a small amount of interest on short-term loans in 1968. Many other companies have prior charge capital, the servicing of which can represent a substantial proportion of the cost of capital. For inter-company comparisons it is usual to show profits before interest and tax (see chapter on Finance and Gearing).

(6) The tax shown in the profit and loss account is a provision by the directors. It can be affected by a transfer to equalization reserve or by the adding back of overprovisions. Where a company trades overseas, tax is payable locally, and can be offset against UK tax. This does not, however, apply to overseas tax credits. It is usual to calculate the total tax charge as a percentage of pre-tax profits, to see whether the charge is normal.

(7) Profits earned for ordinary capital are applied to the issued equity capital, and shown either as a percentage or in shillings and pence per share. This should be calculated with the actual tax charge, and with tax at the standard rate.

(8) Dividends are charged gross (that is, before allowing for tax payable by shareholders in their personal capacity), but actually distributed net after withholding tax at the standard rate (41·25% at the time of writing).

(9) From the point of view of shareholders, the actual disposition of sums carried forward or transferred to reserves is not very important. For them, undistributed profits are a measure of dividend-paying capacity, and internally generated growth.

Notes to the Balance Sheet

As before, the actual Tesco balance sheet has been amended and amplified. The comparable figures for the previous year, which all balance sheets must show, have been omitted for simplicity.

(1) Notes on share capital must show the terms on which the company has power to redeem preference capital, any arrears of fixed cumulative dividends and details of any shares under option.

(2) Notes on reserves must show movements during the year. The main distinction between capital and revenue reserves is that capital reserves are not available for distribution through the profit and loss account. Any share premium account must be shown separately. This is a capital reserve, and is the difference between the proceeds of any issues of shares and their nominal value. It can, incidentally, be paid back to shareholders free of tax.

(3) Loan capital consists of debentures and loan stocks, including

Tesco: Consolidated Balance Sheet, 1968

Liabilities

	£000	£000	£000	Notes
Share capital				
Preference	Nil			
Ordinary	11,174	11,174		(1)
Reserves				
Capital reserves	2,370			
Revenue reserves	3,555	5,925		(2)
Total, capital and reserves		17,099		
Loan capital	Nil			
Long-term provisions				
Deferred tax	4,233			(3)
Minority interests	Nil	4,233		(4)
Total, capital employed		21,332		
Current liabilities				
Creditors	15,440			(5)
Overdrafts	Nil			
Other short-term borrowings	Nil			
Current tax	2,143			(6)
Dividends (gross)	894	18,477		
		39,809		

Assets

	Notes	£000	£000	£000
Fixed assets				
Freeholds	(7)	13,222		
Leaseholds		3,377		
Plant, fixtures and fittings		8,651	25,250	
Intangibles				
Goodwill	(8)	Nil		
Trade investments	(9)	22	22	
			25,272	
Current assets	(10)			
Stocks		11,149		
Debtors		2,060		
Cash at bank and in hand		1,328	14,537	
			39,809	

Note

	Notes	£000
Commitments for capital expenditure	(11)	1,727
Capital expenditure authorised but not contracted for		1,122
		2,849

those with options to convert into equity capital. Terms of repayment
must be shown in the notes.

(4) Long-term provisions. The distinction between provisions and
current liabilities is not hard and fast. It is partly a question of time
(i.e. liabilities not falling due within twelve months are normally
classed as provisions) and partly a question of the degree of certainty
of the amount due.

(5) Minority interests appear in both profit and loss accounts and
in balance sheets. They represent the proportion of profits and net
assets respectively attributable to outside shareholders in subsidiaries.

(6) Current liabilities (generally due within twelve months) do not
include long-term debts which will soon fall due for repayment. They
do include items such as overdrafts which may not *necessarily* fall due
within a year.

(7) Fixed assets are usually shown in the main balance sheet net of
depreciation and amortization. The notes give gross costs, up-to-date
valuations where appropriate and accumulated depreciation. Ideally
this information is presented so as to show gross additions during the
year and realizations from sales. Details of leaseholds are given, split
between those with more and less than fifty years to run.

(8) Intangibles include goodwill, patents, royalty agreements and
capitalized expenses which have no physical existence. Under this
heading comes any difference between the cost of shares in subsidiaries and the book value of the net assets attributable to them.

(9) Trade investments are shown at cost, with notes on market
value or, if unquoted, directors' estimates of value.

(10) Stocks are generally valued at the lower of cost or market value.

(11) Future capital spending, whether actually committed or merely
authorized by the directors, must be shown in the notes to the
accounts.

trend of earnings on capital employed, and second, the build
up of assets as a source of income growth. Actually both should
ride in harness; good figures for one without the other are
suspect. If the trend of earnings on capital is upwards, without
any supporting rise in assets, there is no solid backing, and it
may turn out to be a chance fluctuation. On the other hand,
if assets are being built up, but the earnings on them are going
down, the extra capital tied up is being used more or less
defensively. The return on it must certainly be very poor. In
neither case is there the stamp of a true growth investment.

To illustrate all this let us look first at the record of an outstandingly successful company of the 1960s, Tesco Stores.
The annual series of significant figures are printed on the
opposite page. The top band, which is extracted entirely
from the balance sheet, shows the items which a company uses

in the course of trading – its premises and plant (net of depreciation), its stock and its current trading account, that is, its debtors net of its creditors. The total of these items, which we call net trading assets, is shown in the left-hand column, and next to that the same figures are given in index form, to illustrate the growth in percentage terms.

Tesco Stores
£000's; Indexes: 1962 = 100

Years to end February	Net trading assets	Index	Premises	Plant	Stocks	Net debtors
1961	5,100	73	2,879	1,058	2,215	−1,052
1962	6,949	100	4,002	1,804	2,778	−1,635
1963	8,290	119	4,921	2,404	3,281	−2,316
1964	9,297	134	5,827	2,711	4,385	−3,626
1965	11,970	172	8,156	3,704	5,595	−5,485
1966	15,411	222	11,007	6,294	7,239	−9,129
1967	18,726	270	13,528	7,257	9,282	−11,341
1968	23,019	332	16,599	8,651	11,149	−13,380

	Profit before tax and interest	Index	Profit as % N.T.A. (previous year)	Earnings index	Dividend index
1961	1,219	86		80	81
1962	1,413	100	27·7	100	100
1963	1,699	120	24·4	117	133
1964	2,450	173	29·6	160	200
1965	3,576	253	38·5	191	238
1966	5,286	374	44·1	260	344
1967	6,669	472	43·3	300	372
1968	8,363	590	44·6	355	383

It is worth noting right away that net trading assets are the same as net tangible assets, except that they exclude cash from among the assets, and make no allowance for short-term liabilities, such as overdrafts or tax and dividends due. This is because we are concerned at the moment simply with the assets which a company uses to make money and not with financing.

You will notice at once that Tesco has been growing at a fair clip. Net trading assets have more than trebled between 1961 and 1968. Yet if you do not mind doing some rough mental arithmetic you will also notice that premises, stocks and, most of all, plant have been going up faster still – over four times in each case. This is made possible because the large negative figure for net debtors in the right-hand column has been growing most rapidly of all. And as this is crucial for understanding Tesco's success, it would be as well to explain it at once.

If you come to think of the way a supermarket like Tesco works, effectively it gets cash over the check-out point for everything it sells. In other words, it is never owed much money (actually its debtors in 1968 represented little more than $1\frac{1}{2}\%$ of its turnover, compared with nearly 25% for Joseph Lucas, of electrical accessories fame, a manufacturing company of roughly similar size). On the other hand, its suppliers, generally the big food groups, would naturally give it normal trade terms, that is a month, in which to settle its bills. As well-managed supermarkets turn over their stock once every two or three weeks, they are in the delightful position of not having to pay for their goods until after they have sold them on to the public. In balance-sheet terms this shows up in the relationship between stocks, debtors and creditors. If creditors less debtors (the same as a minus quantity for net debtors) more than cover stocks, effectively the store's suppliers are financing its day-to-day transactions, and the money in the till is available to pay for expansion.

Actually, as you can see from the table, Tesco's stocks were only half covered in this way in 1961. But the relationship has improved steadily ever since, with break-even coming in 1965. If you recall that increasing size would also enable the Tesco management to negotiate better prices for bulk supplies you will realize how brilliantly they have exploited their growing market power.

Going back to the table, the second horizontal band shows profits, both in money terms and in index form, and relates them to net trading assets. Profits are shown before interest as well as tax, because we are trying to isolate what the trading assets alone are producing. If the company has a deposit account at its bank that is not relevant. In our opinion the relationship of profits to net trading assets is probably the most meaningful way to show earnings on capital employed. The exact method of calculation is really a matter of choice. We prefer to relate the year's profits to the previous year's assets, that is, the position when the trading year began. Other people work it on an average between the assets at the beginning and end of the year. One advantage of our method is that it allows a rough arithmetical check of profits' forecasts arrived at on other grounds.

The fact that Tesco's return on capital is so high may not necessarily mean very much. It is, of course, partly explained by the fact that suppliers are putting up so much of the money. If one adds back their contribution the return on the funds in the business, irrespective of ownership, is more like 20%. But all this only emphasizes the notorious difficulty of interpreting earnings on capital-employed figures. So much depends on what industry a company is in and how far brains, which do not feature in any balance sheet, are responsible for earnings. As a general guide, most stores and manufacturing companies should show 15–25%; if it gets down near the 10% mark the company will have difficulty paying interest on any new money it may need to borrow.

Another point is that it is often sounder to go for a company with a good average figure which keeps very steady. As long as the build-up of assets is progressive, earnings will benefit accordingly. The trouble with high and rising earnings on capital is that they attract competition. And though there is no reason why total earnings should not rise every year for decades, there is a practical ceiling on earnings on capital employed. One's admiration for exceptional increases should therefore be salted with suspicion.

The last two columns in this band of the Tesco table show earnings and dividends per share in index form. It is useful to compare their progress not only with each other but with profits' growth as well. In any case, from the point of view of shareholders, earnings per share is a highly important item. There isn't much joy for them in profits' growth if it does not work its way through to dividend-paying capacity. However, this takes us on to a completely new aspect of balance sheets, the division of profits among owners of different classes of capital. We leave this for detailed discussion later on, in the chapter on gearing. At this stage it is worth checking how the analysis of assets and profits can help investors choose between one company and another.

A Tale of Three Stores

The food-distribution industry is a particularly suitable one to have under the analytical magnifying glass, because so much depends on management. The post-war growth in food sales, at $1\frac{1}{2}$–2% a year, has been slow even by the sluggish standards of the British economy. The dynamic expansion of the Tescos, Pricerites and so on has been achieved at the expense of less responsive competitors, notably the torpid Co-ops and the under-capitalized, one-family grocers. Against such a commercial background, mistakes are costly. Food-store managements – and investors who back them with their money – cannot simply wait for the next indiscriminate boom to float them off. No such boom may ever materialize.

One might imagine, in these competitive circumstances, that size was strength, as conventional wisdom so often assures us. So let us examine the record of the largest grocery chain, Allied Suppliers. This giant can trace its origins back to the grand old days of the Home and Colonial, and Sir Thomas Lipton, who went boating at Cowes with Edward VII. Backed by the Unilever colossus, its sales in the early 1960s, when supermarketing was in its infancy, were already some £160 million, from 3,000-odd outlets. Its ramifications included a wide range of food wholesaling and meat manufacturing, to say nothing of a couple of tea plantations.

But quite a perfunctory examination of its financial history would have shown that it could not possibly be such a good growth investment as Tesco. Let us compare their positions as they would have appeared at the beginning of July 1966, the peak point before the market slump in the late summer and autumn of that year. The table opposite gives the key figures for Allied Suppliers. For convenience, the corresponding ones for Tesco are reprinted alongside.

You can see clearly that Allied's growth is nowhere near as fast as Tesco's, either in assets or in profits. In spite of some improvement in the earlier years, the stock/net debtors relationship remained virtually unchanged from 1963 to 1965. No doubt these uninspiring figures owe a good deal to the manufacturing interests – only about two-thirds of group sales were in retailing at the time. But the suspicion remains that small, unprofitable outlets and inadequate stock control also had something to do with it. As the comparative figures for

Allied Suppliers and *Tesco*
£000's; Indexes: 1962 = 100
(Years to January 1st and March 1st respectively)

	Allied Suppliers		Tesco	
	Net trading assets		Net trading assets	
	Actual	Index	Actual	Index
1961	37,767	87	5,100	73
1962	43,612	100	6,949	100
1963	44,751	103	8,290	119
1964	45,850	105	9,297	134
1965	47,500	109	11,970	172
	Stocks	Net debtors	Stocks	Net debtors
1961	18,517	−7,292	2,215	−1,052
1962	20,953	−8,055	2,778	−1,635
1963	22,460	−11,359	3,281	−2,316
1964	23,278	−11,626	4,385	−3,626
1965	23,582	−11,191	5,595	−5,485

	Profits before interest and tax			Profits before interest and tax		
			As % of N.T.A.			As % of N.T.A.
	Actual	Index	(previous year)	Actual	Index	(previous year)
1961	4,267	86		1,219	86	
1962	4,968	100	13·2	1,413	100	27·7
1963	5,419	109	12·4	1,699	120	24·4
1964	5,783	116	12·9	2,450	173	29·6
1965	5,901	119	12·9	3,576	253	38·5

return on capital employed plainly indicate, Allied was not using its resources nearly as efficiently as Tesco, and that should be reflected in the price of the shares.

In fact, both shares fell sharply in the imbroglio that followed. As so often happens in bear markets, people were not very discriminating about the finer points of investment rating. But once recovery started – both shares reached their best July 1966 levels in the late spring of 1967 – quality began to tell. And, as we write in summer 1969, Tesco have trebled, and Allied Suppliers are only up by about 50%.

You may well argue that all this does not prove anything

very startling. To be sure, supermarkets à la Tesco were a
better bet than Allied's mixture of self-service and other
grocery outlets, but you could see that well enough in any High
Street, without grubbing about in balance sheets. We would
answer that it emphasizes the difference and helps to quantify
its significance. In any case there are plenty of broadly similar
firms in other industries whose different methods of operation
are much less clear-cut. This type of analysis pin-points the
existence of dissimilarities, and prompts the investor to investigate them.

Besides, one can take the argument a stage further by using
these techniques to analyse two directly competitive firms –
Tesco and Victor Value. They started in business about the
same time; they both weathered the move into self-service;
and they both effectively exploited the abandonment of resale
price maintenance on groceries in 1958. By the early 1960s
Tesco was ahead, in terms of size, but Victor Value's stock
control looked superior against a background of scarcely less
impressive growth.

Victor Value

£000's; Indexes: 1962 = 100

Years to December 31st	Net trading assets	Index	Premises	Plant	Stocks	Net debtors
1960	1,243	47	586	660	955	−958
1961	2,212	84	1,066	1,223	1,522	−1,599
1962	2,636	100	1,289	1,392	1,738	−1,783
1963	3,373	128	1,292	1,755	2,342	−2,016
1964	3,529	134	1,703	1,883	2,248	−2,305
1965	3,611	137	1,990	2,278	2,272	−2,929
1966	4,849	191	3,052	3,425	2,841	−4,469

	Profit before tax and interest	Index	Profit as % N.T.A. (previous year)	Earnings index	Dividend index
1960	528	78		87	64
1961	619	91	49·8	100	80
1962	678	100	30·7	100	100
1963	684	101	25·9	117	120
1964	764	113	22·7	120	132
1965	705	104	20·0	122	132
1966	548	81	15·2	74	132

Note: For comparable Tesco figures, see table on page 77.

But as you can see from the analysis of assets and profits,
Victor Value stumbled in 1963. By a coincidence, the two super-
market groups produced their accounts in the same week in
June 1964 (they were, of course, the 1964 accounts for Tesco,

as its financial year ends in February, rather than the previous December). The differences were crucial. Tesco was swinging forward at a 20% growth rate on all fronts, Victor Value's asset growth was there, but profits' growth had ground to a halt, and the return on net trading assets was falling sharply.

From then on the group seemed to be beset with difficulties, such as assimilating the unprofitable Anthony Jackson (Food-fare) and extricating itself from unhappy experiences with trading stamps, first King Korn, then pink stamps. Profits never again caught up with assets growth, and the return on capital continued to slide. In the process its trading image somehow seemed to weaken, just when the real need was for supermarkets to upgrade. The end of the story came in the summer of 1968, when Victor Value was absorbed by its old rival for an addition of barely 4% to the Tesco equity.

In summing up we must point out that there are weaknesses in this approach. For one thing, the asset values of super-markets are exceptionally amenable to this sort of treatment. Their premises and plant are usually well sited in good shop-ping areas, and their stocks – all of them goods for sale – are worth, by and large, what they say they are. One cannot al-ways assume as much with the asset value of old textile mills in Lancashire, and stock valuation in heavy engineering groups, with long production cycles and huge ranges of spare parts, is notoriously arbitrary. As so often in investment, one must be prepared to do nine routine statistical assessments which end up meaning very little for every one that is significant and help-ful. For all that, when a light does shine through the gloom of figures it can shine very brightly indeed. Better to be guided by that light than the persuasive tip in the saloon bar.

CHAPTER NINE

Ordinary Shares: Finance and Gearing

INVESTMENT WOULD be easy enough if it were simply a question of assets growth. In practice, matters are more complex; growth must be properly financed.

The techniques which analysts use for assessing company resources are getting steadily more sophisticated (to say nothing of the extra enlightenment they are receiving from annual accounts). However, we are still a long way from having all the information published in a readily accessible form. The ideal is a financing table showing, in as much detail as possible, the sources of funds coming into a business, and the uses to which they are put. However, constructing such a table oneself can involve laborious hours of ferreting and cross-checking among balance-sheet notes. We shall therefore concentrate mainly on a rough-and-ready guide to company liquidity, such as anyone can apply from normal balance-sheet material. After that we will go on to a simplified form of financing table, as an outline of the principles involved.

The obvious place to begin an assessment of a company's finances is to examine the net cash position in the balance sheet (this is cash and short-term investments less any outstanding overdraft). As a further measure of liquidity, you should check the relationship between current assets and current liabilities. Not, it must be admitted, that the figures mean much in isolation. A lot depends on the business the company is in. A shipyard, for example, would have a very different financial profile from a supermarket like Tesco. But as a rather coarse-grained indicator, in the right context, the current assets/liabilities ratio is of some value.

Whatever broad deductions you can draw from one set of these figures, they become far more revealing over time. If net cash has been running down for years, or if the ratio of current assets to current liabilities is deteriorating, you may be sure something will have to be done about it. To guess how drastic the action may be, you can consider the supply of funds being generated within the business, and the possible calls on them as well.

There are two main sources of funds which arise from a company's day-to-day business. One source is profits – or rather that part of them which is not distributed in dividends. The other source is the allowance for depreciation of assets. Obviously, the assets which a company uses wear out over time, so part of its profits really represent consumption of capital. Tax authorities everywhere allow for this by permitting businesses to provide for replacement out of profits before assessing how much tax has to be paid. In practice, though, replacements are not geared to annual depreciation provisions. Directors spend money on new assets as and when they think fit. Depreciation simply becomes part of a company's resources.

These two sources of funds, depreciation and undistributed profits, make up a company's net cash flow (purists like to modify this further to take account of changes in provisions for future tax, because in the interval between setting tax aside and actually paying it, a company has the use of the money. For present purposes, however, the unadjusted version of cash flow is good enough).

For manufacturing companies there is another important source of potential funds, the official investment grants from the Government. This system, introduced in January 1966, enables companies to claim a proportion (currently 20%) of their spending on capital investment. As their name implies, these grants are an outright present, paid over by the State six months after a claim has been established. Naturally, payments on this scale have become a significant incentive for firms to invest.

On the demand side, you can assess from a balance-sheet note what a company's future spending is going to be. The information comes in two parts – one, what is traditionally known as capital commitments, the amount which a company's board has actually contracted to spend, and two, its authorized expenditure, which reflects the board's decision about future spending. The second part is an innovation resulting from the

1967 Companies Act, and therefore is only available on the most recent sets of accounts. Obviously, it has helped to get company intentions into sharper focus, but even before that capital commitments were of no little assistance.

To illustrate all this, let us look at four years in the life of a vigorously expanding company, Grand Metropolitan Hotels. This concern, the creation of Max Joseph, owns hotel and restaurant chains in London and the provinces, notably the May Fair, the Piccadilly and St Ermin's. Here is the position for the previous two years, as you would have seen it just after the 1965 results were published.

Year to September 30th	Increase in net trading assets, £000	Capital commitments, £	Net cash, £000	Cash flow, £000	Current assets/ liability ratio
1964	1,786	65	1,264	454	0·98 : 1
1965	5,171	441	522	1,002	0·75 : 1

From this you would have realized that here was a company with an extremely ambitious expansion programme. The increase in net trading assets in 1965 is vast in comparison with internally generated resources (in fact, it was financed very largely by £3½ million of fixed-interest stock). A cautious investor might well have decided to wait before committing money to such a venture, and the 1966 figures would scarcely have reassured him.

Year to September 30th	Increase in net trading assets, £000	Capital commitments, £	Net cash, £000	Cash flow, £000	Current assets/ liability ratio
1966	5,180	2,276	−2,409	989	0·56 : 1

Investment had continued on the same prodigious scale, and there was plenty of evidence that it wasn't going to stop, but cash flow remained quite unequal to the existing cash deficit, let alone future growth. In the event, there was another fixed-interest issue (to raise £1,600,000) in 1967 and the inevitable rights issue (to raise £5,300,000) the year after. All this led to a worthwhile improvement in net cash, particularly as a rationalization of recent acquisitions meant a net reduction in trading assets in 1967. But generally the company's appetite seemed to grow with feeding. And if the new (more revealing) figures for capital-spending intentions for 1969 are anything to go by, another mammoth capital-raising operation can only be just round the corner.

Year to September 30th	Increase in net trading assets, £000	Capital commitments, £	Net cash, £000	Cash flow, £000	Current assets/ liability ratio
1967	−913	3,750	−443	961	0·67 : 1
1968	10,109	9,739	603	1,243	0·84 : 1

Note: Surpluses arising from revaluations of fixed assets have been excluded. In 1968 only, capital commitments includes authorizations.

Before considering the investment implications of all this, there are two points of detail to be made. First, there is no mention of investment grants, for the simple reason that Grand Metropolitan, for all its contribution to the tourist trade, is a service company and does not qualify for them. Secondly, the current assets/liabilities ratio is exceedingly low – for most businesses a figure of $1\frac{1}{2}$ or 2 to 1 would be normal. No doubt this is largely a reflection on Max Joseph's abilities as a convincing financier, but if it also persuades you not to pay much attention to this statistic in other companies so much the better. Generally speaking, it should be looked on as a flashing light, indicating caution. If the company decides to raise money by a rights issue there is a definite possibility that this results in a dilution of earnings per share. We cannot illustrate this by reference to Grand Metropolitan's July 1968 rights issue because there has not yet been time, as we write, for this to be reflected in earnings per share. However, the point comes across clearly enough if we consider the record of Pillar Ltd., the aluminium and engineering group. Between 1964 and 1967 the company just about trebled, from £8¾ million to £25¼ million, in terms of capital employed and better than doubled, from £860,000 to £1,900,000 in terms of pre-tax profits. Yet earnings per share (on a corporation tax basis) actually fell from 47¾ to 36½%.

There were a number of factors involved in this, including trouble with unprofitable companies in the group, but part of the explanation undoubtedly was that the board was very free in issuing new shares. A good many of them were handed out to finance acquisitions of other interests, but there were also two rights issues, neither of them on particularly generous terms. The consequence was a very dreary earnings record until the benefit of the new money, and the new interests, worked their way through to shareholders in 1968.

As a rule, therefore, you must not be surprised if equity financing has a dampening effect on a share price. This holds good, especially if company directors, aware that investors do not like repeated calls for fresh funds, decide, once an issue becomes inevitable, to provide for their needs a good way ahead. In such circumstances the new money does not immediately earn its keep on the same scale as existing resources. The reception of rights issues can, however, vary enormously as a result of the market's mood. In times of ebullience they are usually well received, but when markets are nervous there can be a sharp reaction.

The methods of taking a company's financial pulse which we have been discussing so far are pretty rough-and-ready. However, the investment community is groping towards a more sophisticated approach to the analysis of corporate financing. Oddly enough, the main impetus in this direction has come from continental analysts. Habitually, and with good reason, they distrust their companies' profit and loss statements, so they have concentrated on assessing balance-sheet changes as some sort of guide to what profits really are. Over here the emphasis has shifted, so that analysts are mainly interested in how companies are deploying their resources, and where they get those resources from. You may well see this referred to as the analysis of sources and uses of funds, instead of, as here, a financing table. Some companies, notably Shell or Unilever, provide tables of their own, but as a rule you must be prepared to construct them painstakingly yourself. This in itself is enough to explain why they are not in widespread use.

The obvious thing to do is to produce some such table for Grand Metropolitan Hotels, to see if it adds anything to the gleanings from our earlier discussion. This table appears on the opposite page. For the benefit of would-be professionals it should be stressed right away that this format is considerably simplified, compared with the Platonic ideal of a financing table as envisaged by the Society of Investment Analysts. Our version is merely to illustrate the principles involved.

Some of the things this table tells us we already know, notably the vast scale of total operating investment compared to cash flow. But it also brings into much clearer perspective the means by which this investment was financed. If you look under the section headed External Changes on the financing side of the table you will see that, in addition to regular infusions of share and loan capital, in three out of the four years there was an acquisition issue. There were also large increases in minority interests probably (though admittedly not necessarily) associated with a policy of buying into other firms. To judge by the surpluses – and deficits – on the sale of fixed assets, the board does not flinch over rationalizing the properties it has acquired. On the other side of the table, the run down in stocks in 1967 and 1968 suggests the same story. But so far, at least, these fruits of internal pruning are quite inadequate to meet the company's investment ambitions.

To sum up, therefore, this financing table does, in a particularly blatant way, the thing which financing tables are best able to do. It enables you to infer the company's liquidity, or rather the lack of it. More, its very pattern carries strong overtones about the company's investment style. With such a table before them shareholders need not be surprised at the record capital spending plans for 1969 and after.

Gearing

The last main item in a company's balance sheet which needs analysis is the capital structure. This determines the distribution of income among the owners of the different classes of capital, and therefore has an important bearing on share values. You may remember from the chapter on fixed-interest stocks that the income and capital entitlements of different classes of stock – loan capital, preference and ordinary capital – can be calculated from a company's balance sheet. To

Financing Table for Grand Metropolitan Hotels, 1965–68

£000

	1965	1966	1967	1968
Income Finance				
Retained profits	860	693	564	932
Depreciation	142	296	397	311
Cash flow	1,002	989	961	1,243
Internal Changes				
Increase in tax & dividends due	−26	−124	546	1,083
Drawing on (addition to) net cash	742	2,931	−1,966	−1,046
Surplus (deficit) on sale of fixed assets	2	25	−419	−52
Other	—	257	−36	66
	718	3,089	−1,875	51
External Changes				
Fixed-interest issue	3,405	265	1,602	83
Equity issue	—	—	—	5,310
Acquisition issue	—	1,938	475	699
Changes in minority interests	999	−10	918	1,645
Total Financing	6,124	6,271	2,081	9,031

	1965	1966	1967	1968
Acquisition of Fixed Assets				
Physical assets	4,102	4,103	2,247	10,244
Trade investments	1,285	853	1,284	460
Intangibles	768	421	1,871	1,286
	6,155	5,377	2,834	9,418
Changes in Other Trading Assets				
Stocks	105	1,204	−256	−352
Trade debtors	364	826	914	1,896
	469	2,030	658	1,544
Less creditors	−500	−1,136	−1,411	−1,931
	−31	894	−753	−387
Total Operating Investment	6,124	6,271	2,081	9,031

Notes: Surpluses arising from revaluations of fixed assets have been excluded.

refresh your memory, we saw that Fortes' priority percentages for income were as follows:

	Net amount required for interest and dividends, £000	Priority, %
5¾% debenture	132	0–8
7¼% debenture	83	8–13
7% preference	105	13–19
7% second preference 4½% preference	199	19–31
Ordinary A Ordinary B Ordinary	625	31–68
Undistributed	550	68–100
Total	1,694	

Now the conventional way of expressing cover for an ordinary dividend would be to say that after meeting fixed-interest commitments there was £1,175,000 available for ordinary dividends (that is the sum of the ordinary dividend of £625,000 and the undistributed profit of £550,000). And if you divide the amount available by the actual payment $\frac{(1,175,000)}{(625,000)}$ you get 1·88 times cover.

Now look back at the priority percentages. You will see that interest and dividends together, including the payment on the ordinary, take the first 68% of total profits. In other words, if total earnings fell by little more than a third the ordinary dividend would be uncovered. This is rather less reassuring than the 88% margin shown by the other method.

The structure of issued capital is referred to as a company's gearing (you may also come across the American term for the same thing, which is leverage). If a company has a relatively heavy load of prior charge capital – debentures, loan stocks or preference shares – it is called highly geared. If it has nothing but ordinary shares it is ungeared. The effect of the difference can be seen most strikingly from a comparison between two companies in the same industry. So let us look at two newspaper and publishing groups – Associated Newspapers, owners of the *Daily Mail*, the *Evening News* and a string of regional papers, and The Thomson Organization, whose main properties include *The Times* and the *Sunday Times*.

The breakdown of some newspaper profits 1967/68

	Associated News		Thomson Organization	
	£000	%	£000	%
Net profits plus net interest	2,689	100	4,291	100
Loan and bank interest (net)	4	—	752	18
Minority interests	59	2	471	11
Preference dividends	67	3	1,335	31
Earned for ordinary	2,557	95	1,733	40

As you can see, the pattern is completely different. In Associated Newspapers' case interest, minorities and preference dividends take only about 5% between them, so 95% of the profits we started with work their way through to ordinary shareholders. In Thomson's case payments on prior charge capital and minorities take a full 60% of profits. By the time we reach ordinary earnings only 40% of our original profits still remain. In fact, had not the group's parent, Thomson Scottish Associates, waived its right to dividends worth over £1 million, profits would not have covered the declared dividend.

The full impact of gearing becomes clear if one then assumes that profits are going to go up or down. The table on the opposite page is worked out on just that assumption – it allows for a rise, and then a fall, of 25% on profits at the top level. Apart from that, everything remains unchanged.

Here Associated News' ordinary earnings rise or fall more or less in line with the overall change in profits, but Thomson's move $2\frac{1}{2}$ times as much. In other words, highly geared companies are fine when prospects are bright, but extremely vulnerable to a setback. Low-geared or ungeared companies are better defensively, but not so exciting when profits get moving.

There is more to the concept of gearing than appears from such conventional balance-sheet analysis. In a sense depreciation is a fairly inflexible charge on profits, which cannot be avoided or glossed over if a company has a bad patch. Also, if you come to think of it the cost of developing a business, or even simply maintaining its position, can effectively pre-empt a first slice of profits in the eyes of management. Development in this sense is a blanket word which can cover basic research, product improvement or even advertising.

In this context further study of Thomson's 1967 report and accounts is illuminating. It is explained in the notes to the accounts that treatment of net expenditure on development of new projects has been reviewed in the light of their expected

Hypothetical Changes in Newspaper Profits 1967/68
Assuming 25% Rise

| | Associated News | | Thomson Organization | |
	£,000	%	£,000	%
Net profits plus net interest	3,361	100	5,364	100
Loan and bank interest (net)	4	—	752	14
Minority interests	59	2	471	9
Preference dividends	67	2	1,335	25
Earned for ordinary	3,231	96	2,806	52
Change % in earnings	+26		+62	

Assuming 25% Fall

| | Associated News | | Thomson Organization | |
	£,000	%	£,000	%
Net profits plus net interest	2,017	100	3,218	100
Loan and bank interest (net)	4	—	752	23
Minority interests	59	3	471	15
Preference dividends	67	3	1,335	41
Earned for ordinary	1,887	94	660	21
Change % in earnings	−26		−62	

Note: Minority interests would probably change in practice, although not in line with overall profit changes. They are left unaltered here for simplicity's sake.

future profitability. Whereas expenditure of this nature had previously been written off against profits when incurred, in 1967 certain new expedients were resorted to. Some £314,000 spent on Thomson Directories was carried forward as work in progress, another £462,000 on new evening papers and so on was capitalized as copyrights, and no less than £892,000 spent on *The Times* was met by a transfer from capital reserves. Taken together, these items tot up to £1,668,000, and if they had been taken off pre-tax profits of £6·15 million, as in earlier years, they would have left a nasty hole.

Now there is nothing phoney about this. It is all down in

black and white, accredited by Thomson's prestigious auditors, Price, Waterhouse & Co. And there is a perfectly respectable argument that a company should show the basic profitability of its existing business, without confusing investors with the capital costs of future developments. However, it does emphasize that the quality of Thomson's profits is very different from the quality of Associated Newspapers' profits. It would be exceedingly glib to say that they should be capitalized at the same sort of rate merely because they are both predominantly in the newspaper game. Thomson *may* have the better prospects. Certainly a high rate of capital formation provides scope for profit increases, given that the management's commercial judgement was correct. Against that, a mistake would prove extremely costly, both in profits' and assets' terms. In particular, the group could run into much more severe liquidity problems than you might imagine from a quick glance at the balance sheet. Retained earnings are not available for capital spending; they have been largely spent already.

Of course, it is not only investors who know about gearing. Finance directors are aware of its significance, increasingly so since the introduction of corporation tax in the 1965 Finance Act. The immediate effect of this measure was to make financing by debentures and loan stocks much cheaper than issues of preference or ordinary shares. Not unnaturally, therefore, there has been a flood of loan capital issues (although the average gearing of British companies is still probably not much more than 12%). Gearing up has also proved a powerful force in the urge to merge. It is not difficult, in a takeover, to devise a suitable mixture of ordinary shares and loan capital which will give shareholders a high gross income without biting too deep into profit retentions. The loser is the Inland Revenue, but that institution, however worthy, has few partisans in the investing community. The difficulty for takeover strategists, particularly in the newly fashionable conglomerate groups of diverse business, is to maintain a properly balanced capital structure. However rude you may feel about the declining value of pound notes, the Government does not have a monopoly in the issue of overvalued paper.

CHAPTER TEN

The Convertible Compromise

PERHAPS THERE is something about convertibles which appeals to the British taste for a cautious flutter. These hybrid issues are a blend of fixed interest and equity – in short, a compromise between income-cum-security, on the one hand, and growth potential, on the other. As so often with compromises, the income, the security and the growth potential are usually a bit watered down compared with more straightforward alternatives. Nevertheless, convertibles have become popular enough to bulk significantly on the investment scene.

With most of the early convertibles, the fixed-interest ingredient was the dominant part of the cocktail. Typically, they were debentures or loan stocks with fifteen- to twenty-five-year lives, with coupons much the same as they would have been if they were normal fixed-interest issues. On top of this, they offered holders the right to convert into a pre-arranged number of shares at certain specified times. As a rule the period of conversion was three to five years ahead, and the prices at which one could convert could well be as much as 20% or more above the ruling price of the equity. Very frequently the terms of conversion deteriorated over time. If one was entitled to exchange £100 of stock into, say, 36 shares in the first year the entitlement could easily have fallen to 32 shares or even 30 a couple of years later. If for any reason the stock was not converted it simply became an ordinary loan issue after the last conversion date was past.

All this meant that the emphasis was on issuing a convertible as a temporary expedient. Company finance directors wanted holders to convert as quickly as possible, no doubt because the company's flexibility over future borrowing would be restricted until it was cleared up.

There is still a fair number of this type of convertible around, and no doubt it often does make sense, particularly for smaller companies, to regard a convertible as a sort of bridging loan while the earnings from a new project build up. However, there has been a marked change of emphasis in the majority of convertibles. Most of them have become much more closely tied to their equities, rather than to fixed-interest rates. One obvious reason for this is because interest rates have become so high. However, corporation tax has probably had more to do with it. This is because loan interest – and convertibles almost invariably are loans – can be deducted before taxable profits are struck. Dividends on ordinary share capital, on the other hand, can be paid only out of taxed earnings. So if a company is contemplating a rights issue it can often be cheaper to issue a convertible instead – cheaper, that is, in the sense that companies can retain more of their profits for every pound distributed to their shareholders.

Of course, the greater emphasis on the equity connection does mean that more care has to be taken to make sure that the conversion option is exercised. A 5% yield on a company's convertible, which is by no means a rarity these days, might well look attractive besides a 2% yield on its equity. But it would show up in a very different light if the conversion option lapsed, and the stock had to stand up in a world where the yields on loan capital were about twice as much. For this reason the conversion terms and timespan of these issues are generally very much less rigorous than on old-style convertibles. In particular, one often finds, as in America, a very long conversion period. Over there it is customary for it to last the entire life of the stock (though usually with some provision to allow the company to enforce early conversion, provided the shareholder does not lose by it). In such circumstances it is scarcely unfair to dub these stocks deferred equities.

At this stage let us take an actual example, and go through the necessary figurework associated with convertibles. Guest, Keen and Nettlefolds, the giant engineering concern, has in issue at the present time £3,450,363 of 6% convertible unsecured loan stock 1988/93. Holders are able to convert all or part of their stock on May 31st in each of the years between

1971 and 1975. The terms on which they can convert remain the same throughout the life of the conversion option – that is, each £100 of stock can be converted into 22·22 ordinary shares. After that, if the stock has not been converted, it reverts to being a straightforward loan capital issue.

As a convertible carries with it the right to exchange the stock for ordinary shares, clearly one can calculate the equivalent price per share after conversion by dividing the price of the convertible by the number of shares you will be allotted. As convertibles are usually quoted in pounds and shares in shillings, you will naturally have to multiply the convertible price by twenty to get the calculation on all fours. For instance, with the Guest, Keen 6% stock, taking the convertible at par, you can divide £100 by the share entitlement as follows:

$$\frac{100 \times 20}{22 \cdot 22} = 90s.$$

If the price of the ordinary shares was 75s. you could then work out how much extra you would be paying if you bought the convertible instead of the ordinary. In this example 90s. is 20% more than 75s. This is known as the conversion premium, and you might think that it looks unreasonably high. But you should remember that one of the things you are buying is time. To get this into clear perspective, imagine that you were thinking of buying this stock in November 1968. You had a $2\frac{1}{2}$-year run until the first conversion date and a $6\frac{1}{2}$-year run to the last.

The conversion premium per year would therefore be $\frac{20}{2 \cdot 5}$ or

8% till the first conversion date and $\frac{20}{6 \cdot 5}$ or 3·1% till the last. Put this way it looks much more reasonable.

In addition, of course, you would be buying extra income. As a rough measure, the difference in the yields at the prices quoted above is 2·9% – 6% on the convertible at par and 3·1% on the ordinary, taking the dividend at 2s. 9·6d., or 14%. You can get a more accurate idea of what this means over time by using the following formula:

The additional income =

(Conversion coupon × Number of years to conversion × 20)

minus

(Ordinary dividend × Number of years to conversion)

(× Number of shares received on conversion)

With the Guest, Keen dividend equal to 2s. 9·6d. per share, the income gained was therefore (6 × 20 × 2½) — (2s. 9·6d. × 2½ × 22·22) or 144s. 6d. per £100 stock till the first conversion date and (6 × 20 × 6½) — (2s. 9·6d. × 6½ × 22·22) or 335s. 6d. per £100 stock till the last. You can make the calculation more sophisticated still if you allow for possible increases in the Guest, Keen dividend while you are holding the convertible, whose rate of interest does not change.

Following up the sums a stage further, suppose now that the price of the convertible was to rise – say to 108. You could work out the new conversion price in exactly the same way, that is $\frac{108 \times 20}{22 \cdot 22} = 97s$. Assuming the ordinary were still 75s. (in practice, they would probably have risen somewhat), the conversion premium would be 29·3% or 4½% per annum to the last conversion date (the gain in income is not affected by price movements).

One other alteration in the calculation would occur if there was a scrip issue on the ordinary while the convertible was still outstanding. What happens is that the conversion terms are amended in line with the terms of the issue – for instance, if Guest, Keen had a one-for-three scrip issue the share entitlement would be increased by a third to 29·63 at the first conversion date and so on. The conversion price and ordinary price would be adjusted down in the same proportion, so the conversion premium would remain unchanged.

This Guest, Keen issue is no more than a representative one, and there are plenty of variations in the terms available to investors. In each case you need to study the provisions carefully so you know what your rights, as a stockholder, would be. One of the types which is probably best avoided is the partly convertible stock; experience suggests that the rump left after conversion has taken place is pretty friendless. On the other hand, one can expect growing interest in stocks where the carrot comes in the shape of warrants or an option to subscribe for ordinary shares at a favourable price. An idea with a more uncertain future is the convertible whose conversion terms actually *improve* over time. This is intended to keep investors in the stock, rather than converting it, to save corporation tax. In practice, they may tend to hold back the price of the equity, which would scarcely be popular.

Having checked on the background of a convertible, how should you set about a sober valuation of it? For old-style convertibles, with coupons reasonably close to the rate of interest, the best thing to do is to split it up into its constituent parts and assess it first as a fixed-interest stock, and secondly, as an equity. You start by deciding what its price would be if it was not convertible. You can refer to a similar stock with the same coupon and roughly equivalent life. If the parellel stock is 97 and the convertible is 105 you can then say that it is standing about 8% higher because it is convertible. In other words, the cost of the option to convert is 8%.

You can get some idea of the current value of this option by checking the difference between the conversion price and the existing price of the ordinary shares. Obviously if there is little difference between them it is worth paying more for the option to convert. But if the gap is wide, so the option may never be worth exercising, the option cost is likely to be much less. Generally speaking, a conversion premium of 20% or over should be valued, in terms of option cost, at well under 10%.

New-style convertibles, whose coupons have been fixed in relation to the underlying equity yield, have little in the way of a safety net in the event of their not being converted. Logically, therefore, they ought to be quoted at levels where their conversion equivalents are the same as the price of the ordinary shares, after allowing for the net difference in the yields, as explained above. Occasionally, though, one finds the convertible lower, so that it offers a cheap way into the equity. The usual reason for this is simply a lack of marketability, and it is something to watch out for in smallish issues – say less than £2½ million.

Although convertible buying can be pretty indiscriminate, there are some special situations where convertibles will be particularly appropriate. Companies in notably cyclical industries, like primary commodities, are one example; smallish concerns which are expanding fast are another. In both these instances the outlook for the equity can be awkward to assess. With overseas stocks it may also be worth paying a conversion premium. It is always harder to supervise investments properly at a distance, and the conversion premium is in some sense an insurance against unexpected developments. It is also fair to say there is a substantial requirement from investors who have a genuine reason for buying these stocks. Not only are they useful yield sweeteners for the income conscious. In many trust portfolios the income and capital belong to different individuals, and a convertible may offer a proper solution to the conflict of their interests. Again, under the Trustee Investment Act convertibles may be included in the narrower range of stocks, that is, in the fixed-interest half of a trust's portfolio. Although the trustees would not be allowed to retain these stocks in the narrower range once they had been converted (they could, of course, be transferred to the wider range if there was room for them) they nevertheless increase, short term, the equity content of a list. Whatever the intentions of the legislators, there are plenty of instances where this is appropriate trustee behaviour.

To sum up, then, there is no doubt that convertibles are here to stay. Not only do they fill a worthwhile niche in the array of goods that stock exchanges have to offer. In a world where the Government seeks to pre-empt the market for true fixed-interest securities, by exempting its own stocks from a capital gains tax which has to be paid on everyone else's, it may well become impossible for companies to issue prior-charge capital without some sort of equity garnishing. In such circumstances it will be all the more important to remember that these issues are not invariably equity alternatives. So far the number of convertibles which have not proved worth converting has been reasonably small. Sooner or later, however, we must expect a sharp, uncomfortable reminder of the risks involved.

CHAPTER ELEVEN

Building A Portfolio

HOWEVER EXPERT you may become at assessing individual equities, fixed-interest stocks or convertibles, it is not enough to rush your money into a few likely looking holdings, and just hope for the best. You need an overall strategy of attack. Unfortunately, it is not possible for us to set down a simple blueprint for you to follow, because so much depends on your personal circumstances. What we can do is discuss alternative approaches and so help clarify your mind about your own problems.

For most people with money to invest the crucial factor in forward planning is time. A couple in their late fifties may want to retire to Mediterranean warmth in four years' time. Another couple in their twenties with a young family to look after may want to feel confident they can meet their bills at the end of the month. Obviously their investment requirements are vastly different. The older couple should take steps to be sure that the capital for a new home will be there when they need it (in practice, this may well mean covering part of the anticipated cost with a government stock maturing at the right moment). The younger couple should balance their immediate requirements against their hopes for the future. In other words, the economically ideal policy of investing for a maximum real return must be adapted to take account of your living situation.

It is not often that people want a definite amount of money at some specified point in the future. More usually they find they must modify a straightforward equity investment policy to take account of income requirements. If so, it is nearly always wrong to argue that you need, say, $5\frac{1}{2}\%$ on your money, and therefore you are going to buy nothing but shares which yield $5\frac{1}{2}\%$. The resulting portfolio will probably look humdrum at best, and at worst downright dangerous. It is more sensible to adapt your approach so that at least part of your fund is aimed at capital growth.

There are two alternative ways of doing this. One way is to tuck part of the money away into high-yielding fixed-interest stocks and put the rest of it into equities. For example, suppose you had just received a legacy of £10,000 and wanted it to produce an income of £600 a year before tax. Nowadays you can get 10% on good-quality debentures or loan stocks, so if you put £3,000 into them that would secure just half the income (£300) with an outlay of only 30% of the capital. With the remaining £7,000 capital you would only have to aim for an average yield of 4¼%. Saving 1¾ points of yield may not seem dramatic, but in practice it is much easier to pick a growth portfolio with yields ranging from 3 to 5% than one with a range of yields from 5 to 7%. Another advantage of accepting a lower starting yield on the equities is that you give yourself a much better chance of future increases in dividends.

The other possibility is to put all the money into equities and make up the difference by drawing on capital. This suggestion can be counted on to draw a gasp of horror from some quarters, but a little figuring shows that it is not all that flighty. Suppose you aim for the average market return on your equities – about 4% as we write. On £10,000 the return is £400 gross or, for a standard taxpayer, £235 net. The comparable net equivalent of a gross income of £600 is £352 10s. 0d. so the annual withdrawal of capital would have to be £117 10s. 0d. This works out at 1·175%, requiring something like 1·4% before capital-gains tax. The market often moves by more than that in a single day, so it is certainly not an unwarrantable gamble to cut back income by two points in an effort to build up your capital by more than 1·4% a year. In practice, to avoid selling shares you have bought a short time before, you should put £235 of your legacy into a building society, to tide over the income shortfall for the first two years.

This is a policy that needs some sophistication on your part. It is rare indeed for equity portfolios to go up consistently year after year, so you must be prepared for times when everything seems to be going wrong – shares slipping, income lower than it might be and perhaps even sales on a falling market to meet living expenses. We can only say that, in recent years, being in on the booms has far outweighed the disadvantages of being caught in the slumps as well.

Given that you are going to have a worthwhile proportion of your fund in equities, how should you set about the delicate business of portfolio construction? Everyone pays lip service to two highly important factors – spread and timing – but in practice one often finds them overstressed.

The point of spread is to diversify one's risk, but people tend to forget how few shares are needed to provide proper protection. It has been calculated in America that 90% of the benefits of diversification can be secured with fifteen shares. For most private portfolios, therefore, one can set an upper limit of twenty shares; after that you will find yourself including shares which are less intrinsically desirable. This works out at about 5–6% of the portfolio in each share. You should not be afraid to let single units go up to about 10%, particularly if they have got there by appreciation. What you should not permit is small fragments. They need watching, just as larger holdings do, but even if they are successful they have practically no impact on the total value of the list. Too many investors fritter away their resources in an over-extended train of tiny holdings.

Industrially, it is a mistake to have something in everything, particularly in a slow-growth country like Britain. That is bound to produce mediocre results. You should, however, think of balance between different kinds of risk. Day-to-day consumption shares – food, beer, stores – provide stability, interspersed with bright spots. In growth areas which are more volatile, like chemicals, building, electrical and electronics, motors or insurance, you should define your objectives precisely. It is necessary to disturb this sort of holding from time to time (e.g. at the time of writing in mid-1969 a blue chip like Royal Insurance has still not regained the peak it reached in 1962). With industries like machine tools, textiles, shipbuilding and metals you can be more or less sure of wide price fluctuations.

Once you go in for any of them, you cannot afford to be caught napping.

Generally speaking, it is wrong to imagine that several shares in the same industry provide proper spread. Obviously your risk is less concentrated than it would be if all the money were in one share. But a universal setback in one sector of the market is much more common than the collapse of a single share in an otherwise prosperous industry. In any case, it is lazy to cover yourself by buying two directly competitive shares. One of them, surely, is better than the other. You should find out which, and back your judgement..

A sprinkling of overseas shares has obvious attractions as a hedge against political or economic setbacks at home. There are two drawbacks, however. If you want to invest outside the sterling area you have to pay a premium for the privilege of buying overseas currency. One might have hoped this burden would ease after devaluation. In fact, it has got worse; the premium has even been as high as 50%. The position has been aggravated by the need to give up one-quarter of the premium to the Bank of England whenever one sells a non-sterling share. This makes switching prohibitive. It also helps to explain the growing popularity of the one major overseas investment market – politically stable and economically progressive Australia – which is inside the sterling area.

The other drawback is more intractable. This is the difficulty of managing investments at long range; locals inevitably have the edge over outsiders. For some reason, even seasoned experts seem to lose their heads when they go abroad; they are apt to move in just when the market's peak is near. Probably the most sensible answer to both these problems is to invest in an offshore fund. These funds, which are generally run by nationals of the country in which the money is actually being invested, are called offshore because they are based in one of the well-known tax havens, usually in Luxembourg or the Caribbean. Although you have to pay the overseas currency premium to get in, and although you suffer from the give-up and from capital gains tax when you get out, the fund itself escapes both. The professionals managing the investments can wheel and deal to their hearts' content, and you can sit back and watch it happen. There are very few distinguishing features to help you choose one offshore fund from another, but your broker probably has connections with one or two of them, and should be able to advise you.

Many investors who dislike paying the overseas currency premium prefer to buy British companies with trading activities abroad, like Shell or British American Tobacco (or for that matter, some of the big South African mining finance houses). For a diversified stake in North America you can also often rely on some of the better Scottish investment trusts.

Jobbing backwards is always a bad habit, but it is particularly pernicious when it puts timing into false perspective. People find themselves carried away with the idea that if you plunge into the market with every penny at Point A, and then sell out completely at Point B, you will achieve spectacularly good results. Looking backwards on the charts of share prices it is easy indeed to see where Points A and B are. But peering forward into the future it is not easy, and you might as well get used to realizing that you are not going to be able to do it.

The point to keep firmly in mind is that in the long run you can only make money by holding shares. You don't see any Fifth Avenue mansions built by bears, as one Wall Street dealer once sagely remarked. The implication is that some at least of the shares you buy should be worth hanging on to, even when prospects in general are grey. If you think the market is looking toppy (to use an expression beloved by brokers) by all means take profits on some of your shares or, better still, cut losses on your failures. But as a general, not-counting-1929, rule you ought seldom to be more than about 30% disinvested.

The point will perhaps become clearer if you imagine that you have made a mistake. If your well-chosen, growth-orientated portfolio gets caught in the downdraught of a bear market, nevertheless, in the fullness of time, it will revive in step with the growth in the economy. But if you sell out in the expectation of a fall which never occurs you will simply have to buy your way in again when prices are higher. And loss of profit through not being invested when markets are moving up is a serious matter. You cannot afford to ignore it simply because it does not show up in your books.

So timing should be a negative factor in your overall market strategy. You should never get into the position where you have to commit yourself to a major decision. This is why one so often hears of people coming fresh to the market with a cash legacy or the proceeds of the sale of their business and investing it all at the wrong moment. Admittedly it is a very human reaction, when one is faced with an unfamiliar problem, to want to tackle it right away and get back to normal. In practice, however, an unhurried approach is almost always more successful. It is not a bad idea to invest the same amount of money at regular intervals over a period of perhaps a year or even more. Although you will not hit the bottom like this, you will not risk committing all your capital at the top either. But the best way is to collect a portfolio gradually whenever a really attractive opportunity crops up.

All this is not to deny that timing is of the greatest importance in each separate decision. More investors come to grief by buying good shares at the wrong price than from any other cause – usually, one suspects, because they are too easily carried away by their own enthusiasm. It is a useful discipline to formulate profit targets and to estimate what earnings per share could be in, say, a year or two's time. The balance-sheet analysis which we were looking at in earlier chapters should help you to assess the quality of the business you are investing in. Furthermore, however confident you may be about the profits prospect of the shares you are buying, you need to be dispassionate about checking relative prices to see you are getting good value for money. Other people may know about those future profits too, so that the share price discounts them already.

Fortunately there are a fair number of useful guides to help you on your way. The *Financial Times*, for example, publishes price indices of forty-odd different market sectors, together with estimated dividend yields and price/earnings ratios for that sector. Remember, if your chosen share has

got above or below average statistics that does not mean it is
cheap or dear without any further argument. It is more a
signal for you to investigate why it is out of line.

Perhaps more helpful, for people who are prepared to do
quite a lot of investment homework, are the charts of the
Financial Times market sector indices. Below you can trace
two years in the life of the composite insurance sector, not
only in its own right but also as a ratio of the market as a
whole. This ratio line deserves special study, because it can
undermine complacency about a share that is simply jogging
along. For example, you might have imagined that your in-
surances were doing all right during 1968 because they were a
wee bit up on the previous year. Relatively, though, they were
down against the market by something like a third – significant
loss of profit in a bull year. Fortunately these relative movements tend to persist, once they get properly established.
Prompt action will often get you out of a sector which is losing
impetus into another which is just getting up steam.

CHAPTER TWELVE

Chart Reading

INVESTMENT IS NOT, on the whole, a controversial subject, but charts are the exception. For some analysts they are indispensable, the most valuable weapons at their command. For others, no less expert, they are virtually beneath contempt. Yet the chartists' claim, if it could be proved true, would be worth anyone's attention. For they believe that by looking at a chart they can sometimes predict, with telling accuracy, how a share price is going to move.

At first sight this looks a remarkable assertion. A chart, after all, is nothing more than the record of past price movements – whether of a single share or a share index – plotted on a piece of graph paper. To predict the future from that would seem to need an astrologer, not an analyst. But there is one particularly powerful support for the chartists' case. The price is always the most up-to-date piece of information about a share. From moment to moment it indicates the point of balance between buyers and sellers, and over a period it indicates the relative pressures between them. As such it reflects the collective wisdom of the market – and remember the market includes the people most closely in touch with a company's affairs, like directors, trade customers, suppliers, and all their relations and friends. However carefully you may study the fundamentals of a company's position – its record, prospects, markets, finances – you will always be working with material which is slightly out of date. The chart alone can tell you what is happening now.

Chartists believe that in these records of price movements certain patterns keep cropping up again and again. With experience, they say, you can predict from these patterns what the next move is going to be. Over time they have built up a set of hypotheses – some of them commonsensical but others highly complex and artificial – to help them in their interpretations. Such methods, it is fair to claim, have produced notable successes. Still, the ratio of costly failures is also high, for the good reason that chart reading is treacherously difficult.

After this brief introduction, let us plunge straight in and look at a chart. The one on the following page represents six years in the life of ICI. You will see that the years are marked off along the bottom, and share prices up the side. The dark bars at the bottom represent the volume of transactions, a useful if not completely essential refinement.

First look very closely at the scale of prices. You will see that the figures do not move up in even steps, as you might expect, but at a decreasing pace. This is because the chart is plotted on a logarithmic scale, on which equal distances represent equal proportions. In other words, the distance from five shillings to ten is the same as from ten to twenty, not from ten to fifteen. The justification for this arrangement is that it is realistic. Share prices move geometrically, not arithmetically – the very regularity of the chart shows that. Besides, proportionate movements are the ones that matter. It is just as good to buy at 1s. 6d. and sell at 3s. as it is to buy at 40s. and sell at 80s., provided you invest the same amount of money.

This special graph paper can be bought if you go to the right stationers, but it is not always easy to find. If necessary you can make your own by marking off the vertical logarithmic scale against the figures on an ordinary slide rule. You must remember, though, that the horizontal scale is normal, with equal distances between each day, week, month or year. For that reason these graphs are called semi-logarithmic.

Most chartists take the middle market price of the shares they are following and join them together with a straight line (adjustments must, of course, be made for changes arising from scrip and rights issues). Others prefer to mark both the top and the bottom of the price range, so they get a series of vertical bars, rather like the volume indicator at the bottom of the ICI chart. For example, if a share moved between 15s. and 16s. 3d. on a single day bar chartists would mark an upright line which was, so to speak, 1s. 3d. long. This method increases the amount of information available, but it also makes it harder to

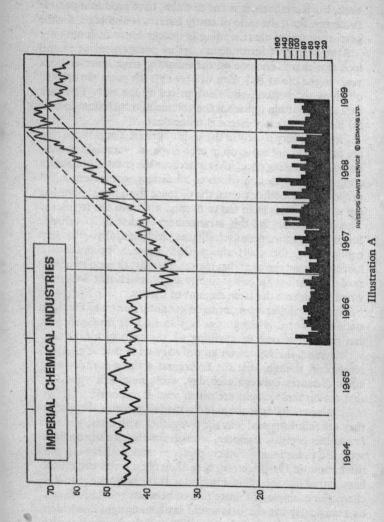

IMPERIAL CHEMICAL INDUSTRIES

INVESTORS CHARTS SERVICE © BEDMANS LTD.

Illustration A

keep a set of charts up to date. Since charts are intended to produce a clear signal that you can act on, there is a lot to be said for stripping down the detail to the essential minimum. For this reason weekly chart entries have a lot to commend them, even though they lack the finer nuances of daily fluctuations.

We mentioned earlier the chartists' creed about patterns which keep appearing. So before looking in detail at the lessons to be learned from a chart it would be as well to consider what principal patterns are involved.

Trend Lines. Stock markets, like the economic events which they reflect, tend to move in cycles. Starting at the beginning of an upswing, share prices first move upwards at the hint of improving economic conditions. Before long the improvement shows up in better company earnings – and share prices respond by gaining still more ground. Finally, buyers begin to discount the future too hopefully, and reaction inevitably sets in.

This is the classic bull market pattern. On the way down it is mirrored, on a smaller scale, by bear developments. Over-optimism gives way to caution, which in due course may be reinforced by setbacks in company earnings. Eventually, pessimism is driven to unrealistic lengths, and the stage is set for a new bull market.

This picture of a market cycle is, of course, grossly over-simplified. Primary trends, both up and down, are interrupted by smaller but significant movements in the opposite direction. The problem is to assess the importance of secondary reactions when they are actually going on. The vital thing you need to know is whether a break in a trend is temporary or final.

Chartists like to measure trends by joining the peaks or troughs as they appear on a chart. If you look back at the ICI chart you will see the trend channel marked over the bullish years 1967 and 1968. In this case it was the line joining the peaks that was most clear cut, but the parallel line running underneath the troughs was perhaps, in the end, more significant. The price kept quite closely to this line for a matter of months in the winter of 1968. When it broke down from

this level in February 1969 that was the end of the two-year
run.

Resistance Levels. If you come to think of it, the peaks and
troughs on this chart represent levels of resistance. At the top
they show where sellers come into the market in enough force

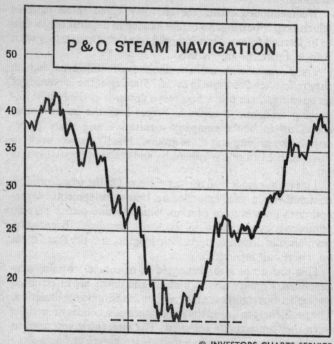

© INVESTORS CHARTS SERVICE

Illustration B: P. & O. Double-bottoming

to reverse its upward progress; at the bottom they show where
buyers are sufficiently attracted to stop a further fall. Sometimes these reactions occur twice, or even more, at the same
point. You then get one of the most indicative of all patterns,
the *double top* or *double bottom*. Although it is difficult to say
how far a share will react away from one of these double

patterns, you can be pretty certain it will start going, even if the movement is not followed through. P & O's behaviour in our chart is a clearcut example of a double bottom.

Two further refinements of resistance levels are worth noting at this stage. Sometimes a *line* occurs, which is when there is resistance to both a rise and a fall within fairly narrow limits. Sometimes the resistance levels are being squeezed slowly together to give a *triangle* effect. There is no basic difference between lines and triangles – both suggest indeci-

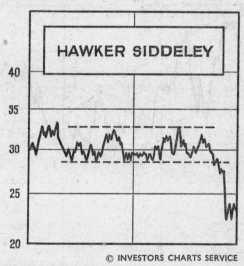

© INVESTORS CHARTS SERVICE

Illustration C: Hawker breaking down from a line

sion. What matters is the way in which the patterns are broken. If a price breaks strongly free, as though it were sweeping aside all resistance, you can be reasonably happy that a new trend – upwards or downwards – has been established. And the longer the line or triangle has taken to form, the more confident you can feel about your interpretation. In the illustration you can see how Hawker Siddeley broke downwards from a line and how Hoover rode upwards from a triangle.

Equipped with these few basic weapons from the chartists' armoury we can now tackle a chart – for example, British Oxygen (illustration E) shown on page 114. The most striking thing about the chart is the way these shares kept surging up-

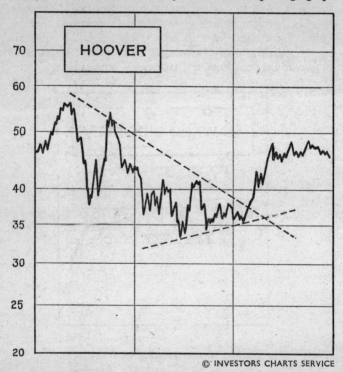

Illustration D: Hoover breaking up from a triangle

wards at the same percentage rate for over three years – from February 1958 to May 1961. This in itself is partial justification for chartism. For if share prices can form such pronounced, well-defined patterns it must sometimes be possible to spot them emerging and act accordingly.

The first big test point for British Oxygen came in August

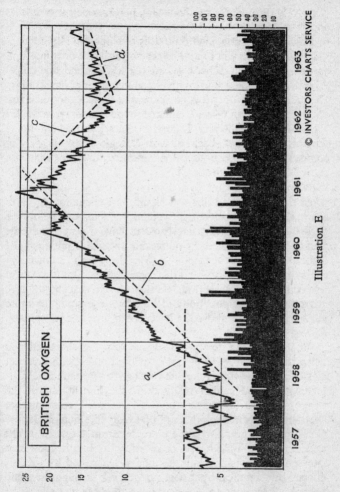

BRITISH OXYGEN

© INVESTORS CHARTS SERVICE

Illustration E

1958. That was when it equalled the peak of the previous summer, so there was a potential double top in the making. Looked at in retrospect, a fair amount of fluttering is evident at this crucial stage (*a*), but eventually the shares broke decisively through the previous high point. A bull market was in the making.

Having got in at a good time (it is too much to ask of charts that they will get you in at the very bottom), the next question is when to get out. This is where the lower trend line helps. You draw a straight line (*b*) just touching, but not penetrating, the various temporary low points on the chart. If you like you can try drawing an upper trend line in the same way, as we did for the Imperial Chemical Industries chart, but it seldom fits as comfortably as that. Besides, with a single share on a rising trend, there is little practical significance, because what you want to know is when to sell.

As you see, the time to sell came in July or August 1961, when the lower trend line was significantly penetrated. (Here again, the system does not get you out till some way below the peak the previous May, but you still have a very handsome profit.) What is particularly noticeable about this selling signal is the abrupt fall to the trend line (May/June 1961) followed by a faint-hearted recovery, and then penetration. This is a typical reversal pattern. Another, no less typical, sign that should have alerted you to the possibility of a fall was the gradually more violent movements above the lower trend line, and subsequent relapse on to it.

What about the downward phase? Can the chart tell you when that is ending? This time it is the upper trend line that matters, because this is the one that has to be penetrated. Unfortunately, you cannot really draw the line at all till the temporary peak (*c*) appears in April 1962. There is another short-lived rally in September of that year, and then just before Christmas, the graph makes a more determined assault on the trend line. This time it goes confidently through it. However, later on it slips back again, as though exhausted by its own efforts. But significantly it does not go back through the trend line; it is beginning to look as though the bear phase is over.

That is not to say that you should rush in forthwith and buy. It is unlikely, in these circumstances, that an enthusiastically strong uptrend will develop immediately. As it happens, British Oxygen actually came up with a fair show of indecision.

Between November 1962 and August 1963 it made a line (*d*) indicating, if anything, an upward tendency, as the low points were on a gently rising trend.

This British Oxygen story gives you some idea, in fairly crude terms, of what can be done with charts. However, reacting to upper and lower trend lines does not always work, and chartists have kept on refining their techniques to try and find something more reliable. One variant is so-called *point-and-figure* charting, which works on the theory that ordinary time – days, weeks and so on – does not matter. The important fact in this system is the length of time necessary to complete a movement, and this is what is measured against the bottom of the chart. Mastering the basic techniques of point-and-figure is more complicated than with conventional charting, and cannot be discussed in so brief an introduction as this one. However, the recommended reading list at the end of this chapter includes references for people interested enough to dig deeper.

One refinement of straightforward charting is an attempt to break down the factors that influence the performance of a share price. The best known of these systems is the measurement of *relative strength*. What is charted here is the ratio of a share price to some index, either an index of all shares or of all shares in the same industry group. From this you can get an idea of how the share is performing in its own right, as opposed to its general (or particular) market context. Performance-conscious investors, who are not too inhibited by tax considerations, often use this technique for measuring industrial groups against the market average. As relative trends, once established, tend to persist, it can indicate whether their funds are in fashionable market sectors. Other ratios which have been much cited in the past are the so-called *confidence indicators* and *yield gaps*. Both of them measure the relative attractiveness of equities and gilt-edged. In recent years the near-total demoralization of the gilt market has undermined some of the value of these concepts. Yield gaps in particular were designed to tell one that something abnormal was happening, but nobody can say now what normality is. Whereas, ten years ago, City experts used to wonder whether the market could sustain a gap of only $\frac{1}{4}$% in favour of ordinary dividend yields, compared with the yield on Consols, nowadays a reverse yield gap of over 3%, between the yield on Consols and the average ordinary share *earnings* yield, arouses very little comment.

Most conventional chartists concentrate attention on critical points at the extreme ends of fluctuations. Statisticians, in so far as they interest themselves in these problems, do exactly the reverse. They like to establish trend lines or, in other words, to fit smooth curves to the centre of the fluctuations. In deference to such ideas, chartists often put in simple trend indicators like moving averages. The trouble here is to know what time period to take. A year's moving average is usually not responsive enough, while a ten-day moving average can prompt overmuch activity. Various ingenious adaptations have been thought up, such as using long-range data with extra weight on the latest information available. However, the fact remains that, by its nature, trend analysis will be helpless in the face of a major sea change in events. And even when it is useful, the profit potential it can produce is limited, simply because it is bound to follow the ups and downs of the market.

A great deal of chartist energy is devoted to trying to establish market turning-points, big and small. This is not surprising. Everyone is interested, and the rewards for success are considerable. Turning-points are also largely a question of sentiment (though some analysts believe there is a link between the performance of the equity market and the index of industrial production). And when it comes to sentiment, chartists are naturally in their element.

The main extra information, over and above the charts for the leading indexes, is the relative strength of buyers and sellers. London's lack of accurate indicators of a day's trading volume is, of course, a limiting factor. But many chartists keep records of the number of shares advancing and declining (the so-called advance/decline line) and of the ratio of new highs to new lows. The raw data is conveniently available day by day in the *Financial Times*, and the usual chart lore can be deployed for interpretation.

Enough has been said to indicate the paraphernalia of charting. Do the results justify the effort and the ballyhoo? As we shall see in the next chapter, there are formidable intellectual objections to charting, so that, for the time being at least, it must be something of an act of faith. Still some hints on living with charts are not out of place. At its most unpretentious a chart is a record of what has happened. And if it records a pattern so striking that it makes you think again, studying it will not have been a complete waste of time.

Undoubtedly the most important thing to unlearn, when you close any book about charts, is the idea that they bring easy profits. All discussions on charts highlight success stories; it is the only way to illustrate the techniques. In practice, the majority of charts you look at will give no clear indication of what to do. And coaxing them with elaborate theories can prove an expensive hobby. For most people their principal use will be as a check of decisions reached on other grounds. More precisely, they can often puncture an impulsive move to buy at the top, or sell near the bottom.

Finally, if your appetite is whetted by an early tasting of charts here is a list of books and articles to read, together with some suppliers of ready-made charts.

Articles and Books

'The Value of Charts for the Small Investor' by A. G. Ellinger (*Moodies' Investment Digest*, 1969, revised edition).

'An Introduction to Technical Analysis' by Edward W. Tabell and Anthony W. Tabell (*The Investment Analyst*, No. 6, Sept 1963).

'Can Technical Analysis Help?' by T. H. Stewart (*The Investment Analyst*, No. 8, May 1964).

'Some Aspects of Technical Analysis' by Peter Freeman (*The Investment Analyst*, No. 18, Oct 1967).

Technical Analysis of Stock Trends by Edwards and Magee (John Magee, Springfield, Mass.).

Suppliers of Charts

Bedmans Ltd, 10 Westbourne Terrace, Budleigh Salterton, Devon.

Investment Research, 36 Regent Street, Cambridge.

CHAPTER THIRTEEN

The Voice from the Ivory Tower

AMID THE claims and counter-claims of chartists and fundamentalists, other voices have started to make themselves heard, and the messages they bring are far from welcome. In academic centres, notably in America but also in Britain, economists and mathematicians have been investigating the behaviour of share prices, and have come up with disturbing conclusions. According to them there is no connection between today's price movements and yesterday's; so what will happen tomorrow is entirely random.

This so-called random-walk thesis depends on mathematical techniques too abstruse for most market men. It is even difficult to find a coherent explanation of the theory in ordinary language which lay investors can understand. Probably the best known in England is an article by Professor Eugene Fama, of the University of Chicago, which appeared in *The Investment Analyst* a few years back.

Fama's starting-point is that stock exchanges are good examples of efficient markets. By efficient, he means a market with large numbers of rational competitors, all of them in possession of important current information. These people, between them, ensure that the price of a share is a good estimate of its intrinsic value.

Of course, in an uncertain world nobody knows exactly what the intrinsic value of a share is. There is room for argument, and the competing actions of buyers and sellers will cause the share price to fluctuate around its intrinsic value. In the same way, if the intrinsic value of a share changes, for good business reasons, the instantaneous adjustment of the share price to take account of the new information will not be exact. It could be an over-reaction, or equally well an under-reaction. Furthermore, the time when the reaction takes place is another quite separate factor. Sometimes price movements anticipate events, sometimes they trail after them.

Taken together, this means that share prices move as though they had no memory – in other words, the past history of the share price cannot be used to predict the future. The business professors have run unnumbered statistical tests through their computers, with results which Fama calls consistent and impressive – and they uphold the random walk.

Now if all this is true the most obvious casualties are the chartists. The random-walk theory implies that the chances of a share following the trend line are exactly the same as the chances of a coin coming up heads or tails: fifty-fifty. It is, in fact, a standard chartist-baiting ploy by business professors to make up charts by tossing coins. If you go up for heads and down for tails you will quite probably turn out a significant-looking point-and-figure chart with all the trimmings.

The implications of random walk are not exactly comforting for fundamentalists either. Analysts are looking for discrepancies between actual share prices and true intrinsic values. Having found out all they can, and tested their knowledge in the light of experience, they plump for a buy or a sell. Given a small coterie of well-informed professionals operating in a market dominated by rule-of-thumb amateurs, this approach will work very nicely. But once the pros become so numerous they get the upper hand their efforts will cancel one another out. Shares will be too near their intrinsic value most of the time.

Naturally, the random-walk theorists have provoked fierce counter-attacks from interested parties. Those skilled in the techniques of equation-infighting should turn to the *Financial Analysts Journal,* a sort of craft union paper for investment professionals in the United States, for the current state of the game. Still, as far as we know, no chartist has taken up Professor Fama's challenge to have his predictions subjected to rigorous statistical testing. And if you have an urge for charting it would be as well to fall back on the dictum of Alec Ellinger, the doyen of British chartists, who simply says he invests better when he uses charts than when he does not.

As for the ranks of fundamentalists, they are in rather better shape after their statistical strafing. An economist working in a Minneapolis bank has found a strong correlation, over a ten-year period, between the rate of company earnings growth and the rate at which share prices rise. And a British firm of stockbrokers, Philips & Drew, have had some interesting experiences with their computer selection programme, which ranks shares according to relative cheapness or dearness. Their system attributes weights to various determinants of share prices – dividend yield, pay-out ratio, past and predicted earnings and dividends growth rates, and so on. For a bit, it did very well. Then, from about the time of the 1966 summer slump, the results deteriorated, though not, they claim, through a fault in the logic of the system. It was more a matter of building poor forecasts into the model. When the sums were reworked afterwards, with actual profits built in as though they were forecasts, the Index once more took a trouncing.

The difficulties of forecasting have been at the back of most fundamentalists' minds ever since Dr Ian Little, an Oxford don, launched an attack on conventional City attitudes about growth shares in an article called 'Higgledy Piggledy Growth'. He claimed to have found that the growth of earnings per share – a vital concept – was largely random. Both this original piece of work and the extended version, with a joint-author, which appeared in book form a few years later, have been criticized for their statistical approach. Still it was probably salutary for investment experts to have their cherished assumptions about good growth shares questioned. As for the more serious implication that there was nothing to choose between good and bad companies, so therefore the Stock Exchange could not be an effective mechanism for channelling capital into the most profitable enterprises, that was, apparently, a minor symptom of the English disease. The sums worked out differently in America.

All this wrangling about the overall workings of the Stock Exchange has, of course, been made possible by the number-crunching appetites of the computer fraternity. Those machines have made a big impact on City life. To begin with,

they were used for obvious chores, much as they are elsewhere
in commerce, such as preparing contract notes, posting ledgers,
churning out valuations and so on. Some firms then extended
the service to cover information retrieval. It is elementary to
programme a computer to list shares with a combination of
required characteristics – e.g. every machine-tool company on
a p/e ratio of under 13 times which has not cut its dividend in
the past ten years. However, Wall Street experience suggests
there is a lowish limit on what people are prepared to pay for
this sort of capability. It may well be just a matter of time
before there are one or two central computers, with subscribers
calling on them for routine information whenever they need it.

It is too early to say how computers are going to work out in
their third City role – the actual selection of shares to buy and
sell. Some Wall Street houses have had successes with limited
sections of the market, like utilities, where small gains over the
index performance – say 2% or so – have been pretty consistently achieved. But the more general systems of equity
selection tried so far always seem to trail off after a bit, however jauntily they begin. Perhaps this underscores the most
important market lesson to emerge from all the theorizing –
however carefully you programme the computers or cultivate
the right people, you will never find the perfect solution to all
investment problems, because it simply isn't there.

CHAPTER FOURTEEN

Speculation

EVERY INVESTMENT has a whiff of speculation. It does not matter who is involved – a bishop buying a blue chip is speculating. It does not matter what the security is – sometimes it is hard to justify buying War Loan on any grounds except speculation. There is one thing in common throughout: buyers are betting on the future and the financial rewards they hope it will bring.

In practice, however, speculation is recognized as something separate, whether to be envied or denounced being a matter of opinion. The difference is that investors are interested in sound value for money, but speculators simply regard shares as gambling counters. It does not concern them what shares are ultimately worth as long as they go the right way today. In short, you are a real speculator if you are doing it on purpose.

Although you will often hear people talking about speculative shares, there is nothing to stop you speculating in any security, however splendid its investment status. The Church Commissioners investing with a fifty-year view, and you hoping for a clear 6d. a share before the end of the account, may well have your eye on the same share. In fact, if you are wise you will concentrate on reasonable investments. There is no better way of keeping the risk in bounds.

Successful speculation is an intensely personal achievement, very difficult for outsiders to fathom. It is doubtful whether good speculators understand it themselves. Even when they hand down their investment philosophy, there is usually an irreducible minimum of flair which they cannot explain. One market operator, at the time of the Black Tuesday of May 1962, sold out everything he had the Friday before. Why? Because he was going away for a long week-end.

Look at Bernard Baruch, a Wall Street office boy at nineteen who had made his first million by the time he was thirty – and in the days when millions really counted, back at the turn of the century. He defined a speculator as a man who observes the future and acts before it occurs. According to him, three things are necessary. First, one must get the facts of a situation or problem. Second, one must form a judgement as to what those facts portend. Third, one must act in time – before it is too late.

Certainly Baruch was a demon for delving to the bottom of a situation, and not only in investment matters. Later on, when he became chairman of the War Industries Board, President Woodrow Wilson dubbed him Mr Facts. But at bottom he lived by near-infallible hunches. There is a story of him sitting on a bench in Central Park late in the summer of 1929, while young protégés clustered round asking for tips. All he would say was 'Buy US Bonds'. 'Sad,' said his friends as they drifted away, 'the old man's past it.' But was he? In a matter of weeks the world's most shattering slump was under way.

Or take John Maynard Keynes, the economist. He relied exclusively on his own analytical abilities and then gambled heavily on foreign currencies or commodities, like wheat or jute, linseed oil or cocoa. For him investment was an intellectual conundrum. For half an hour in bed each morning he would absorb the news and the circulars from his brokers. Then he would take decisions. Often they would fly in the face of common sense, but with triumphant success. Friends like to tell of the time during the first war when Keynes was handling foreign currencies for the Treasury. 'There was urgent need for Spanish pesetas. With difficulty a smallish sum was raked up. Keynes duly reported this, and a relieved Secretary to the Treasury remarked that at any rate for a short time we had a supply of pesetas. "Oh, no!" said Keynes. "What!" said his horrified chief. "I've sold them all again: I'm going to break the market." And he did.'

Speculators of this calibre understand the ground rules of the game by instinct. But for other people it may be worth pointing out the sort of situation which provides speculative opportunities.

Every now and again a major rising trend gets established in the market as a whole. The summer of 1968 is a golden collective memory for investors, just as the summer of 1969 is for sunlovers. Deciding when the market is due for a long rise is really a matter of common sense – at least one calls it common sense for want of a better term. In practice, it seems rather rare. For some reason people think they have to be outstandingly clever to be good speculators. But it is not a matter of outwitting opponents. What you have to do is to gauge the average reaction of the investing public, which requires insight but not necessarily brains. Charts are useful to check the progress of the market as a whole; indeed, they are probably more reliable for this purpose than any other.

Once you have made up your mind that the market is on the upswing, choose a share which seems to be making the running. At that stage of market development the pickings are in shares that are rising at above average speed. Shares that have got left behind may not start catching up till later, if at all.

Sometimes it is worth backing recovery when the market as a whole is extremely depressed. Patience, of course, will be essential, even if you are justified in arguing that things are bound to get better sooner or later. What you are going for is economic revival, so you ought to choose a share which will reflect it quickly. A natural market leader like Marks and Spencer would fit the bill. So would a consumer-durable company like Hoover, because it is the sort of share which responds to an upturn in personal spending. Later on, when a boom starts working its way right through the economy, you should switch to the shares of companies supplying capital goods to industry. That is the way to play the business cycle.

Not that there is any rule of thumb to tell you when the market is bumping temporarily along the bottom. Still less can you expect any unmistakable warning that a rising trend is just getting established. But it should help to remember that the economy has moved in a cyclical pattern for most of this century. Since the war this cycle has tended to rise and fall in four-year waves. Typical symptoms of the low point are short-time working in the factories and deputations of beleaguered industrialists to the Chancellor of the Exchequer. He has probably damped down demand in defence of the balance of payments. And unless the country is to slide into depression, he must eventually ease off the pressure.

When you are staking your judgement on market trends you are going for a comparatively large percentage rise over a fairly long period of time. Short-term opportunities in the market as a whole are rare. They occur usually under the impact of some sudden shock. Wall Street shook with spasms whenever President Eisenhower choked on blueberry pie. As he recovered, so did the market. The shares to watch on these occasions are the active blue chips, particularly those which have fallen exceptionally far.

As a rule there is more scope for gambling on individual shares than on the market as a whole. Shares get out of line for reasons of their own, whether it is because of a recent offering of rights or because it suits some large shareholder to sell. Here you should be out for a small, quick profit, with the minimum of risk. Rights issues provide somewhat exceptional opportunities. At the beginning of their lives you can deal in them nil paid, that is before the new money which the company is raising has actually been subscribed by shareholders. Sometimes rights change hands at only a few pence premium, in which case a jump of a shilling or so would obviously make a major difference to a speculator.

For example, suppose a company whose shares were standing at 10s. offered a one for two rights issue at 8s. 6d. a share. The ex-rights price, you will remember, would be calculated like this

For every 2 shares at 10s. each	Cost 20s.
You are entitled to 1 at 8s. 6d.	8s. 6d.
Total 3 shares	28s. 6d.
	or 9s. 6d. a share

Before the 8s. 6d. call had actually been paid, allotment letters would change hands at 1s. premium – the difference between the call and the ex-rights price. A rise to 1s. 6d. premium would not mean much in terms of the long-term movement of the share's price. But from the point of view of a speculator who had bought at 1s. it would mean a 50% profit, before expenses.

The trouble is, this type of manoeuvre is particularly difficult to judge. The shares might fall, leaving you with a call for a large sum of money which you cannot afford to pay. The first rule, if you are dealing in nil or even partly paid shares, is to make sure you have enough resources to pay the call if necessary. Not that it is always the most sensible thing to do. If the premium on a rights issue runs off altogether it could be extremely dangerous to pay the call. Far better to write off your original stake altogether than to risk a bigger loss by going in deeper. That would be a vintage example of throwing good money after bad.

Perhaps the commonest form of speculation is gambling on a company's results. Higher profits and dividends are, after all, a compelling incentive for buying a share. The trouble is, results have got to outstrip market expectations if a gamble of this sort is to pay off. When results are good, but no better than anticipated, the shares often fall under pressure from speculators who are anxious to cash profits. Potential new buyers hold off, arguing that there is nothing to go for. For this reason the best way to speculate on results is to buy about two or three months early and sell just before the figures are announced. If the shares rise in anticipation of good results you will be at the head of the queue. You will be able to take a profit with much less risk, before other speculators are trying to take their profits too.

Speculators getting out after results are announced provide you with a different opportunity. Their operations hold back the price when, on other grounds, a rise would be justified. You should not be too frightened about moving in when you think a share price has reacted too sluggishly to good news.

Even if you are not, at heart, a speculator, you may find yourself tempted from time to time by tips. Someone may claim to know the inside story on a takeover, or some other sensational development, which is going to put a share up by a fat percentage in practically no time. As a rule, tales of this kind should be scrupulously ignored. Listen to Baruch's advice, written in memory of some blunder of his own:

'It taught me one thing about tips, namely, that people sometimes drop remarks calculated to bring the little minnows into the net to be served up for the big fish. I had been a little minnow.

'The longer I operated in Wall Street the more distrustful I became of tips and "inside" information of every kind. Given time, I believe that inside information can break the Bank of England or the United States Treasury.

'It is not simply that inside information often is manufactured to mislead the gullible. Even when insiders know what their companies are doing, they are likely to make serious blunders just because they are in the know.'

Still, suppose you are satisfied there might be something to it. Remember the golden rule about only buying investments which are sound in themselves. Before you go ahead, check whether the shares are reasonable value on other grounds, so that even if the gamble fails you will not be exposed to too much risk.

In recent years investors have made a good deal of money out of buying the shares of companies coming to the market for the first time – stagging the issue, to use the City slang. The experts who bring a company to the market are naturally anxious that its shares should get off to a good start. They tend, therefore, to fix a pretty attractive opening price. In that case people who are lucky enough to get an allotment of shares find themselves with a healthy profit as soon as dealings begin.

By this time, of course, the investing public is thoroughly awake to the possibilities, and new issues are often heavily over-subscribed. It is so much a matter of luck whether you get any shares that many professionals no longer bother with stagging. But if you do decide to have a go, be discriminating. Sentiment over new issues can change remarkably suddenly. After weeks of successful launchings a company can get off to a bad start for no very obvious reason. Incidentally, this emphasizes the need for care in gauging the size of one's application. When stagging interest is running high applications are usually scaled down drastically. You may get only a token number of shares. The obvious response, provided you have enough funds available, is to put in for much more than you really want, in the hope of getting a worthwhile allotment. But this, of course, is when it is most important to be discriminating. To misjudge the response to an issue and be landed with a large block of shares can result in disastrous losses.

Very often the best advice over new issues is to wait until dealings begin. It is quite usual for them to make good progress once a broader market starts to develop. If you get in quickly at this stage you may do very well out of it.

These are the sort of opportunities for speculation which you might be able to exploit. But if you are to make the most of them there are a number of general rules which are worth bearing in mind. Perhaps the commonest problem arises when you simply get stuck. The shares you have bought just do not seem to attract any interest at all among the investing public. You are left holding on to them, possibly with a small loss after allowing for expenses. How can you guard against an awkward situation like that? The first rule to remember is always to keep well within yourself financially. If you get carried away and plump everything on a single share you leave yourself no room to manoeuvre if things go wrong. There are occasions, obviously, when your timing is at fault, and there is no alternative but to wait and see if your judgement is justified in the end. In that case there is nothing more galling than to let sure-fire opportunities slip simply because you are already over-committed. In your long-term investment policy you probably think in terms of a suitable amount – perhaps 5 or 6% of your total capital – to invest in any one share. For a speculative fund 10% is a more realistic figure, with 15 or 20% the upper limit.

Next you should remember that your eventual success as a speculator depends on two things: your average profit and your rate of turnover. There is little to be gained by jacking up your profits by a few percentage points if it means you only have two coups a year instead of twelve. Far too many speculators hang on for an extra shilling, perhaps for some utterly irrelevant reason like getting up to a round figure, when their resources would be much better employed elsewhere. The point to think about is whether there is still a useful rise to go for, in percentage terms. If you think there is, by all means run your profit. Otherwise be cynical about your own abilities to hit the top. Baruch says it can't be done – except by liars. Remember also the saying attributed to an early Rothschild with a reputation for getting out too soon: sell, regret – and grow rich.

When things go wrong be quick to cut your losses. In the stock market, as Baruch observed, the first loss is usually the smallest. Ask yourself whether your original reason for buying is still valid. If it is, you may simply have paid rather too high a price for a good speculation, and there should be no harm in waiting unless some new factor intervenes. Otherwise you should sell. To try and find other reasons for hanging on could be a very expensive exercise in rationalization. And besides, you must be prepared to make mistakes. Once more according to Baruch, if a speculator is correct half of the time he is hitting a good average.

So far we have been dealing with what one might call soundly-based speculation. At every point we have been urging you to check back to normal investment principles and see whether your prospective dabble measures up properly against them. Still, there is nothing to stop you indulging in pure speculation if you want to.

What this amounts to is following a share which seems to have established a strong upward trend. Typically, this sort of share has the glamour of a well-known business name, or is mixed up in some futuristic project. Recent examples are English & Overseas Investment Trust or Channel Tunnel. English & Overseas was unheard of until John Bloom of Rolls Razor, riding high on the washing-machine boom, took control of the company. Then the shares bounded ahead, far beyond the levels which could be justified on assets or earnings, because it was believed Bloom would use it as a vehicle for his future enterprises. Once the going got harder for the washing-machine business, with fatal results for the Bloom empire,

English & Overseas plummeted downwards as fast as they had risen. In the same way, Chunnel shares soared on hopes that the company would be cut in on the cross-Channel tunnel, only to drop again when the hopes faded.

In cases like these you know perfectly well that the rise will come to an end, probably sooner rather than later. Obviously you have to be careful not to come in too near the final stages. To a large extent this must be a matter for your own judgement, though charts should help you to spot signs that the rise is nearly over. A more practical way of protecting yourself is a device very common among speculatively-minded people in America, known as a stop-loss order. This means that you instruct your broker to sell automatically if the price of the shares falls below a certain level. In this way you can at least keep losses within reasonable bounds if there is a catastrophic collapse in the market. On the other hand, it needs skill to fix your order so that you are not shaken out by some minor fluctuation on the way up. And, last but not least, stop-loss orders are not well regarded in the City. It is doubtful whether many brokers would accept them.

This technique, or rather a highly personal version of it, is the one used by Nicolas Darvas, the dancer who made a fortune on Wall Street without ever going there. His approach is technical, in the sense that he only buys stocks which are showing a convincing pattern on the charts. What he likes to see is a solid-looking advance, backed by a rising volume of activity in the stock. But he also blends this fairly conventional chartism with an insistence on the sort of glamour which stirs people's imagination for the future. To quote from his book *How I Made $2,000,000 in the Stock Market*:

'I carefully watched stock market quotations in this general bracket of expanding stocks in tune with the jet age. I was not interested in the company's individual products, whether it was metals for rockets, solid fuel, or advanced electronic equipment. In fact, I did not want to know what they made – that information might only inhibit me. I did not care what the company's products were, any more than I was influenced by the fact that the board's chairman had a beautiful wife. But I did want to know whether the company belonged to a new vigorous infant industry and whether it behaved in the market according to my requirements.'

Once satisfied that he has found a stock to his liking, he more or less backs it with his shirt. He seldom holds more than two or three stocks at a time. The idea then is to hang on as long as the stock is rising, but to flee, as he himself says, 'like a disturbed burglar' if ever the trend is reversed. The possibility of flight is provided by a stop-loss order placed at a sensitive distance below the current quote. As the share price rises, so the stop-loss order is kept trailing along behind. Like that, he never lets a profit run off altogether.

All this sounds disarmingly simple, but the selection of stocks and the setting of stop-loss orders both require effort and flair. If you choose the wrong stock and get sold out on your stop-loss order before there has been any appreciation at all you stand to lose about 10–15% of your capital on each operation. In London, where dealing expenses are higher than in New York, the dangers are correspondingly greater. Besides, the technique depends on active markets, or at least on active stocks. In a bear market, or just a dull phase, it need not take long for you to be rubbed out completely.

Another way of gambling on price movements pure and simple is the bear sale. This consists of selling shares you do not own in the hope of buying them back more cheaply later on. This is much more of a needle operation than a speculative buy. In the first place, you can only keep it open for a fairly short time – for most practical purposes until the end of the account – because then you will have to deliver the shares you have sold. Secondly, and more importantly, you risk much more. For while your potential loss on a purchase is limited to the amount of money you put up, there is in theory no limit to the amount you could lose on a bear sale. Certainly the shares could rise to a price many times what you sold them for.

It is possible to clothe bear transactions with a slightly spurious air of sobriety by dealing only in shares you do in fact possess. This is known as a covered bear. It means that you sell shares you own in the hope of buying them back more cheaply, just as you would in an ordinary bear sale, except that if the price moves against you there is no risk of your being squeezed when you have to close the bargain. The trouble with this is that if the shares fall you may well wonder whether you ought to buy them back at all. On the other hand, if they rise you must buy them in at a loss or go without. Either way it leaves an unsatisfactory taste in the mouth.

Options

For many people options – the right to buy or sell shares at a stated price within a stated period – are the quintessence of speculation. This is not just a matter of popular imagination; it is widely supported in some sections of the City itself. So strong was the opposition to options within the Stock Exchange Council that the practice of dealing in them, abandoned at the beginning of the war, was not resumed until as recently as 1958. What the Puritan element has always dreaded is that options will give the City a bad name as a casino. For example, taking out steel options before the 1964 election was a simple way of gambling on the Conservatives, and with pretty good odds – the more so, since you could cover the cost of the option by betting on a Labour victory with the bookmakers, and still have something to go for. But there is a distinct air of hypocrisy about such moralizing. If the capitalist, free-enterprise system has proper economic justification, then speculation plays an intrinsic part in it, by reducing price fluctuations and easing the operations of the market. If you do not like options you are on much stronger grounds if you argue against their prudence, rather than their morality.

Options work like this. You can either *give for the call* (which means you acquire the right to buy within the option period) or you can *give for the put* (this is the right to sell). If you are thoroughly undecided, except that you expect a good deal of activity in the share of your choice, you can take out a two-way option, so that you can either buy or sell during the option period. Not unnaturally this privilege costs twice as much.

The normal option period is three months. It can be less, but this is slightly academic, because you can close a normal option at any time during its three months' life. Once on each account, usually on the first Thursday, there occurs what is known as declaration day, on which you can exercise your option.

The cost of an option is generally about 5–10% of the price of the shares you want to deal in. Option rates for the leading counters are quoted each day in the *Financial Times*, but dealing facilities are freely available in other securities as well. The rates fluctuate roughly in accordance with supply and demand. To quote again from 1964 election experience, the cost of steel options tended to rise when more and more people started taking a view on Conservative prospects of re-election.

The actual option price does not represent the whole cost of dealing in options. This is because an option is granted at a special price known as the striking price, which is not the ordinary buying or selling price in the market. For example, if ICI were quoted at 45s. to 45s. 6d. these prices would not be the striking prices for put and call options. The striking prices would be somewhat lower – say 44s. 6d. – for put options and somewhat higher – say 46s. – for call options. In theory, the difference represents the option dealer's cost of financing the shares for the duration of the option. In practice, however, he uses it as a device for widening his margins. Realistically, you should reckon that your shares will have to move about 10–15% before you start making a profit on an option.

If the main disadvantage of options is their cost this is perhaps not altogether surprising. After all, they provide the opportunity of speculating without capital and, as so often in life, things are more expensive for people who cannot afford them. At least there is the compensating advantage that options limit the amount one can lose. For this reason you might have thought that they would appeal to bears, whose potential losses are so much greater than bulls'. Another consideration is that they let you keep a bear position open for as long as three months. Ordinary bear sales must usually be closed within the account. Yet, oddly enough, around 90% of all options are call options.

As we saw earlier, it is comparatively expensive to be on one side of an option bargain, so you can fairly argue that it must be comparatively lucrative to be on the other. Who is in this happy position? Well, it could be you, provided you are rich. In practice, though, there are a number of institutions which make the market in options. Most of the deals are handled by one of five firms of brokers who specialize in options under licence from the Stock Exchange Council. Your own broker, if he will consent to deal in options at all, will get in touch with one of them. These specialists know who is prepared to go long or short in a wide range of shares. As a rule, the institutions concerned are content to take a very long view of the shares they trade in, while picking up a useful living on option money. If they are taking for the call – that is, if they are guaranteeing to let you have stock at a certain price – they are usually happy to part with their holdings if the option is exercised. On the opposite tack, they are no less ready to buy, should occasion demand it. And, as well over half the options taken out are never exercised (except in strong bull markets), trading in options has so far proved well worth while. Incidentally the institutions are not alone in the option market. With rare or unpredictable stocks the institutions are unlikely to be interested, in which case the dealers themselves will take on the option, usually covering themselves by the classic device of laying off half the bargain.

One final point needs to be made on the tax status of options. Options do not come within the net of capital gains tax unless they are exercised. One curious anomaly arises out of this rule. As the cost of unexercised options cannot be offset against taxable gains, it sometimes pays to take up an unprofitable option and sell your shares at a loss, for tax reasons. In that case the loss on the whole operation – including the option cost – can be set against any taxable profits you may have available.

CHAPTER FIFTEEN

New Issues

THE STOCK EXCHANGE, as its champions like to point out, is the perfect place for borrowing money. Year by year huge sums of fresh capital are raised from the investing public. The 1968 total, for example, was a bit over £850 million, not counting the Government's own funding programme, which is too involved to disentangle properly.

Most of the private money is sought by companies whose names are already well known in the City. They offer new shares to their existing shareholders by way of rights, or issue prior-charge stocks like debentures. But on top of that there is a smaller but no less important flow of issues from newcomers who are after a quotation for the first time.

This process of floating a new issue for an unknown company is subjected to very careful control, and rightly so. Otherwise the scope for high-pressure salesmen unloading worthless securities on to an innocent public would be almost limitless. For this reason, the various Companies Acts lay down that a prospectus must accompany all offers of securities to the public. They go into very great detail about what should appear in these documents; furthermore, the Stock Exchange Council insists on certain extra disclosures as a condition of granting a quotation. As a result, you will be able to find out from a prospectus a wide range of information about a company's business, management, assets, earnings, dividends and outlook before you need make up your mind whether to buy its shares. In many respects the standards of disclosure required in a prospectus are higher than those of companies already publicly quoted.

Investment interest in new issues is always lively, because of the widespread feeling that newcomers are likely to be attractively priced in order to gain the necessary support. There is certainly a good deal of truth in this. Indeed, new issues are often so cheap that people who manage to get any shares find themselves with a good profit overnight. As we have already seen, new issues attract a special class of speculators, known as stags, who play an important, if occasionally invidious, part in the mechanism of company launchings.

Before considering how to assess new issues, it is worth getting clear in your mind the different ways in which a company's shares can be brought to the market. There are three main methods – an offer for sale, a placing and an introduction. Whichever method is used, at least 35% of a company's share capital must end up in the hands of the public.

An *offer for sale* is the most usual method, and the one most favoured by the Stock Exchange Council. Under this system some sponsor organization in the City, like a merchant bank, buys a block of shares and then invites the public to apply for them at a fixed price. The issue is widely advertised in the newspapers, together with the prospectus and a coupon which any potential applicant can cut out and send in. When all the applications have been received – a day is set by which they have to be in – the shares are allotted according to the state of demand. When, as so often happens, an issue is over-subscribed, allotments have to be scaled down below what people asked for, or sometimes even put into a ballot. On the other hand, some issues are not fully subscribed. In that case any shares not applied for have to be taken up by a special class of investors known as underwriters. These long-stops, who are usually institutional investors, are arranged in advance. For a small fee they each agree to absorb a certain number of shares if by some chance the issue is a failure.

To illustrate how the process works let us consider the offer for sale of part of the equity of Martonair International, manufacturers of pneumatic control equipment.

In January 1969, 1,310,000 Martonair Ordinary 4s. shares were offered to the public by a merchant bank at 20s. per share. The response was extremely enthusiastic, with applications for over 130 million shares. This more than assured the success of the issue. What actually happened was that people who had put in for less than 20,000 shares had their names put into a ballot and those successful received shares in the proportion of

100 shares for applications for less than 1,750 shares and 250 shares for applications for less than 20,000 shares. The remaining applicants, those who had gone for more than 20,000 shares, received about 1% of the number they applied for.

A *placing* is suitable when an issue is small or unlikely to arouse much public interest. What happens usually is that a sponsor organization buys the shares which are to be issued and then places them, at a slightly higher price, with clients of its own choosing. A Stock Exchange regulation lays down that 25% of an ordinary share placing must be offered to the public by way of the jobbers. With fixed-interest stocks the proportion is only 10%, though with another 10% which has to be provisionally placed on call if there is public demand for it. The point of this is to try and get a reasonably wide spread of ownership, not least so that the market should be orderly when dealings begin.

Sometimes a company's capital is sufficiently widely held to allow an *introduction*. Here the quotation is a convenience; a reasonable distribution of the shares already exists. In this instance no published prospectus is necessary under the Companies Act, because no capital is being offered for sale. However, the Stock Exchange insists on the preparation of a similar document for circulation by the Moodies and Exchange Telegraph statistical services. An introduction is very much a matter of circumstances. The Council refuses to say in advance what number of shareholders, or spread of holdings, will provide a passport to an introduction. It may well be that existing holders will be expected to make some of their shares available to the market when dealings begin. Certainly the brokers to the issue will be under pressure to satisfy any demand reported by the jobbers. In the case of overseas securities with established quotations in their own countries an introduction is the natural method, because there is already a market to which jobbers can turn for stock. The same is true of provincial securities coming to London for the first time.

The newest and most controversial method of marketing shares is an offer for sale by *tender*. Here the information and apparatus is exactly the same as with an ordinary offer for sale, except that the price is not fixed in advance. Prospective subscribers are invited to name their own price, subject to a minimum. To be precise, the technique is not entirely new. It has been the established way of marketing water stocks for some years. But since all water companies have maximum dividends, and their operations are very similar, tendering is largely a matter of an intelligent appreciation of current market circumstances. In consequence, the highest and lowest tenders for a water stock tend not to be too far apart, and it is perfectly logical to start issuing stock to the highest bidder and work on down the list until the stock is exhausted.

The novelty about tenders for ordinary shares lies in the adaptations which are necessary to make the system fit in with the Stock Exchange's requirements for conventional equity launchings. Most importantly, allotments have to be made on a different basis. For though applications are counted off from the top until the entire issue is absorbed, just as they would be with water stocks, the usual arrangement is for everyone to pay the lowest price accepted. In practice, however, this sometimes has to be modified, mainly in order to ensure a wide enough spread of holdings when dealings begin. After all, taken to its extreme conclusion, a situation could arise where one individual could acquire the whole issue by bidding the highest price. In consequence, there is often some scaling down of applications, and sometimes balloting, even with tenders.

This time let us take Rentokil as our illustration, which was offered for sale by tender in March 1969. Its excellent reputation in the field of pest control and insecticides, combined with an impressive record of profits growth, suggested that demand for the new shares would be heavy. But there were several features about it which sounded a note of caution. In the first place the minimum tender price of 20s., giving a prospective price/earnings ratio on estimated 1969 earnings of 18·9 times, was hardly over-generous, and in a weak market this could have proved discouraging. Secondly, there were memories of the touch-and-go Wilkinson Sword tender in 1964, though the factors which upset that particular issue –

a powerful and hostile competitor, and a rather cumbersome package of voting and non-voting shares – were not present in this case. In such a situation the success of the issue remained delicately poised on a knife edge until the very end. As it turned out, Rentokil's past record and future prospects were a powerful enough attraction to ensure that the issue was comfortably oversubscribed, sufficient to allow a striking price of 25s. When dealings began, the shares opened at a small premium.

Are any of the varied methods of launching companies superior to the others? No doubt an offer for sale ought to fit the bill on most occasions. From the point of view of members of the public it is fair, because anyone can apply. From the point of view of the owners of the company on offer there is the advantage of having the widest possible market. The trouble lies in the fixing of the price at which the offer is made.

Now there is no doubt that the price and timing of a new issue are genuinely difficult factors to assess. Market conditions can change so rapidly that even the soundest-seeming plans go awry. The judgement and experience of the merchant banks and stockbrokers who handle the majority of new issues are invaluable in helping companies to avoid the worst hazards of the market place. Still, these expert institutions are sensitive, possibly over-sensitive, about being party to an issue which gets off to a slow start. In recommending issue prices they sometimes seem more anxious about their own reputations than the financial interests of their clients. One can say, with the benefit of hindsight, that in recent years a lot of issues have been made at unrealistically low prices. One test is the number of times an issue is over-subscribed, and in some instances many millions of pounds have been put up for very small issues. Another test is the premium over the issue price which the shares reach when dealings begin. Here again it is not unknown for shares to double in a single day. The obvious objection is, some lucky people make a killing in practically no time, and what could be more casino-like than that? More subtly, the parcelling out of tiny allotments keeps serious, long-term investors away. They cannot get the stock they want, and a tiny fragment is merely a nuisance.

Both these undesirable features have been mitigated, though not eliminated, by the tender system. Issues by tender have usually opened only a little way above the price fixed for the sale. There have therefore been fewer fat profits about for the stags, and even if the size of allotments has not greatly increased, this need not be such a deterrent for medium-term investors. The very fact that tender issues do not go to such fantastic premiums means that it is relatively easy to round up a small holding by buying in the market without substantially affecting one's average cost.

Tenders have attracted a good deal of criticism, mostly out of fear that they will be used to wring the last penny out of investors. In that case new issues would start life at very small premiums or even at discounts. The backlog of goodwill among stag-minded investors would then be frittered away, and the flow of new issues would have to be curtailed. This is a very real danger, but it can be avoided if the issuing house fixes the minimum tender price at a generous level. Then if prospective buyers, as a body, can only keep their heads there is no reason why they should not get a bargain. Admittedly, investors are collectively excitable and often inclined to bid up prices too high. But the theoretical advantages of tenders remain substantial. A shrewdly judged minimum tender price can leave the stags with something to go for. But if the issuing house has under-estimated bullish sentiment, at least it is the vendors who benefit most. All in all it is a good thing that tenders look like having come to stay.

What are the best tactics for approaching new issues? Before answering that question we ought to give much closer consideration to prospectuses. And as a preliminary it will be helpful to take a look at the work which goes into them.

When a company wants to come to the market its first step is to find some financial sponsor in the City. In most cases this will be a merchant bank, though some stockbroking firms provide a similar service. For simplicity's sake, let us divide the functions of issuing house and issuing broker.

Now City institutions are very careful about their reputations. They do not like their names to be associated with failure, dishonesty or even the breath of adverse rumour. You may be sure, therefore, that when a merchant bank backs a new issue it has taken considerable care to satisfy itself that there is nothing wrong with the project. A director will as a matter of course go round any company his bank is thinking of launching. No doubt he will also prepare a confidential report for his colleagues before any decision is reached. This is the background to the advice you so often hear in the City to look at the names of the institutions associated with a new issue. It is advice which we gladly repeat, though it takes experience, unsuitable for print, to know how to use it.

Once satisfied, the issuing house is responsible for shepherding the company to the market. It will commission a firm of accountants (possibly the company's own auditors) to prepare an independent report on the company's affairs. It will advise on any reorganization of the company's capital which may prove necessary. Many firms coming to the market are private, and their transformation into public concerns provides an opportunity for adopting a suitable capital structure. Incidentally, the same is often true of many other details, such as articles of association, directors' service agreements, arrangements for share registration and the like. In any issue there is always a good deal of work to keep solicitors busy. Through the brokers to the issue, the issuing house will also keep the Stock Exchange in touch with developments. Every prospectus has to be submitted to the Share and Loan Department for vetting before a quotation can be granted.

By the time a prospectus appears, it has been sifted through many processes, discussed by many experts and run through many proof stages. As a result there is a good deal of material which you can take more or less on trust – for example, various statutory declarations, general information, contracts not entered into in the normal course of business and so on. All this detail is essential if the investing public is to be properly safeguarded against dishonesty. Paradoxically, however, the very fact that these forms have been observed is a large measure of protection. Read them by all means in the small print at the end of the prospectus. More particularly, read what the professional commentators have to say about them, if anything. But do not be surprised if they are of little help to you in putting a value on the shares.

By tradition, a prospectus appears in a set shape, with what you really need to know coming about a third of the way down. The heart of the matter comes in six paragraphs, as follows:

History and business

This explains what the company does, how long it has been doing it and states the relative importance of its activities if there are more than one.

Management and labour

This gives the names, ages and positions of the directors, the arrangements for continuity of management, including service agreements, and details about the labour force.

Plant and premises

This sets out the company's factories and other main buildings, with details of tenure.

Statement on working capital

This either states that there is enough working capital or if not explains how it is to be provided. It gives details on any new issue of ordinary shares during the last two years, including the use to which the money is being put.

Accountants' report

This is, in effect, an extract from the much longer outside report which, as already mentioned, the issuing house will have commissioned. The statutory details it has to include are given below. (It should be noted, however, that the provision of records for ten-year periods, where available, is a Stock Exchange requirement. The 1948 Companies Act stipulates five years.)

1. Ten-year profit record (if available).

2. Assets and liabilities. One year's balance sheet, consolidated and for the parent company alone, if this is appropriate.

3. Separate report on any business which is being bought with the proceeds of the issue, including a ten-year profit record (if available).

4. Ten-year dividend record (if available).

5. If the accounts are more than three months old there must be a statement that no subsequent accounts have been prepared. (The accounts in any case must not be more than nine months old if they are to be acceptable to the Stock Exchange. Failing that, special half-yearly accounts would have to be prepared.)

Profits, prospects and dividends

This is a statement on current trading and a forecast of profits, dividends and earnings cover, subject to unforeseen circumstances.

Compared with what the majority of companies print in their annual reports, prospectuses provide a reasonable amount of extra information. By New York standards they may be thin (one American expert has remarked that there is not much to choose between a British prospectus and an entry in the telephone directory). But by studying the details on business, management and premises, prospective investors can get a closer insight into a company's operations than they can usually hope for. A weakness is the fact that only one year's balance sheet is published, so in this respect conventional analytical methods cannot be usefully applied.

This apart, there need not be much difference between your approach to a newly issued company and an established Stock Exchange counter. You should perhaps pay more attention to trends in a new company, rather than year-by-year changes, when you are considering the profit record. Private companies, which do not have to worry about their image with the investing public, feel freer to make exceptional write-offs against profits, whether because of research, promotion expenditure or the costs of a move. But if there is a severe interruption in an otherwise healthy profits trend, ask your broker if there is a convincing reason. After all, if that should happen again it could be very sharply reflected in the company's status.

So much for the contents of a prospectus. Let us now go back to the actual process of an issue and see how the timetable works. The key moment, of course, is the day when permission is granted to deal in the new shares. This is either a Wednesday or a Friday. Perhaps a week before that, word starts getting around that an issue is on the way. There may, for example, be a press conference; and the arrangements for underwriting the issue would certainly be going ahead. A day or so later the prospectus is published. It must appear (together with an application form) in at least two daily national newspapers; many companies decide to use more. This is your opportunity to study the company's record and prospects and lay your application plans.

At least forty-eight hours must elapse between the publication of the prospectus and the granting of permission to deal. Anything from a day to a week after that the application list for the issue opens and closes. It may be that this list will remain open all through the business day. More often than not, however, the issue will be over-subscribed, in which case the list will close a minute after it has opened. For this reason it is wise to make sure your application is in by the first post, or perhaps even the day before.

The next sequence of events follows as quickly as possible. The applications are sorted, then the basis of allotment decided upon and announced to the Press. A day or so may elapse before letters of allotment are posted but, generally speaking, dealings should begin within a week of application day. For the first few weeks of a new issue's life the shares change hands by allotment letter. During this period, by a special concession, the normal 1% transfer stamp duty does not have to be paid. As with other new issues, such as scrip issues and rights issues, if you are the person to whom the shares were originally allotted you can dispose of them by signing a special form of renunciation which is usually on the back of the allotment letter. If you prefer, you can sell part, in which case special split allotment letters can be obtained for you from the company's registrars. If you decide to hold on to the shares all that is usually necessary is for you to keep your allotment letter in a safe place. In good time – about ten weeks after the original granting of permission to deal – the share certificate will be sent to you without further action on your part. Otherwise, during the initial six weeks of grace, renounced allotment letters simply pass from hand to hand in settlement of any bargains that take place. The people who own allotment letters at the end of this period fill in the registration application form (usually in the middle of the allotment letter) and send it in to the company's registrars. In due course their certificates will be sent to them.

The whole process may sound complicated, but the text of an allotment letter usually explains quite clearly what you have to do. Even if you do not understand it, your stockbroker or other professional adviser will be there to help you. To prevent you throwing away good money by mistake, all documents which may have any value must be so marked at the top of the front page. That is why it is always worth inspecting the contents of any boring-looking envelope that comes your way.

Does the timetable of a new issue have any bearing on your tactics if you decide you would like to apply? With a placing it certainly does. The only way of getting any of the shares which are being placed with the market – as you may remember, with ordinary shares that is a quarter of the issue – is to ask your broker to apply to the jobbers who are going to deal in them. It may be that some of his other clients will have asked the same thing, in which case he may have to share out his quota among all of you. It may even be that he will not get a quota at all, if the issue is a popular one. Either way, it is a good idea to get one's claim in early. This is a case where you should make up your mind as soon as possible after the prospectus is published and get the wheels in motion right away.

With offers for sale and tenders it will often pay to wait until the last moment before acting (with an introduction there is really very little choice except to ask for a quotation as soon as dealings begin). The problem with an offer for sale is to guess the weight of applications. If there is clearly going to be a fair amount of interest – you can judge this by the comments in the Press or by asking your broker to find out what the market thinks – you may have to consider stepping up your application beyond what you would really like.

If you decide to have a go at a popular issue your first concern should be to try and make sure you will get something. It is very tiresome to go to the trouble of making an application only to have it returned without any allotment. It can be expensive too, if you are borrowing the money. It is worth remembering therefore that, in all but the most popular cases, the larger applicants usually get something, even if it is only a minor fraction of what they wanted. That is an argument for putting in one large cheque. On the other hand, if you have misjudged the issue and you are allotted everything you have applied for you may be in a very awkward position. An issue of that kind will almost certainly get off to a slow start, and you may have to get out at a loss. Another alternative is to put in lots of smaller applications, in the hope that at least one of them will turn up trumps if there is a ballot. The trouble with this is, many issuing houses frown on such practices and throw out any multiple applications they are sharp-eyed enough to spot. Yet again, you can try to improve your chances by picking some slightly odd number of shares – say 2,200 – in the hope of getting into a higher balloting bracket than if you simply applied for 2,000. This has been known to pay off; but it may be scotched by a sensible approach which some City houses now use. By this method the issuing house chooses some set numbers of shares – say 100, 500, 2,000 and 5,000 – as the only amounts which it will accept on application forms. Not only is this much quicker and easier for everyone concerned. It also makes hair's-breadth attempts at out-foxing rival applicants irrelevant.

With tenders, the amount you should apply for is less important than the price. There are two lines of thought about that. One way you can argue that you should put in a very high bid, on the grounds that you are sure to get something. So you are; but sooner or later we shall see a bad flop with a tender, and then your fingers really will get burned. Alternatively, you can bid what you would be prepared to pay for the shares as a medium-term investment. Like that you will at least have few regrets over any allotment you get. Incidentally, you can keep in touch with reality by asking your broker to check with the market to see what price is expected. Press indications tend, reasonably enough, to be on the conservative side.

Finally, do not forget that you can always move into a new issue after dealings have begun. It is surprising how a price can hang around for an hour or two after the opening, no doubt because stags are taking quick profits. Later on a better trend becomes established. It is also worth keeping tabs on issues which are a few months old. Interest dies down and stags cash their holdings so as to try for another new issue.

CHAPTER SIXTEEN

Keeping Abreast

CYNICS LIKE to say that when you become a shareholder you need a bigger letter box and a bigger waste-paper basket. The outsize letter box, for receiving the large, glossy annual reports which many companies publish nowadays, will doubtless come in useful. But any shareholder prepared to take an intelligent interest, as well as a financial one, in the companies in which he invests should find the experience absorbing enough to make extra waste-paper facilities unnecessary.

Communications between companies and their shareholders rise and fall in an annual rhythm. Basically, the legal requirement is that firms should send out each year a report by the directors and a properly audited statement of their accounts. Provisions exist to prevent these reports lagging too far behind the accounting period to which they refer. One feature of reports is that they contain notice of the annual general meeting of the shareholders. The meeting must be at least three weeks after the date on which reports are mailed to shareholders, to give time for even the busiest investor to brood over them. Between meetings there is no legal compulsion for companies to be in touch with their shareholders except in matters affecting their rights, but under pressure from the Stock Exchange Council a growing body of firms are taking greater pains to keep their shareholders well informed on their progress and performance.

Improvement has come in two ways: frequency and detail. The custom has grown up among firms of paying dividends in two instalments – an interim some time during the trading year and a final immediately after the annual general meeting. Increasingly, boards of directors have been accompanying their interim payments with some sort of statement about how they are getting along. Since the autumn of 1964 such reports have been made a requirement for admission to quotation. And since this requirement refers to all new issues, whether from companies new to the Exchange or from long-established firms raising fresh funds, it is clear that half-yearly information is likely to increase. Even so, British practice will continue to fall below the standards exacted from American companies quoted on the New York Stock Exchange. Over there they are compelled to publish quarterly figures.

A further advance in the standards of corporate disclosure has been prompted by the 1967 Companies Act. However, from a strictly analytical viewpoint some of the extra information is of interest simply as lunch-room gossip (e.g. directors' salaries or political and charitable contributions). And the Act scarcely goes far enough in its requirements on turnover or valuation of stock and work-in-progress. On the credit side, the Act obliges companies to list their principal activities (though the breakdown of turnover and profits between the separate parts of the business is left to the discretion of their boards) and to put more realistic values on fixed assets and unquoted investments. In spite of not inconsiderable gaps, the Act has made some contribution to the raw materials at the investor's disposal.

On top of the regular bulletins which companies issue to shareholders, there are other communications which are less frequently encountered. Some publicity-conscious firms send you a glad-to-have-you-aboard letter when your name first appears on the shareholders' register, usually accompanied by the latest copy of the accounts. Others more usefully get in touch with you when you sell shares, saying that someone purporting to be you has signed a sales transfer, and if there is a mistake this is your last chance of correcting it.

In between whiles, companies sometimes write to explain financial manoeuvres affecting the standing of your shares. They may have decided to enlarge the issued capital by handing out a free scrip issue; they may have decided to raise fresh capital by offering new shares by way of rights, or by floating a new debenture; they may even wish to tidy up the company's articles of association, which set out its objects and administration. In such cases it is usual to receive one document giving the formal details which shareholders are being asked to approve and another to explain what the proposals involve. It is the second of these two papers which you, or your professional advisers, ought to study. If you approve of the idea, as explained to you in a straightforward way, it is obviously a waste of time to worry about its legalistic formulation.

Enclosed with any document requiring the assent of shareholders will be a proxy form, typically a postcard addressed to the company by business reply service (i.e. you do not have to stamp it). This will authorize one or other of two directors to vote on your behalf at the meeting called to consider the resolution under discussion. Provided you return the card, properly filled in, at the appropriate time you will be able to record your opinion just as though you were at the meeting in person. In most cases there is a time limit – your proxy must be in forty-eight hours in advance of the meeting – and the directors reserve the right to vote either way unless you specifically instruct them what to do. But a conscientious shareholder can, without trouble, make his views known by a proxy card.

Some of the documents which reach you in this way will be of financial value. In that case this has to be clearly marked at the top of the first page and sometimes on the envelope. If you do not understand why, there will be a recommendation for you to consult your professional advisers. Under no circumstances should you fail to take action of some sort. Otherwise you could be literally throwing money away. For that, if for no other, reason you should never dispose of letters from your companies without first reading what they have to say.

Unquestionably the most dramatic communications you may receive will occur if a company of yours gets caught up in a takeover. Here again the offer usually comes in two parts: the formal proposal, whether for merger or takeover, and a letter explaining what is going on. More often than not, the implications will take a little time to digest. The crucial piece of information to extract (apart from the terms you are being offered) is the period of time you have in which to make up your mind. Having done that, you can relax, comparatively speaking.

As a general rule, you should wait until a very few days before an offer expires before doing anything about it. There is nothing to be lost, and an incalculable amount to be gained, by waiting, like Micawber, to see if anything turns up.

So much for the communications you can expect direct from companies in which you have shares. But there is a good deal more to investment than that. Agile investors need to keep their eyes skinned for new opportunities to deploy their funds. The obvious way of doing so is to study the financial Press.

The long-sustained equity boom of post-war years has greatly enhanced the quality and quantity of City information available from the columns of the Press. All the main dailies now devote important sections to business news. And the influence of Sunday columnists on Monday-morning share prices is enormous. Still, it is hard to dispute the overall leadership of the one specialist daily in the field, the *Financial Times*. On its unmistakable pink pages one can find a remarkable variety of news and comment on industry, commerce and public affairs. Even the arts page is excellent. At the back there is a unique record of some 2,000 share prices at the close of the previous day's business, together with details of dividends, earnings and price ranges during the past year. This is a service which the quoted companies are prepared to pay for, currently at the rate of £250 a year. For other securities you can consult the complete record of Stock Exchange dealings, also published daily in the *Financial Times*.

It is worth taking a closer look at this record of Stock Exchange transactions, even though, unlike the detailed and comprehensive statistics available in New York, the British system is very imperfect. It works like this. When brokers deal they may, if they wish, record the price at which the bargain took place. This list of prices, known as marks, is published each day, but each price is only given once, regardless of how many deals have been recorded at that figure.

There are, of course, serious weaknesses in the marking system. It is not an accurate guide, because marking is not compulsory. Besides, there is no means of knowing how many transactions took place at any given price. Finally, the marks give no record of volume, because they can equally well apply to 50 shares as 50,000. All anyone can really hope for from a study of marks is an idea of the pattern of activity.

Some sophisticated investors find this useful both in relation to a particular share and to the market as a whole. As we saw earlier when looking at charts, increased activity when markets or shares start moving in one direction is a sign that the trend is becoming established. If activity falls in the same circumstances the movement will probably peter out.

In recent years total activity on the London Stock Exchange has fluctuated between about 8,000 and 35,000 marks a day. Over 25 marks in a single share is evidence of very considerable interest. An average figure for an active stock (according to the daily lists in the *Financial Times*) would be more like 15.

Many private people find it expensive to take the *Financial Times* at a cost of 8*d.* a day, particularly if they are too busy to do much more than glance at it. The Business News section of *The Times*, now also 8*d.*, caters for this market as well as for a growing readership interested in industrial news. In addition, there are one or two specialized financial weeklies, notably *The Investors Chronicle and Stock Exchange Gazette*. This is a paper of record. At weekends it publishes a near-complete list of dividends announced during the previous seven days; reviews company accounts, new issues, offers and other stock-market happenings; and in general acts as a sort of parish magazine for the financial community.

All these papers devote a fair amount of space to share recommendations – almost invariably buying recommendations. On balance, their advice is pretty successful, though not unnaturally it needs careful sifting. A more frequent target for criticism is that once having tipped a share, they often do not mention it again, least of all to tell you to sell it. This can be infuriating, but public bearishness is nevertheless a dangerous game to play. This is not just because companies resent bearish stories and can make their displeasure felt in their advertising appropriations. Editors must also protect themselves against the wrath of their own readers, the very people they are supposed to be helping. If a paper recommends a sale at the wrong moment sellers commit themselves to something much more final than buyers who time their purchases badly. It may be irrational, but people can live with the hope of recovery much more easily than they can forget sacrificed opportunity.

It would be tedious to list other sources of comment, tips, investment systems, advertising and advice which circulate in the City and round its fringes. There is no doubt that some of the subscription sheets (like the *IC Market Newsletter*) have more than paid for their keep in the hands of some shrewd investors. If you think you are the kind of person to benefit from such advice there is only one way to find out. Try it and see.

So far we have been considering specialized investment information. But the market is also extremely sensitive to general economic events. Nowadays it is easy to keep a close watch on changes in such important items as output, employment, wages, prices and the international balance of payments. All these can exercise a considerable influence on the course of market prices, not only in themselves but also in so far as they foreshadow action by the Government to keep the economy on an even keel.

If you are prepared to work really hard at the statistical basis of investment you can track down all these figures in their original source books – official publications like the *Monthly Digest of Statistics*, the weekly *Board of Trade Journal* or the *UK Overseas Trade Accounts*, which show imports and exports in considerable detail about four weeks in arrears. You can go further by probing into the details of individual industries. Many of the trade associations collect and publish statistics of output, sales and the like. As long as they are not too technical in emphasis, trade journals (stocked by many public libraries) can keep you in touch with new developments. Of considerable interest are the annual reports of some of the major state organizations that are big customers for capital goods. The Coal Board, for example, gives details of its equipment expenditure, the Post Office publishes its spending plans in advance and the Central Electricity

Generating Board analyses its annual commissionings of new plant.

For most private investors, of course, such detailed burrowing is impracticable. People have their own work to do without straying into the territory of full-time investment analysts. Still, it is worth everyone's while to remember the increasing professionalism of investment studies. More and more buying decisions are being taken on the basis of thoroughgoing information and analysis. The result is a greater concentration on outstanding growth situations, and less indiscriminate confidence in big companies that have merely been all right so far.

This is not to say that the days of amateur flair are past. Some of the best research is sparked off by comment in the daily Press, and anyone can learn to read their newspapers with investment eyes. Above all, no amount of hard pounding can replace the gift of foresight. By the time a new development is so clear that anyone can see it the investment opportunity is hopelessly lost. For the market is always casting into the future, trying to discount events that are just round the corner. When they actually arrive there is often no market reaction whatsoever. You can probe and plan as carefully as you like, but your labour will be lost unless you remember this crucial rule: it is not tomorrow's facts that decide tomorrow's prices, but the expectations of the day after that.

CHAPTER SEVENTEEN

Investing at One Remove: Investment Trusts . . .

'TAKING IT all in all,' said Montaigne, the essayist, 'I find it is more trouble to watch after money than to get it.' You may feel like a wry smile at such a thought. But among the investing public there is a substantial and growing minority who agree with him. For them the problems of gathering information and taking decisions about their portfolios are a heavy burden. Whether they are uninterested in investment or too busy with their own affairs to give the matter proper attention, they are glad to turn to experts who can provide them with ready-made portfolios. There are several ways of doing so, both in and outside the market. In this chapter we shall be concerned with two methods which still involve your buying shares on the Stock Exchange, whether through investment trusts or under the guidance of professional investment managers. In the following chapter we shall turn to unit trusts.

Investment Trusts

The confusing thing about investment trusts is that they are not really trusts at all. They are ordinary limited-liability companies, whose managements are trying to invest a pool of resources for the maximum benefit of their members. Their capital structure is just like any other company's. They can have prior charge capital, such as debentures or preference shares, as well as ordinaries. In other words, their capital can be geared – a factor of major importance in their results. Like other companies, they can raise fresh capital when they want to, by having rights issues in the usual way. They can also plough back part of their earnings, although since the 1965 Finance Act they have had to pay out 85% of the dividends and interest which they receive. Generally speaking, however, the funds at their disposal are pretty stable. As the Americans would say, they have closed ends.

From the point of view of investors, the main advantage of investment trusts is that they provide a carefully chosen spread of interests without holders having to bother about investment decisions. Yields may not be particularly exciting; you may get only about 3% at the time you buy. But given a portfolio of well-selected trust shares (and this is a significant proviso, because choosing the right trusts in the first place requires some skill) you should be able to look forward to a steadily increasing income, combined with acceptable capital growth. Like this you can have a quiet life investment-wise.

You might imagine that holding shares through the indirect medium of an investment trust would mean paying capital gains tax twice over – once by the trust when it takes a profit on its holdings and again by you when you cash your shares. By a special concession, however, you can offset your share of the profits on which the trust has paid tax against your own liability. Each year, usually with the voucher for the final dividend, the trust provides you with a certificate showing what its net realized gains were. This can be added to the original cost of your shares, so when you cash your holding your tax liability is reduced by that amount. Since the trust pays long-term gains tax at the personal rate, it does not make much difference for gains tax purposes whether you hold shares direct or through an investment trust.

If an investment trust is to qualify for this comparatively favourable capital gains tax treatment, it must comply with certain requirements. First, as we have already seen, it must pay out at least 85% of its income as dividends. Secondly, not more than 15% of its assets may be held in any one share. Finally, at least 35% of the equity must be in public hands. The object of these provisions is to prevent people from using the form of an investment trust for purposes other than the general management of securities.

The British first thought of investment trusts, and to this day have remained well pleased with the idea. It has been extensively copied in other English-speaking countries, though in Australia the fact that gearing for investment trusts is illegal has robbed the movement of one of its principal advantages. Over there most saving of this kind has therefore been channelled into unit trusts, and development of investment trusts has been spasmodic. In Britain, and still more so in America, there was a prolonged, rueful phase between the wars while the after-effects of the slump were being worked off. Once confidence in the market was regained, however, the formation of investment trusts started up again.

Many powerful City names are tied up in some way or other in the investment-trust game. Merchant banks find trusts fit in neatly with their other interests in securities, especially issuing-house business. When Schroders was merging with Helbert Wagg or Kleinwort with Robert Benson Lonsdale the investment trust networks of each of the junior partners were tempting features in the deal. Private industrial reputations, moreover, have been founded on investment trusts. The late Harley Drayton, the financier of buses, laundries and Rediffusion, traced his commercial roots back to the trusts of 117 Old Broad Street.

Away from London there are investment trust outposts in cities like Newcastle, Swansea and Birmingham, but the movement achieves its finest flowering north of the border. Of the ninety-odd major trust management groups, no fewer than twenty-six are Scottish. Some of them, it is true, have colonized London. For the most part they prefer to brood at a cautious distance from the hectic fashions of Throgmorton Street. Brokers ambitious for trust business must take themselves, like mountains going to Mohammed, to Edinburgh and Glasgow, Dundee and Aberdeen.

Investment trusts have a comforting ring about their name, and many companies like to use the title even when their activities have nothing to do with owning Stock Exchange securities. Shareholders who simply want to rid themselves of their investment problems should make sure that the investment trusts they buy are properly diversified. Broadly speaking, you should exclude trusts which are known to have a disproportionate holding in any one company, whether it involves an unduly large proportion of the trust's funds or an unduly large stake in the company's equity. (In practice, qualification as an investment trust for capital gains tax purposes is a reliable enough safeguard on this score.) It does not constrict the field unduly. In 1969 there were over 300 conventional investment trusts, each with portfolios worth more than £½ million, which investors could choose from. In addition, there was a handful of trusts which have straightforward investment portfolios, but whose capital is split into income shares and assets shares.

In the circumstances amateurs might expect to have to pick their trust holdings with a pin. But City analysts have developed techniques for sorting out the relative merits of individual trusts. Detailed methods of approach vary from firm to firm, without any of them being convincingly superior.

With a properly diversified trust portfolio the main influence on its performance is the performance of share prices as a whole. No one can be completely insulated from market occurrences. Another factor of crucial importance is the skill of the trust's management in outdoing the averages. In particular, the distribution of the fund – in equities or fixed-interest stocks, at home or overseas – will have a major bearing on the results. How far all this is reflected in the trust's own share price depends partly on the gearing of its capital structure and partly on changes in the relationship between the share price and the value of the underlying assets.

Each of these factors can be isolated and used to decide whether the shares look cheap or expensive. It is worth considering them in closer detail, taking the ten largest trusts by way of illustration.

Broadly speaking, investment trust funds are invested in the ordinary shares and fixed-interest securities of British and North American companies. Obviously, proportions vary from one trust to another (e.g. in the table on page 162 Witan has none of its money in fixed interest, but Alliance has 11%). One has to arrive at an average for all major trusts and then, on the basis of the usual published share indexes, calculate a sort of composite index as a measuring rod. Over the decade mid-1959–69 this composite index rose by about two-thirds.

Turn now to the individual trusts and work out the changes in the value of their portfolios. (To be strictly fair, one has to take some account of net dividends, because it is part of a trust's business to earn a return on its assets as well as increasing their capital value. The management ratings quoted in the table in fact make appropriate allowances.) You can then divide the index of individual portfolios by the composite index, to get an idea of how far above or below average they are. For instance, if a portfolio had risen $2\frac{1}{2}$ times while the composite index had doubled one could attribute the extra to good management. So Alliance, the biggest and one of the very best trusts in the table on the next page, has enlarged its fund 1·34 times as fast as the average over the past ten years: testimony of excellent management. One can, of course, go through this calculation every year. The purpose of the ten-year record is to check the consistency of a trust's record, to make sure the last year was not a fluke.

Reasonably enough, good management does not come for nothing. Directors and their staff have to be paid for their skill in choosing investments, not to mention the routine administration of the fund. It is usual to check these costs against the income or capital of a trust, to make sure that they bear a realistic relationship to the sums of money involved. In the larger trusts, where economies of scale can be expected, expenses as a percentage of assets tend to be well below the average figure of 0·18%. With smaller trusts the ratio can sometimes be twice the average. Before investing in such trusts it is worth remembering that the cost of personal supervision of one's investments is not more than 0·5% (though admittedly that cannot be offset against tax).

So far we have been dealing with overall portfolio performances. The management record refers entirely to the success or failure in choosing investments. But from the point of view of investment trust equity holders, what matters is the effect on their shares, and that can be influenced by gearing. Of course the gearing is a reflection on the managers in one

Investment Trust Analysis
(The figures are those available in October 1968)

Name	Total size assets, £m.	Five-year Management record	Gearing, %	Priority earnings taken, %	Portfolio breakdown		
					Fixed interest, %	North American, %	Discount, %
Alliance	108	1·34	9	15–89	11	46	10
Foreign & Colonial	97	1·19	15	35–101	3	46	15
Mercantile	92	1·21	8	21–91	6	34	18
Industrial & General	89	1·22	7	13–98	6	21	22
Witan	89	1·45	17	41–102	—	38	12
Cable & Wireless	88	1·26	5	5–81	6	18	26
Globe Telegraph	84	1·27	3	5–78	3	17	24
British	82	1·18	12	21–99	—	44	16
Philip Hill	70	1·26	8	12–97	5	17	21
British Assets	64	1·17	20	42–92	1	56	1

sense, because they decide what it is to be. For analysis, however, it is more convenient and precise to keep these two factors separate.

The gearing, as shown in the table, is the percentage of the trusts' funds attributable to the fixed-interest prior charges. That does not mean to say that it is simply the amount of such capital in issue. The significance of prior-charge capital depends on current interest rates. Suppose a trust had in issue £150,000 of 7½% debenture and at current interest rates it was possible to get a return of 10% on debentures bought in the market. The trust would merely have to invest £112,500 in order to get an income of £1,125 to cover the interest on its own debenture. The remaining £37,500 would, in effect, be available for the trust's equity holders. For this reason, the gearing figures shown in the table take the prior-charge capital at realistic market values.

Gearing can also be affected by the composition of the trust's portfolio. For example, if a trust has 15% gearing, but has 15% of its assets in fixed-interest stocks, the gearing is cancelled out. In the table it looks as though Foreign and Colonial (15%) is more highly geared than British (12%). In fact, their effective gearing is the same because Foreign and Colonial has 3% of its assets invested in fixed interest, which has an offsetting effect. British Assets shows the highest gearing figure, while Alliance is actually negatively geared (9% − 11% = −2%). The priority percentages in the following column show the effects of gearing and distribution policies on the trusts' incomes.

Although gearing can have a profound effect on trust equity prices, it is naïve to think of it as a good thing without any qualifications. Gearing works both ways. When prices fall, a highly-geared equity is rapidly exposed to danger, as trusts discovered to their cost in 1929. A matter of months before the Great Crash, trusts were being launched with 50% gearing. That meant that when prices halved – and it did not take them long to halve – the trusts' equities were worth nothing at all.

Once a year, in its report and accounts, an investment trust discloses the market value of its investments as at the last day of its financial year. After allowing for gearing one can calculate the net asset value of its equity by dividing the assets by the number of shares. This, in theory, is what the market price of the shares ought to be. In practice, it is usually lower; the shares are said to stand at a discount. The last column in the table shows some typical discounts in the share prices of large trusts. Oddly enough, the range is extremely wide, stretching from a 26% discount on Cable and Wireless to only about 1% on British Assets.

It does, however, sometimes happen, particularly in bull markets, that investors are prepared to pay a premium over asset value to obtain the benefit of the expertise of some of the better trusts.

These differences between break-up values and market prices are obviously of vital importance in assessing the prospects for investment trust equities. The public is not going to let a share stay badly undervalued for long unless its management has somehow blotted its copybook. Unfortunately, official break-up values are generally published only once a year. The rest of the time one has to guess what effect subsequent market movements must have had. Brokers deal with this problem by noting changes in the main indexes – ordinary, fixed-interest and North American – and applying them to each trust in proportion to the breakdown of its portfolio. For illustration, suppose fixed-interest stocks had fallen by 5%, ordinary shares were up by 20%, and North Americans down by 12%, since the last valuation was published. These are what the apparent portfolio changes would have been in British Investment and Cable and Wireless:

(1) Category	(2) Change, %	(3) Index number	(4) Weight British	(4) Weight C. & W.	(3) & (4) British	(3) & (4) C. & W.
Fixed interest	− 5	95	0	6	0	570
Ordinary	+20	120	56	76	6,720	9,120
North American	−12	88	44	18	3,872	1,584
					10,592	11,274

If the portfolio breakdowns remained the same as they were at the last balance-sheet date – and investment trust portfolios are pretty stable – British Investment's net asset value should have moved up by about 5·9% and Cable and Wireless by 12·7%. In this imaginary example British's heavy commitment to North America has dragged it back, and Cable and Wireless's attachment to UK equities has pushed it forward. Incidentally, this exercise also shows that names of investment trusts do not mean very much.

The next step is to check whether these changes are more or less reflected in market prices. If not, that is an argument for doing something about it. Armed with the appropriate statistics on the breakdown of a trust's portfolio, and given access to routine share indexes, any investor can work these sums out for himself – or get his broker to do them for him.

With the advent of the computer these asset-value calculations have become a much simpler proposition; so much so that several broking firms now produce daily sheets showing the current position for large numbers of leading trusts. This has taken a great deal of the guesswork out of the day-to-day valuation of trusts, and it is now possible to tell at a glance whether a trust is cheap or dear (in terms of discount on asset value) when compared either with its long-term management record or with its average discount over the last year.

But it is not just a matter of discounts on assets. The market tends to value highly trusts with good long-term records, even to the extent of putting them at a premium on asset value, but there are occasional anomalies which can be profitable if you can spot them first. Provided one can avoid trusts whose management is genuinely deteriorating, and where this has been spotted by the market, this approach will be a considerable help in choosing which one to buy. In this connection, it is worth noting that investment trust managements generally are becoming more performance-conscious. There is a greater willingness to take a positive approach, both by concentrating lists into 40 or 50 holdings, and by going liquid by up to 20% or so of the total fund, when a bear market is judged to be in the offing.

Turning to split capital trusts, detailed refinements vary, but essentially the dividends from these funds accrue exclusively to income shareholders, while the assets shareholders enjoy most, if not all, of the capital appreciation. Typically, these trusts have a winding-up date about 20 years off. Otherwise, they would, in effect, imply an indefinite loan from the assets to the income shareholders. As it is, high and low taxpayers can play one another off to mutual advantage.

Valuing these trusts is not easy, so it may take some time before a sophisticated market develops. The position of the assets shares is straight-forward; there is a high premium on good investment management, because their gearing is so high. The income shares present a more intriguing picture. They offer similar prospects, in capital terms, as any 20-year industrial debenture, but hold out the hope of increasing income over the years. In terms of price, there is the problem of balancing rising dividends against eventual redemption at, or near, par, possibly involving a capital loss. But the divergent requirements of investors with different tax positions open up a prospect of a healthy two-way market.

Investment Counsellors

If you find investment trusts uninspiring you can, at a somewhat higher charge, enjoy the benefits of personal supervision. Expert advice comes in a good many shapes and sizes, some of it as a sideline of professions like accountancy and the law. Among the specialists there are the City merchant banks, offering a full-dress service for people with six-figure capital accounts. There are also the joint-stock banks. Their function usually is to provide a link between clients and a sound stock-broking firm, but in addition they run executor and trustee departments handling many millions of pounds. In between come the ultra-specialists, the independent firms of investment counsellors.

Investment counselling traces its origins back to Boston just after the First World War. Since then it has become thoroughly established in the States, where there are now several thousand firms, handling some $20,000 million between them. Bernard

Baruch, the Wall Street millionaire, has given them his blessing:

'What of the man or woman with modest savings' [he has written] 'who is simply looking for a fair return on his or her savings and who cannot give full time to a study of investments? My advice to such persons is to seek out some trusted investment counsellor. The emergence of this new profession of disinterested and careful investment analysts, who have no allegiance or alliances and whose only job is to judge a security on its merits, is one of the more constructive and healthy developments of the last half century.'

The idea has also spread rapidly in Canada and Australia, but it is only in the last few years that it has begun to catch on in Britain. It is doubtful, in fact, whether counselling has yet reached its final form in this country. After all, anyone can set up shop as an adviser, whereas in America a firm with more than fifteen clients has to register with the formidable Securities and Exchange Commission, the watchdog of the investing public. Over here the Jenkins Committee on Company Law has recommended some action on investment advice, but so far, at least, legislation is not even on the horizon. For this reason you should be careful about choosing a counselling firm. Many of them are pretty small, and it is worth looking into the standing of the people behind them.

Investment counsellors aim to provide their clients with a progressive investment policy properly adapted to their personal circumstances. If you consult them they will typically go to some lengths to show you what they can do, giving you a free opinion on your portfolio and making some suggestions on how it might be improved in the light of your income requirements, your tax situation and your overall objectives for your capital. Once in operation, they usually ask for discretion to make changes in your portfolio without referring to you for your approval. You may jib at this on the grounds that you are losing control of your own money. But, from their point of view, constant reference is not practicable. All their clients would suffer if they spent too much time sending routine letters to and fro. Most counselling firms will in any case agree to consult you before selling a favourite security. And they also take a lot of trouble to keep you in touch with what is going on in your portfolio, reporting changes whenever they occur, and providing an up-to-date valuation and full-scale review at periodic intervals.

An investment counsellor's job is to manage, not to handle cash, or take over the functions of a bank. In fact, you should beware of firms which claim otherwise. As a rule, therefore, counsellors simply give buying and selling instructions to your brokers. The exchange of cash, certificates, transfer deeds and the like goes between you and your brokers in the normal way. If you want to be rid of the chores of paperwork the best thing is to have your securities registered in the name of a bank nominee company and let bank, brokers and counsellors sort out the settlements between them.

What does all this cost? It varies from firm to firm, but a complete management service would usually be about $\frac{1}{2}\%$ a year of the capital sum involved, with a minimum of perhaps £40 and reductions as the amounts get larger. An advisory service, where the counsellors know what is in your portfolio and write to tell you what to do, would cost less. But this, of course, means you have to give orders to your broker yourself, and in the time lag since the letter was written to you share prices may have moved against you. Some firms charge by results, so you do not have to pay anything unless you make above-average profits. At first sight this is attractive, but if things go right the charge can skim off a big slice of your profits. Besides, in a bear market, when your counsellors face the possibility of making no money for themselves at all, they may be tempted to speculate. The conventional method of charging – a small percentage on the capital and nothing else – should be sufficient incentive to managers to try and keep the value of your portfolio moving upwards.

You may feel that $\frac{1}{2}\%$ (which you cannot offset against tax) looks high beside the 4 or 5% you can expect your portfolio to yield. The logical thing, however, is to regard it as a charge against capital. After all, if your managers cannot increase your wealth more than that they are not worth anything. You may also feel that it looks high beside the ⅛% which some of the joint-stock banks charge. The reason for the difference is that counsellors try to outdo the banks in personal attention. Most of all, you may feel you could save the charge altogether by giving your broker discretion to act for you. No doubt such an arrangement can be a success if you know your broker well. But many brokers do not like it. In principle it is doubtful whether you ought to give discretion to someone whose financial interest is in keeping your portfolio active. Either he may be tempted to deal to earn commissions for himself; or he may refrain from justifiable dealing for fear of seeming money-grubbing. To keep themselves off the horns of this dilemma, many investment counsellors refuse to share commission.

How much do you have to have to interest a counsellor? Few firms would take on a client with much less than £5,000, though they sometimes run their own unit trusts for the benefit of smaller investors. Their main market niche seems to be in the £20,000 and upwards range. Certainly they welcome people who would be turned away by most merchant banks. In addition, the bigger firms, which can provide a full-scale analytical service, accept some institutional business, including pension fund management.

Finally, how well can you expect a counsellor to do for you? It is difficult to get them to promise any rate of growth, though you are clearly entitled to expect them to outperform the averages. But there is one last thought to bear in mind. Investment counsellors are human, and like everyone else they can make mistakes.

Chapter Eighteen

. . . and Unit Trusts

HOWEVER SUCCESSFUL the investment-trust movement has been, its growth has been far outpaced by unit trusts. In mid-1969 there were some fifty unit-trust management groups, offering holdings in about 200 different trusts. In money terms, they controlled around £1,500 million, catching up fast with the £2,500 million for investment trusts. Yet little more than a dozen years earlier there was only a handful of trusts, and fewer still were the far-sighted people who saw much future for this brand of popular capitalism.

How is it that unit trusts have expanded so fast? To begin with, they are very easy to buy. It is simple to fill in a coupon, pin your cheque to it and post it off – much simpler than to establish a working connection with a professional adviser, particularly if you don't have much capital to invest. Secondly, unit trusts can advertise their wares, an advantage they have not been backward in exploiting.

Perhaps because of the very power of their advertisements, which unsophisticated amateurs can read just as easily as City solicitors, unit trusts are strictly controlled. In fact, although unit trusts are basically the same animal as investment trusts – both of them are investing with the object of benefiting members as much as possible – the supervision of unit trusts has always been much more detailed. This is partly a matter of legal status. Investment trusts, as we have seen, are straightforward limited-liability companies, and as such come within the scope of ordinary company law. Unit trusts, on the other hand, really are trusts, and there is a special department at the Board of Trade looking after them.

Actually, with unit trusts, there are three quite separate parties involved – the trustees, the managers and the Board of Trade as a sort of public watchdog. The trust deed, which is the legal document setting up a unit trust, is an agreement between the trustees and the managers. It covers virtually every aspect of running a trust. But it has to be approved by the Board of Trade, and in practice, when a new unit trust is formed, it is the Board and the managers who thrash out, between them, what goes into it. The trustees usually take a back seat till after the trust is formed. Then they act as police-men, to look after the cash and securities and to see that the provisions of the trust deed are not infringed. Their other functions include checking the calculation of unit prices from time to time; keeping an eye on transactions to see that the trust's income is not unnaturally boosted by buying shares just before a dividend and selling them just afterwards; and ensuring that an adequate reserve fund is set up so that the trust could keep going if anything happened to the manage-ment.

The main things the trustees do not do are to choose the trust's investments, or to take any responsibility for the per-formance of the fund. Both these functions fall to the managers, who also usually make the market in the trust's units.

The dominant position of the Board of Trade in the framing of unit trust deeds means that there is a high degree of con-sistency in them, as between one trust and another. In practice, unit-holders need not bother much with most of the details in trust deeds, except for obvious distinctions, such as whether a trust's income is distributed or accumulated. The Board of Trade also makes sure that the managers are suitable people to run a trust, and have adequate financial resources to do so. In theory, the Board has to approve the trustees as well, but since the trustees have to have paid-up capital of over £500,000, and are usually banks or insurance companies, this is purely a formality.

If you want to invest in a unit trust you have to go through a process which is quite different from buying shares. Instead of getting units from the Stock Exchange you contact the trust's managers. (Your bank or broker will do this for you if you like.) Alternatively, you can apply in answer to one of the block-offer advertisements which appear regularly in the papers – there is no particular advantage either way.

It is the managers' responsibility to sell units or buy them back from the public in whatever quantities are necessary. They do this at prices which they compute themselves, in accordance with the provisions of their trust deeds, as laid down by the Board of Trade. At regular intervals, daily as a rule, the managers value the underlying securities in the trust and divide the total by the number of units in issue. This results in a raw value per unit — or more accurately in two values, because there are different underlying prices for buying and selling. These values are then adjusted to take account of the costs of dealing, accrued income in the trust and the initial charge which the managers are permitted to make. The point of this is to prevent the rights of existing holders from being affected by other people's transactions. Finally, the managers, in fixing buying and selling prices, are permitted to round them off usually by 1% or 3d. whichever is lower.

Taken together, all this means that there is a wide spread between buying and selling prices for units. If we take the middle market price of the shares in the unit trust portfolio as 100 we can then follow the various pluses and minuses that go to make up the final prices of the units:

Middle market price 100

For BUYING add	Amount, %	Running total	For SELLING subtract	Amount, %	Running total
Buying price (jobber's turn)	½	100½	Selling price (jobber's turn)	½	99½
Broker's commission	1¼	101¾	Broker's commission	1¼	98¼
Transfer duty	1	102¾			
Unit trust settlement duty	¼	103			
Initial charge	5	108			
Rounding up	1	109	Rounding down	1	97¼

You can see from this that the permitted formula for calculating the price can produce a spread of up to about 12%. In practice – and unit trust managers like to claim it is a result of healthy competition – the usual spread is about 5%. Of course this spread can be anywhere within the permitted 12% spectrum. It might be from 97½ to 102½, in terms of our table, or from 104 to 109. This is known as pricing the units on a bid or an offered basis respectively. Obviously it can make a substantial difference to unit-holders where the price is at the time when they deal. Broadly you can expect better-known trusts to be on an offered basis in bull markets. And if, when things turn sour, your units seem to clatter down even faster than the market it may be that the price has been moved on to a bid basis to discourage sellers.

One item in the table which has not been explained in detail is the initial charge, which is one of the charges made by the managers to defray their expenses. By law, these charges are fixed at a maximum of 13¼% over a period of twenty years. Unit trusts have some discretion as to how they split this up, but most of them impose an initial charge, generally in the range of 3–5%, and a smaller annual charge, generally about ⅜–½%. (The trusts with a 5% initial charge cannot have an annual charge of ½%, or their twenty years' total would add up to 15% – more than the maximum.) There is, incidentally, nothing to stop managers from charging less if they like. Some of the funds designed to attract four-figure amounts usually do.

It will be noticed that, however you take them, these costs are quite considerably higher than the 0·2% of asset value which is the average for the big investment trust groups. This prompts the question, are unit trusts worth the extra? To answer that, we must consider the differences between the two types which have a bearing on their performance as investments. To begin with unit trusts are necessarily democratic; each unit ranks equally with all the others. Investment trusts can arrange their capital structure how they like. In practice, this means that they can raise part of their funds by issuing fixed-interest securities. Afterwards they can invest the money in ordinary shares so that their own equities are geared. It is rather like an ordinary investor buying a few more shares than he can pay for by borrowing from the bank. For this reason, an investment trust (provided it is geared) is a better shareholding than a unit trust with an identical portfolio so long as share prices are rising. If they start falling the unit trust is the better defensive holding. In fact, the various comparisons which people publish from time to time show that investment-trust equities as a class have done better than unit trusts in the boom times since the war, just as one would expect.

Another factor which compounds the advantage of investment trusts is that they usually plough back a small part of the dividends they receive for reinvestment in other securities. There is no law to prevent a unit trust from doing the same; in fact, some unit trusts plough back all their dividends in this way. But there is one good reason why unit trust managements should distribute all or nothing. The Inland Revenue insists that all a unit trust's dividends should be regarded as taxable in the hands of unit holders in the year they are received. This means that if all the earnings were not distributed the management would still have to provide a warrant for the whole of each unit holder's divided entitlement, regardless of the amount actually paid out, and surtax payers would be assessed on the income retained as well as what they receive in cash.

So far the advantage lies with investment trusts, and in fact if you have enough capital to acquire a pretty permanent stake in a handful of investment trusts you should do so in preference to buying units. Against that, unit trusts are freely marketable at all times at a price which reflects the underlying value of your investment, whereas selling an investment trust depends on finding a buyer – not always an easy thing in a bear market. Unit trusts also have the advantage as a channel for savings into equity investment. Many of them run regular savings plans, so you can put money into them on a regular monthly or quarterly basis. In such circumstances the extra cost, compared with investment trusts, is not a serious handicap. Not that the charge is all that high by American standards. The loading charges on their version of unit trusts – known as mutual funds – are often as high as 8%.

There is one point where the treatment of unit trusts and investment trusts is exactly the same: capital gains tax. Both of them have to pay the tax, at the personal rate of 30%, and both of them can frank it on their holders, so that tax does not have to be paid twice. One valuable feature, from the point of view of unit trust managers, is that there is no distinction between short- and long-term tax. Tax is therefore no bar to active management.

If you decide you would like to buy unit trusts by instalments you should consider one of the many schemes which link unit trusts and life assurance. In that way you can combine the advantages of insurance cover and tax savings on premiums with a full-blooded equity investment policy. Most of the main unit trust groups have started schemes of this sort. Unfortunately, it is not possible to discuss the relative merits of individual schemes, because the terms that managements are prepared to grant depend on the personal circumstances of savers, including their age. Anyone contemplating making use of one of these schemes must either do his homework very carefully in advance or turn to an insurance broker for advice. The following table, however, gives a general idea of the sums involved, assuming a steady uptrend in share values.

Annual Savings	£100
Tax relief on two-fifths or	£40
Equals at 8s. 3d.	£16 10s.
So net cost is	£83 10s.
Value of units purchased	£90 to £92 10s.
Period of scheme	20 years
Life cover	Nearly £2,000 plus changes in capital value
Eventual total net cost	£1,670
Cost of units purchased	£1,800 to £1,850
Value in 20 years, assuming about 5% p.a. compound appreciation	£3,500 to £4,000

There is, of course, no certainty about capital appreciation of this order, or indeed any capital appreciation at all. At the end of the policy (unless you die earlier) you get your units, and their value is your affair. If you are really more interested in life cover without risk, as against equity investment at a discount, you should perhaps opt for a conventional life-assurance policy.

Apart from frills like assurance-linked schemes, how should you set about selecting a unit trust? There is by this time an enormous range of trusts to choose from, many of them pretty new. This means that it is not always possible to apply the test of past performance. In any case, you should be cautious about short-term records, such as the annual league tables favoured by the Press. It is not just a matter of possible chance effects over a brief period; records can be distorted in the short run if a trust is moved from a bid to an offered basis. We think it is better to look at management groups, not single trusts, and if possible over periods of five years as well as one. It is also helpful to see how managers have performed in bear markets, particularly if you are drawn towards a go-go fund. You should look for a consistently good record in varying market conditions.

The potential uniformity of unit trusts has led some management groups to devise gimmicky ideas to attract the attention of the investing public. Some trusts are angled towards special industries – usually scientifically based industries – others towards special areas, whether at home or abroad. Emphasis on any particular section of the market carries obvious weaknesses. No industry or area can go on booming for ever, and a deliberate restriction of the managers' choice of investment is bound to be a handicap sooner or later. The moral is, if you go for specialized trusts you must be prepared to spread your risk and even switch about if necessary. If you want an utterly trouble-free life you should concentrate on trusts with general investment portfolios.

You will still find yourself with a wide choice between various management philosophies and investment policies – the degree of risk they are prepared to take and how much emphasis they place on income compared with capital growth, to give obvious examples. If you look for a trust which suits your own requirements, and which is run by managers with a successful investment record, you should sooner or later feel that warm glow inside when you inspect the price of your units in the newspaper.

PART III
UNQUOTED INVESTMENTS

CHAPTER NINETEEN

Cash with Interest

IF YOU have some cash which you want to keep safe and on tap there are three main outlets for it: the government-sponsored Post Office and Trustee Savings Banks, the big joint-stock banks and the building societies. From all these institutions you can get your money back intact and more or less on demand. Each of them have attractive features of their own. Banks offer services, particularly loan facilities, and building societies provide especially good rates of interest. The Post Office is competing increasingly with both, with its new investment accounts and giro system.

Post Office and Trustee Savings Accounts

Great pains have been taken to make Post Office Accounts both simple and safe. Anyone over seven can have an account, with any sum of money between 5s. and £10,000. Some 21,000 post offices – that is all except the very smallest branches throughout the United Kingdom – are available for paying in money or withdrawing it. All that need be produced is the pass book, in which all transactions, including the payment of interest, are entered. Admittedly there are some restrictions on the amounts that can be cashed. The limit is £10 a day on demand, but for most purposes this is perfectly serviceable, particularly as larger sums can be withdrawn within a matter of days.

As far as interest is concerned, the rate is low – it is still the same 2½% that was fixed when W. E. Gladstone founded the Post Office Savings Bank in 1861. The first £15 of interest is free of income tax, so given the present tax rate of 8s. 3d. in the £ that means the effective return on an investment of up to £600 is the equivalent of £4 5s. 1d.% before tax. An attractive feature of Post Office Savings interest is that it is on a monthly basis. Two and a half per cent is the same as a halfpenny per pound per month, and that is how the Post Office calculates it. Interest starts to accumulate from the first day of the month following the deposit and stops from the first day of the month in which it is withdrawn.

Since the summer of 1966, anyone with at least £50 in a Post Office savings account can open an investment account. You simply take your savings bank book to a post office which handles this sort of business, and you can open an investment account (with a minimum of £1) straight away. You can, if you like, transfer money from your savings account to your investment account, provided you still have a balance of £50 left in your savings account. Interest, which is currently at the rate of 6½%, is added at the end of each calendar year; though liable to tax, it is credited gross. If you want to withdraw cash, you must give one month's notice.

The Trustee Savings Banks cover the same ground as the Post Office Savings Bank, and if they are not quite as straightforward they offer certain extra advantages. Most Trustee Banks are divided into three departments: ordinary, special investment and government stock departments. It is the ordinary departments which overlap with the Post Office – interest is the same, the tax concessions are the same (though you cannot get them from both institutions at once), and the arrangements for opening accounts, and the amounts you can keep in them, are also the same. An advantage is that you can draw up to £50 on demand. Against that, there is the drawback that the eighty trustee banks have only about 1,350 offices. Withdrawals when you are away from home take a little more trouble to arrange.

The other departments extend the range of services which Trustee Banks provide. In the special investment department up to £5,000 can be deposited, the rate of interest varying from bank to bank, but generally of the order of 6%. It is worth noting, however, that special depositors have to have at least £50 in the ordinary department and that the £15 income tax concession is not available. Among the other services available are the buying and selling of government securities, safe keeping of documents and standing orders for regular payments like insurance premiums and so on. In January 1968 the Trustee Savings Bank started a Unit Trust, for the general public as well as depositors, and a life-assurance-linked savings scheme.

Banks

The main advantages of a bank account lie in the services which your bank can provide. The interest you can earn on your money is a subsidiary matter. In fact you will find, more often than not, that you are paying a small charge to your bank for handling your affairs. It is a charge which many people find worth while.

If you do not have a bank account it may be for reasons of deep-seated distrust; in some quarters the banks are regarded as forbidding, snooty and expensive. Besides, their hours – from nine-thirty in the morning to three-thirty in the afternoon – may take little account of the realities of your working day. Recently the banks, stirred into a new consciousness of their image, have started putting gay advertisements in the papers and backing them up with friendlier premises. This is a reflection of their anxiety to attract a new kind of custom. So even if your local branch still looks pillared and formal, remember they need you as much as you need them and go boldly inside.

Banks are a safe place to keep money, to save you the worry of keeping too much around the house. You can get the money out again by writing yourself a cheque and presenting it at your own branch. By previous arrangement you can cash cheques at any other branch, though usually only a certain amount each day. Alternatively, it might suit you better to apply for a cheque card, which most banks provide for customers of suitable standing. This will allow you to cash cheques of up to £30 at other bank branches generally. It is a rather different animal from the credit card, such as Barclaycard or Diners' Club, which effectively gives you a month's credit in a wide range of hotels, shops, airlines and so on. You only pay for this service if your account is overdue. Its running costs come out of the retailer's margin, because payment is guaranteed. As cheque cards involve no cost to the payee, you may find them rather more welcome in business circles.

Cheques come in two kinds – open and crossed. Either way they cost twopence, government stamp duty. Open cheques are for drawing out cash; crossed cheques are for making payments to other people. The point of crossing them is to make them safer, as they can only be paid into another account. They are safer still if you write 'a/c payee' between the cross lines, because then they can only be paid into the account of the person to whom the cheque has been made out.

Your bank will make payments for you in two other ways: by standing order or by credit transfer. Standing orders are suitable for regular payments, like rent, hire purchase payments, insurance premiums and so on. You sign a form and the bank automatically transfers the money once a month, once a year, or whatever it is. Credit transfers provide an economical method of paying a lot of bills at the same time. For each bill you fill in a standard slip showing your own name, the name of the account you want to pay and details of the bank and branch where that account is kept. For the convenience of customers, gas boards and the like attach credit transfer forms to their invoices. You then add up the bills and pay one cheque for the total amount to your own bank. The bank does the rest. With credit transfers you save stamp duty on cheques, but you will have to pay something for handling. How much depends on your other charges, but fourpence is the upper limit. Incidentally anyone can hand in credit transfers at any bank. But in that case you have to pay cash and there is a charge of sixpence.

When it comes to paying money in, it may be that your wages or salary will be given you as a cheque or transmitted direct to your bank account. You can also have interest or dividend payments credited to your account. In fact, most companies prefer it that way. If somebody has given you a cheque you do not necessarily have to pay it in at your own branch. You can present it at any branch of any of the big banks, fill in an appropriate form, and be sure that the money will reach your account in due course. It is worth remembering that this process of clearing cheques takes three working days.

Among the other facilities offered by banks are safe-keeping of valuables, including share certificates, for long or short periods, the transmitting of funds abroad, and travellers' cheques if you expect to be away from home. You do not have to be a customer to buy travellers' cheques. There is also a range of auxiliary services, many of them directly connected with investments. The banks run executor and trustee departments, handle the paperwork of investment through their nominee companies, and in some cases provide investment advice. Some of them also have their own unit trusts, which are on sale across their counters.

If you simply want somewhere to keep money and nothing else, a Post Office Savings account will suit your book. But as your affairs get more complicated a bank account will make life easier for you. Admittedly it will cost something – it is difficult to say what, because charges depend on the amount of work you make the bank do and the amount of money you have in your account. Generally speaking, the service is cheap enough for it not to be worth keeping a large average balance in your account simply in order to avoid charges. You could certainly gain more by putting the money in a building society.

If you put your money into a deposit account, which means that you agree not to withdraw it with less than seven days' notice, the bank will pay you interest on it. The rate is low – 2% less than Bank rate. This is never competitive with the return on building society shares. You should think of it entirely as a temporary expedient. There is the advantage that bank interest accrues from the day of deposit to the day of withdrawal and is credited to your account gross. Tax is payable, however, and in fact your bank will make a return to the Inland Revenue whenever it pays interest of more than £15 a year.

A more valuable aspect of a bank account is the availability of an overdraft. This is, of course, a sore subject, because you cannot expect an overdraft as a right. You have to tell your bank manager a convincing story, and back it with security for the loan you want. Stocks and shares with a ready market, life assurance policies with surrender values and deeds to property are the sort of security banks like. Do not forget they have to be worth a lot more than the amount you hope to borrow. From the bank's point of view, the security may have to be realized in a hurry for the most it can get. There must be some margin in case of emergencies. For example, a life policy will generally command an overdraft of about a third of its surrender value.

Another more expensive form of accommodation favoured by some banks is a personal loan, which has the advantage that you do not need any security. In a way, the banks offering these loans are competing with hire purchase companies. They grant them for purposes like buying a car or installing central heating and for periods of two years or so. The sums involved are not large – probably not more than £500 – and repayments are usually arranged at so much a month. Personal loans are a bit cheaper than hire purchase because rates are lower, but more expensive than a normal overdraft because you pay interest on the original loan, not on the fluctuating balance you owe.

Banks regard themselves as short-term lenders. It is a mistake to think of overdrafts as a permanency. Your manager will certainly review your overdraft half-yearly, keeping an eye on it in the meanwhile for periodic reductions. Anyway, it is in your own interest, if you want good working relations with your bank, to be as co-operative as possible over repayments. One thing that can lead to bad feeling is the side-effects of credit squeezes. A directive may go out from head office to cut down on overdrafts all round as part of the Government's credit policy. However sour you may feel about it, it is not the manager's fault.

If you want to open a bank account the question arises which bank to choose. In practice, this is largely a matter of personal preference. All the main banks offer the same rates, their differences being confined to services. We recommend one of the so-called clearing banks, English, Scottish, or Irish.

Giro

The giro system which the Post Office introduced in autumn 1968 offers many of the advantages of a current account at a bank, and quite often more cheaply. To operate this system, the Post Office has equipped a highly computerized giro centre at Bootle in Lancashire. It is almost as though everyone with a giro account had an account at the same branch of a joint stock bank. The main difference in operation is that payments go round the other way. Suppose you want to pay your gas bill. Instead of your sending the Gas Board a cheque, and their clearing it through the banking system, you send your giro form direct to the giro centre, and they clear the payment and then notify the Gas Board. Arrangements are, of course, available for drawing cash, making regular payments by standing order and similar services. However, no interest is paid on deposits, and there are no overdraft facilities.

Unlike a bank account, the cost of the giro does not necessarily rise in step with the number of transactions passing through your account. Transfers between giro accounts, deposits by account holders and postage are all free. Inpayments by non-account holders cost 9*d.* each; transfers to a bank account cost 6*d.* Such a service is pretty cheap. In particular, it competes with, and possibly even replaces the GPO's own postal order business for sums over a guinea. The 9*d.* charge for a giro inpayment is a penny cheaper than the 6*d.* cost of a postal order over a guinea, plus 4*d.* postage. There is a charge for giro forms and envelopes, but it is only 7*s.* 6*d.* for 50 forms.

Building Societies

Some people, particularly in the North, treat their building society pretty much like a savings bank. They drop in for some cash on their way into town. But the main advantage of a building society investment – its higher rate of interest – comes into play with bigger sums, even when they are invested only for shortish periods. True, we are on less safe ground here, because building society investors depend for their security on the proper and prudent conduct of the society's affairs. Still, the majority of societies are for all practical purposes entirely sound. Before you invest there are some minimum standards to look for, and these are dealt with in the next section. But once you are satisfied about the security of the society of your choice, you can enjoy a usefully higher return.

The main form of investment in building societies is in shares. Accounts of any size can be opened, with an upper limit of £10,000 down to perhaps £1 at the lower end. Interest starts within a matter of days from when money is deposited, and is usually credited up to the time of withdrawal. The rate of interest varies in accordance with national rates, except that it does not necessarily respond to every fluctuation of Bank rate. As a broad generalization it can be said that the Building Societies Association likes to make sure that recommended rates are fully competitive with those offered by the Post Office and Trustee Savings Banks. For example, at the time of writing the standard building society rate is 5% tax paid, or £8 10s. 2d. grossed up at the standard rate of tax. Some societies, generally those in close competition with the giants of the movement, offer $\frac{1}{4}$% more than the recommended rates. Although it is perfectly possible to find reputable investments among such societies, they should be specially carefully vetted for security.

With building societies, cash is often paid over the counter – in or out. For though they usually reserve the right to, say, a month's notice of withdrawal, most of them will pay at least £50 on demand and larger sums in emergencies. In practice, therefore, they can be as flexible in their arrangements as Savings Banks, with one drawback, that they do not have as many outlets as the Post Office.

A point to bear in mind about building society interest is that it is distributed in tax-paid form. Societies pay their tax direct, at a special rate agreed with the Inland Revenue. This so-called composite rate is an estimated average of what investors would pay if they were assessed direct. It is 32% as we write, but will probably go up. Obviously this is a valuable concession for the movement as a whole, but it is a snare for people who pay tax at less than the standard rate, because they cannot reclaim any of the tax paid by the society. So although building society shares are a comparatively high-yielding investment for standard taxpayers it is not safe to recommend them indiscriminately to everyone. Surtax-payers, incidentally, are assessed for surtax on the gross equivalent interest; that is, if you have £1,000 in a building society at 5% net, your interest for surtax purposes is £85, not £50.

To sum up, therefore, building societies are outstandingly suitable as a temporary home for relatively large amounts. They also provide an avenue for savings, which we discuss in a later chapter (see page 201).

Minimum Standards for Investors

During the late fifties there was a mushroom growth of building societies which offered above-average rates of interest and used their funds for property dealing. This boom ended with the crash of the State Building Society in 1959. Since then there has been extensive legislation governing the conduct of building societies, most of which is consolidated in the Building Societies Act, 1962. In consequence, there is a simple check which anyone can apply as a test of the security of any building society. The point to find out is whether the society has qualified for trustee status.

Under the Trustee Investment Act, 1961, the shares and deposits of building societies are trustee investments, provided they have been so designated by the Chief Registrar of Building Societies. To achieve trustee status a building society must:

(a) have assets of more than £500,000;
(b) have liquid funds, at market value, representing not less than 7½% of total assets;
(c) have free reserves, taking investments at market value, representing not less than 2½% of total assets.

There are some other minor conditions of trustee status, which is, in addition, at the discretion of the Chief Registrar.

On the whole you should invest only in a building society which has qualified for trustee status.

To be fair, however, there are some local societies which fail to qualify merely on grounds of size. Such societies can, if they wish, become members of the Building Societies Association, which also insists on the same minimum standards of liquid funds and free reserves. If you have some special reason for investing in a small society which is in the Association – for example if you want to promote home ownership in your own area or if you would like a loan from the society yourself – we have no objection to such an investment.

We recommend you *not* to invest in a building society which has neither achieved trustee status nor is a member of the Building Societies Association.

The reasoning behind the minimum liquidity and reserve ratios, on which trustee status is conditional, is as follows. Most of a building society's money is in mortgages, usually of twenty or twenty-five years' duration. In other words, it is in long-dated investments and cannot be readily cashed. On the other hand, individuals lending money to building societies like to feel it can be cashed at short notice. The reason why a society needs liquid reserves is to enable it to repay lenders without having to call in mortgages. The $7\frac{1}{2}\%$ ratio is the minimum level suggested by experience. In practice, most societies have higher liquidity ratios, 10 or 12% being not uncommon. The money is invested in short-dated government securities and local authority loans and mortgages. Market values are taken in case the society has to sell quoted securities at a time when they are temporarily depressed.

The reserve ratio is required as a cushion against possible losses. Losses are unlikely, because most societies are cautious in their lending policy, and in any case they can, as a last resort, take possession of a property whose mortgagor is not meeting his payments and sell it in the open market. The possibility remains, however. The reserve ratio is calculated after taking market values of investments into account, because the society would have to meet losses out of actual liquid resources. Again, the $2\frac{1}{2}\%$ reserve ratio is the minimum level suggested by experience. Again, most societies in practice have higher reserve ratios, 5% being not uncommon.

Investors often ask about the security of societies which have trustee status but offer above-average rates of interest. The point to remember is that societies which pay higher interest will also have to charge more on their mortgages if they are not to eat into the surpluses they use to build up reserves. Obviously home-owners will try and get the cheapest mortgage they can. Anyone who has to pay over the odds is probably not able to offer quite such good security. With the introduction of the selective employment tax it is no longer possible to make detailed estimates of the mortgage rate which societies would have to charge if they are to pay interest of, say, $5\frac{1}{4}\%$ net, but it would not be less than 9%, compared with $8\frac{1}{2}\%$ for the leading societies.

This represents an approximate measure of the extra risk implied by higher rates of interest to investors. In our view, investors can feel confident about lending to medium-sized societies with trustee status which offer $\frac{1}{4}\%$ tax paid more than the national giants. We should prefer to see liquidity and reserve ratios substantially higher than the minimum requirements and management expenses below the national average.

Hire Purchase Company Deposits

At this point we ought to mention the hire purchase companies, many of which accept deposits from the public. Unfortunately there are several drawbacks from the point of view of private investors in that some do not accept small sums. United Dominions Trust, however, now accepts as little as £1. Even when the big companies do take smaller amounts, the rates of interest they offer for money at short call are usually pretty finely pitched. For most investors, therefore, hire purchase deposits are not as attractive as building society shares, neither is their underlying business as solid. One exception to this is that hire purchase companies pay interest gross on deposits taken out for periods less than a year. But this advantage is available elsewhere, notably from British Savings Bonds and government stock on the Post Office register.

Minimum Standards for Investors

The forty-odd main hire purchase companies are grouped together as members of the Finance Houses Association. Conditions of membership do not involve any requirements for the protection of depositors, but in practice the FHA would be anxious to avoid taking on a company which could not meet its obligations. As a general rule, therefore, you should stick to FHA members when making a deposit with a hire purchase company.

If you do decide to consider making a deposit with any other hire purchase company, you should subject the balance sheet to certain minimum tests. The Industrial Bankers Association, before its merger with the FHA, used to lay down, as a condition of membership, limitations on total borrowing and minimum liquidity ratios. To help you in assessing the balance sheets of hire purchase companies we give below the requirements which the IBA used to insist on:

(i) Total borrowings were related to a company's paid-up capital and reserves. When these were less than £100,000, borrowings were not to exceed five times their total; between £100,000 and £200,000 the limit was six times their total; above £200,000 the limit was seven times.

(ii) Holdings of cash or Treasury bills had to equal 30% of deposits payable within fourteen days, or 10% of the total of all deposits, whichever was the greater.

CHAPTER TWENTY

The Savings Movement

IN THE last chapter we discussed the best outlets for money which had to be safe and easily cashed at short notice. Now let us see if there are any worthwhile alternative outlets for funds which must still be safe and available for cashing at all times, but which you will probably not need for a few years.

No doubt the wares of the National Savings movement are designed primarily to fill this market niche. The optimum holding period for National Savings Certificates and British Savings Bonds is five years. With the new Save As You Earn scheme it is, in effect, the minimum. In practice, however, the inflexibility of the old-established issues has told against them very heavily in recent years. At a time of rising interest rates five-year investments issued on fixed terms have naturally been quickly overtaken by events. In particular, the building societies, which are free to change the rates they pay on shares, have proved very competitive in such circumstances. You may argue that it is not safe to assume interest rates will go on rising. But if you believe they may actually come down, or even stay the same, it would certainly be worth your while to check the yields available on short-dated government stock. At the time of writing it is not difficult to find two-, four- and seven-year issues with higher annual yields, and much superior redemption yields, compared with British Savings Bonds. The National Savings movement also offers Premium Bonds, but as some holders win no prizes, and therefore receive no return on their capital, they are somewhat apart from the mainstream of investment. In the same way, the Save As You Earn project introduced in the autumn of 1969 is designed to compete with life-assurance-linked unit trust schemes, rather than as a home for capital.

National Savings Certificates

There have been a good many issues of National Savings Certificates since they were first introduced in 1916, but only one issue is on sale at a time. Currently the issue on tap is the twelfth. With this issue you buy a certificate of 20s. It does not pay you any interest as such, but increases in value over the next five years to 25s., which works out at a compound rate of interest of £4 11s. 3d.%. This is free of income tax, surtax and capital gains tax, so if you gross up this figure at the standard rate of tax of 8s. 3d. in the £ – that is, if you work out the gross equivalent you would have to receive if you are to end up with £4 11s. 3d.% in your pocket after income tax – you get a return of £7 15s. 4d.%.

This compares poorly with £8 10s. 2d.% on building society shares when their rate of interest is 5% tax paid, or £8 19s. 9d.% when it is 5¼%. There is also one rather unappealing feature about the interest on Savings Certificates. In the first two years it builds up rather slowly, and it is only during the third year that it reaches its maximum. In fact, the progression goes like this:

Year 1. At end of year	6d.
Year 2. At end of each four months	3d.
Year 3, 4, and 5. At end of each four months	5d.

To exploit Savings Certificates you therefore ought to hold them for not less than three years, and probably nearer five. Of course, you can cash them earlier if you want to. It is guaranteed that you can get your money out at eighteen days' notice, and as a rule eight working days is enough. The trouble is that if you take the money out soon after you have put it in you have very little to show for it. In fact, if you take it out before a year is up you get no interest at all.

All this adds up to a rather unattractive picture. In any case it is difficult to see whom they are supposed to appeal to. Some of their characteristics, like the fact that you can buy them in dribs and drabs and cash them at face value whenever you like, seem designed for very small savers. But if small savers

TABLE A

Issue	Dates of issue	Period for which certificates may be held from date of purchase	Purchase price per unit	How each unit increases in value	Maximum holding, units
First	Feb. 21st, 1916–Mar. 31st, 1922	Indefinitely	15s. 6d.	1d. for each complete month	500 in any combination
Second	Apr. 1st, 1922–Sept. 29th, 1923		16s.	1d. for each complete month	
Third	Oct. 1st, 1923–June 30th, 1932		16s.	1d. for each complete month	
Conversion	Jan. 1932–May 1932		16s.	1d. for each complete month	
Fourth	Aug. 2nd, 1932–May 31st, 1933		16s.	2½d. for each complete 3 months	
Fifth	June 1st, 1933–Feb. 28th, 1935		16s.	2½d. for each complete 3 months	
Sixth	Mar. 1st, 1935–Nov. 21st, 1939		15s.	3d. for each complete 3 months	
Seventh	Nov. 22nd, 1939–Mar. 31st, 1947	35 years	15s.	3½d. for each complete 6 months up to £1 7s. 6d. at 22 years. Then 3d. for each complete 3 months, with 6d. bonus at end of 29th year when the value is £1 15s. Then 5d. for each complete 4 months up to the end of 30th year, then 6d. for each complete 4 months up to the end of 35th year, when 3d. bonus is added, making value £2 4s.	
£1	Jan. 11th, 1943–Mar. 31st, 1947	29 years	20s.	1d. for each complete 3 months up to £1 7s. at 22 years. Then 3d. for each complete 4 months up to the end of 29th year, when 1s. bonus is added, making value £1 13s. 3d.	250
Eighth	Apr. 1st, 1947–Jan. 31st, 1951	25 years	10s.	1½d. for each complete 3 months up to 18s. at 20 years. Then 2d. for each complete 4 months up to £1 1s. 6d. at 25 years.	1,000

TABLE A *continued*

Issue	Dates of issue	Period for which certificates may be held from date of purchase	Purchase price per unit	How each unit increases in value	Maximum holding, units
Ninth	Feb. 1st, 1951–July 31st, 1956	22 years	15s.	1½d. for each complete 2 months up to £1 10s. 3d. at 10 years. Then 3d. for each complete 4 months up to the end of 17th year, when 6d. bonus is added, making value £1 16s. Then 4d. for each complete 4 months up to the end of 22nd year, when 6d. bonus is added, making value £1 11s. 6d.	1,400
Tenth	Aug. 1st, 1956–Mar. 12th, 1963	15 years	15s.	2d. for each complete 3 months during 4th and 5th years 3d. for each complete 3 months during 6th and 7th years, with an extra 6d. at end of 7th year making value £1 3d. for each complete 4 months till end of 15th year, when 6d. bonus is added, making value £1 6s. 6d.	1,200
Eleventh	May 13th, 1963–Mar. 26th, 1966	6 years	20s.	5d. at end of 1st year 2d. for each complete 4 months during 2nd year 3d. for each complete 4 months during 3rd year 4d. for each complete 4 months during 4th, 5th and 6th years, with an extra 4d. at end of 6th year making value £1 5s.	600

Note: A month is reckoned from the day of the month in which the certificate is purchased to the corresponding day in the following month, e.g. a certificate purchased on June 15th has been held a complete month on July 15th.

are the same as substandard taxpayers these advantages are outweighed by tax disadvantages. A net return of $4\frac{1}{2}\%$ with no possibility of a tax return is not really competitive with other savings media. On tax grounds Savings Certificates seem designed for surtax payers, and no doubt there are some people – liable to surtax now but not likely to be in five years' time owing to retirement – who will find them mildly attractive. But most surtax payers will obviously prefer the much bigger prizes which equity investment or short-dated gilts could bring over a period like five years. On balance, therefore, we do not believe Savings Certificates are competitive, though changing circumstances after publication of this book may make them so.

Earlier Issues

There is a certain amount of confusion among the investing public about their earlier issues of Savings Certificates. Let us begin with a record of all earlier issues of Savings Certificates, the dates of their issue, the terms and price of units, and the maximum number of each which can be held (see pages 192–3).

If you hold any of the back issues of National Savings Certificates you ought to check carefully when you bought them. From that you can see which issue they are and so work out the return you are getting on your money. Unfortunately this is quite a complicated business. As Savings Certificates are always growing in value, the yield on them is always changing too. Here is an example to make this clear. Suppose you have inherited some certificates of the first issue bought way back in the twenties, which have now grown to be worth 60s. each. They will still be appreciating, the rate being 1s. a year. This year, of course, your yield will be 1s. divided by 60, or £1 13s. 4d.%. By next year, however, the shilling increase will come on top of a certificate worth 61s., so the yield will be 1s. divided by 61 – only £1 12s. 9d.%.

Obviously this yield is unrealistically low in current conditions, and any certificates from that time should be cashed immediately. The same in fact applies to all issues bought before the war; that is, up to and including the sixth issue. With the seventh, eighth and ninth and one-pound issues, steps have recently been taken by the authorities to try to persuade holders to hang on in the expectation of a big bonus after a certain number of years. Details are readily available from the National Savings deskbook for investment advisers, and you should check them if you have a worthwhile sum locked up in any of these issues. Broadly speaking, what is on offer is a single year of quite high interest – generally $4\frac{3}{4}$–$5\frac{1}{2}\%$ free of all tax – some time between 1972 and 1978, depending on when the certificates were bought. We can only say we should be rather surprised if that was worth waiting for.

With the tenth, eleventh and twelfth issues – those on sale since August 1956 – it is worth waiting till the original life is completed. These issues last seven, six and five years respectively. After that they should be cashed.

British Savings Bonds

British Savings Bonds, the successors to National Development Bonds and Defence Bonds, are really only suitable for substandard taxpayers. Their yield – 7% for bonds on sale since April 1969 – is not competitive with the return available to standard taxpayers and surtax payers from building societies. The attractions for substandard taxpayers are, first, that interest is payable without deduction of tax at source and, secondly, that they are safer than hire-purchase-company deposits.

British Savings Bonds are slanted towards medium-term holders, because if you keep them for five years your capital is repaid at 102%. This means there is a gross redemption yield of £7 6s. 9d.% free of capital gains tax. Even so, you can, with a certain amount of inconvenience, cash your holding whenever you wish. You have to give a month's notice in writing, and if you want your money back within the first six months you sacrifice any interest you may have earned.

At the time of writing British Savings Bonds are markedly inferior in yield to short-dated gilt-edged stocks. Furthermore, the security is the same, capital gains tax treatment is the same (after a year) and, as long as you buy stock on the Post Office register, you still get your interest gross. Of course, this may not last, as gilt-edged prices fluctuate, but it is certainly worth checking the position before you commit yourself to British Savings Bonds. Their only compensating advantage is the utter dependability of capital at all times. It is also worth noting the maximum holding is £2,500. With gilts on the Post Office register you may only buy £5,000 nominal of any particular stock at any one time. As, in practice, it would probably pay you to spread your purchases over a number of stocks with different redemption dates, this is not necessarily very significant.

Defence Bonds and National Development Bonds

None of these issues are competitive in current circumstances, and you should consider cashing them immediately. Unfortunately, there are complicating factors, particularly for Defence Bonds. In the first place, with Defence Bonds you have to give either three or six months' notice of withdrawal (depending on the issue involved), the penalty for immediate withdrawal being a $2\frac{1}{4}\%$ deduction from the value of the bonds. Secondly, all bonds are eligible for a small premium at the end of their lives. If you cash your bonds only a few months before this premium becomes due, obviously the effective redemption yield which you are giving up is that much higher. As most of these bonds are redeemable in 1970 or 1971, you might well prefer to sit tight. National Development Bonds, on the other hand, require only a month's notice of withdrawal, so if they have much more than a year's life to run it is possibly worth getting out at once. You should compare the $5\frac{1}{2}\%$ annual interest and the 2% capital addition at the end of five years with returns available on short-dated gilts.

Premium Bonds

Premium bonds provide a mild gamble for investors who would like some fun but cannot afford to lose a penny of capital. They work on the same principle as state lotteries, with prizes going to holders whose bond numbers come up in a weekly draw. But there is one important difference. You cannot lose your original stake. The capital subscribed towards premium bonds does not go into the prize pool. It can be withdrawn on demand under government guarantee and is every bit as secure as any other National Savings issue. What goes into the draw is the interest which would otherwise be paid on the bonds. Effectively, therefore, you are gambling not with your capital but with the income you could earn on it.

Premium bonds are as simple to buy as Savings Certificates. You can get them, provided you are over sixteen, at your bank or any post office. Bonds are £1 each, and you can hold up to £1,250 of them. When you have bought them you have to wait three months before they go into one of the monthly draws. After that, however, they are eligible for every draw until they are cashed. Even if they win a prize in one draw they can go on and win again in another.

Ernie, an electronic device for selecting digits at random, picks the winning bond numbers. Draws take place on the first working day of every month, and weekly for one £25,000 prize. Eligible bonds each contribute a month's interest to the prize fund at a rate equivalent to one-twelfth of the current annual interest rate of $4\frac{5}{8}\%$.

The prize fund is split up like this:

First £25,000 weekly; the remainder monthly as follows:

Each complete £100,000			Each complete remaining £10,000		
	1 prize of £5,000			1 prize of £1,000	
10	„ „ £1,000		1	„ „ £ 500	
10	„ „ £ 500		2	„ „ £ 250	
20	„ „ £ 250		3	„ „ £ 100	
30	„ „ £ 100		20	„ „ £ 50	
150	„ „ £ 50		268	„ „ £ 25	
2,580	„ „ £ 25				

Any residue is divided into £25 prizes.

Taking each complete £100,000 of prize fund, the contributions of 21·6 million bonds are split into 2,810 prizes. The distribution of prizes is slightly more favourable with the remnants of the fund, so altogether the chances of winning a prize are about 1 in 9,700.

This may look a very long shot indeed, but if you hold the

maximum stake of 1,250 bonds your chances are improved to rather better than 7 to 1. And as there are twelve main draws a year, you might reasonably expect to win at the rate of six prizes in four years or so. This may be gambling, but the odds are certainly very acceptable.

What sort of return are you likely to get on your money? Over time, of course, you could expect to get $4\frac{5}{8}\%$, the rate of interest which bonds contribute to the prize fund. In practice, however, you might get very much more (because you had won one of the big prizes) or somewhat less (because you had only won £25) or of course nothing at all. As about 90% of the prizes are £25 ones, the probable rate of return on an investment of £1,000 is £25 every 9·7 months, or about £31 a year. This means a yield of 3·1% a year. Prizes are free of income tax and surtax, so for comparison they should be grossed up. Taking the standard rate of tax, a 3·1% net yield equals about £5 5s. 0d.% gross.

If you feel like buying premium bonds you should be more than usually clear about your objectives. If you want to treat them as a serious investment you ought not to have much less than 400 bonds. The odds then are that you will win a prize – probably £25 – every two years or so. This is a reasonable expectation, and there is the added spice of the possibility of a big prize. If you cannot afford £400, or don't feel like investing that much with the possibility of no return at all, you ought to think of premium bonds as a way of taking a tame flutter. Just how much you can afford to lock away with little hope of any return is obviously a personal matter. As a rough rule of thumb, you should be prepared to hold your bonds for half as long again as the time in which you can expect to win a prize. For example, with 800 bonds you can look forward to an annual win, so give them an eighteen months' run if your luck is out. Of course, this guide has no bearing on your chances of winning. The odds against your winning a prize next month are exactly the same whether you won last month or whether you have come away empty-handed for the last five years. We suggest it merely as a reasonable period for patience. With that in mind, you may find the following table interesting:

With this number of bonds	You can expect to win in this number of years (approx)
100	8
50	16
20	40
10	80
5	160
1	800

Local Authority Loans

Alongside the unquoted securities of the Government, there is an extensive range of stocks issued under the names of the country's local authorities. To understand the situation properly, it would probably be as well to look quickly at the ways in which local authorities raise the money they need for housing, roads and schools. Part of their funds come from the Exchequer through a body known as the Public Works Loan Board. In other words, they have access to part of the Government's credit. But in recent years they have been encouraged to turn to the market for money.

Confronted with the need to tap the market, the local authorities have adopted three main lines of attack. First, they have issued loans on the Stock Exchange. More accurately, this method is pretty well confined to major cities and counties whose needs run into millions of pounds. Their securities, being dealt in on the Stock Exchange, are liable to price fluctuations, and are therefore part of the normal armoury of quoted stocks.

Secondly, local authorities have sought money through the discount market. They offer to borrow for short periods like three months, six months or a year, with slightly rising interest rates for longer periods. Alternatively, the money is simply at seven days' notice, either borrower or lender being able to terminate the agreement at will. But these arrangements are really only suitable if you want to find a home for comparatively large sums of money for comparatively short periods of time. The minimum sum is usually £5,000, and the rate offered for money at seven days' notice is somewhere around $\frac{1}{2}$% less than Bank rate, although it can be higher.

The third method is the one most likely to interest people in search of a risk-free investment offering a pretty generous return. Local authorities at all levels, including rural and urban district councils, advertise for money on mortgage for fixed periods at fixed rates of interest. Typical periods range between two and ten years, and interest rates are higher than you could expect from a comparable government stock. The main advantages of the mortgage loans are a good yield and the absence of any dealing expenses. Even the main disadvantage, the fact that your money is tied up for a set length of time, can sometimes be eased in cases of emergency.

There are a good many variations on the basic theme of local authority loans. Some are offered below par, so that in effect they offer a capital gain on repayment at the end of their lives. Others include escalator clauses, so that loans left outstanding for more than a certain period receive a higher rate of interest. Others again carry bigger returns on larger sums.

Generally speaking, these mortgage loans are attractive for income-minded people, particularly if they can gauge the time horizon of their projected investment in advance. They can appeal to smaller investors, because in many cases sums down to £100 or even £50 are accepted. True, interest is paid net after deduction of tax, but there are no complications about reclaims for substandard taxpayers. If you would like to buy a local authority loan of this type you should check the advertisements in your local paper. For many people the thought of helping to finance development in their own district is an added attraction.

Savings Schemes

On October 1st, 1969, a new Save As You Earn scheme was introduced to provide for regular contractual saving.

The idea is that you can make regular monthly savings of between £1 and £10. It will be possible to do this either via the National Savings movement or with building societies. Arrangements have been made for the sum to be deducted from your pay by your employer, if you like. For every monthly £1 you save over a period of five years you will be able to draw £12, free of all tax. In other words, if you sub-scribe £60 (a pound a month for five years) you will get £72 at the end of that time. If you leave it in for a further two years you get another £12, to make the total £84.

In terms of rate of interest this works out at $7\frac{1}{4}$%, free of all tax, if you keep your money in for the stipulated five years, or $7\frac{3}{4}$% if you keep it in for the full seven. You can withdraw your money earlier, if you like, but then the rate of interest drops to $2\frac{1}{2}$% tax free, unless you hold for less than a year, in which case you get no interest at all. If you hold on for five years, the rate of interest goes up to $4\frac{1}{2}$% free of tax.

We saw earlier that National Savings investments as a whole have suffered from being inflexible, but unfortunately this scheme is more inflexible than ever. Once you start, you really are committed for five years, or else you lose quite badly, compared even with Savings Certificates. More unfortunately still, the main alternative outlet for short-term savings has exactly the opposite quality. It is at its most attractive as a two- to three-year investment, as well as being comparable over a long period.

Basically this alternative scheme works like this. You take out an endowment insurance policy, paying a monthly pre-mium, and the money is invested by the insurance company in building society shares. Effectively this is exactly the same as life assurance linked to unit trust schemes, except for the way in which your premiums are invested. At the time of writing the existing schemes stipulate minimum investments of £3 to £4 a month (with no maximum), but it is expected that other similar arrangements will be announced before long.

As these schemes involve life insurance, tax relief is available on the premiums, although it can be limited, as explained in the chapter on insurance, if the premiums exceed one-sixth of your income. Subject to that qualification, the relief available for standard taxpayers is $16\frac{1}{2}$%, so every £100 subscribed costs, in effect, £83 10s. As the cost of the life insurance part of the package is typically 8%, with the balance of 92% being invested in the building society, you are getting a cheap investment.

Ignoring the life insurance benefit, and treating the scheme simply as an investment, the return is £6 9s.% net, or £10 19s. 7d.% grossed up at the standard 41·25% rate. Although this is lower than the SAYE yield over its full five-year life, it does not depend on your staying in for the whole period. There is a penalty of one month's investment if you get out during the first year, but you can stop investing, and get your money out, whenever you want to.

To sum up, we think that life assurance linked with building societies is an excellent outlet for short-term savings. There are one or two reservations. As life insurance is involved, people who are sick or over 55 may encounter difficulties, and the scheme is not suitable for substandard taxpayers (as always with building societies). Furthermore, if you go round to your favourite building society anxious to sign on you may get a rather discouraging reception. By law, building societies cannot take the money direct from you themselves. The funds have to be channelled through an insurance company, and your building society may not be geared to handle this sort of business. Even so, we believe the scheme sufficiently attractive for it to be widely available before long.

This latest saving scheme has rather undermined the long-standing arrangements for saving through building societies. Still, if you are saving to buy a house, and would like to get the best possible treatment from a building society when it comes to your turn to get a mortgage, there is something to be said for subscription shares. Under this system you agree to invest a set sum of money every month, for three or four years or even longer. Interest is credited in the usual way, but if you complete the programme you get a bonus. Conditions vary from society to society, but an increase from 5% tax paid to 5½% would be quite typical. On the other hand, should you fail to complete the programme or even withdraw your investment you would sacrifice the bonus and part of your normal interest rate as well. The sums involved are always small – seldom more than £25 a month. At the lower end of the scale they are usually about £1.

The other two methods of saving with building societies are both by deposit. Deposits offer extra security, because they have a first call on profits and assets and can only be accepted up to two-thirds of a society's mortgage assets. For this reason, the interest they bear is usually $\frac{1}{4}$ or $\frac{1}{2}\%$ less than on shares. Now that the shares of all the major societies carry trustee status the extra safety of a deposit account has become rather pointless. If a society is worth investing in at all you can be quite confident about sticking to its shares. The same sort of argument applies to term deposits, which in any case are offered by only a few societies. They suffer the same restrictions as subscription shares, but their interest rate is not as high.

CHAPTER TWENTY-ONE

Life Assurance

MANY PEOPLE feel, at an early stage in their investment plans, that they ought to make some provision against death or disaster. They want to be sure that their dependants will be looked after, financially speaking, if anything happens to them. Naturally enough they turn to life assurance for protection.

At first sight life assurance may seem outside the scope of investment. Premiums on a life policy, it can be argued, are much like those on any other insurance policy. These are regular small payments made to guard against a much larger financial risk – anything from the 'fire, explosion, lightning, thunderbolt, earthquake' of a normal householder's policy to the arrival of twins. With life assurance the risk is simply that of somebody's death.

There is, however, one essential difference between car or household insurance and the endowment or whole-life policies favoured by the great majority of people who take out life assurance. In these instances the question is not whether the insurance company will have to pay up, but when. Sooner or later the policy will mature and the sum assured will have to be paid. With an endowment this happens at the end of a fixed number of years or on earlier death; with whole life simply on death. Incidentally the reason why life policies are called assurance, rather than insurance, is because of the certainty of payment at some stage.

Naturally enough you have to pay higher premiums for life assurance. After all, you are sure to get something back for your money eventually. But the extra contributions are not really insurance in the conventional sense. Of the regular instalments which you pay on, say, an endowment policy, only a small part is deducted to cover the risk that you may die prematurely. This deduction, together with the cost of the assurance company's expenses and profits, might total only about 10% of your contributions. The remainder is being invested, to the best of the assurance company's ability.

Now if the greater part of your assurance premiums represent straightforward savings, with the true insurance element comparatively small, clearly you must think of your policy as an investment. You must be satisfied that it is attractive as such, not just as a means of insuring against death. Otherwise you should consider covering the mortality risk by taking out a so-called term policy. This will give you life cover for a certain number of years – say ten or twenty years. And since payment is not inevitable, it will cost you less. Meanwhile you can invest your savings elsewhere.

If assurance policies are to be worthwhile investments they must stand up in comparison with, say, unit trusts or investment trusts. This means, of course, that they must offer some degree of participation in equities which, as we have seen elsewhere in this book, provide the most attractive form of long-term investment. Fortunately, some such arrangement is possible, because all assurance companies offer with-profit policies. With these you share in the fruits of successful investment (and better than average mortality experience). Most people should avoid the other alternative, non-participating policies, for although they give a better guaranteed minimum return, there is no hope of any improvement. In this way, the two different types of policy are akin to equities and fixed-interest stock.

How attractive are life policies as investments? Apart from the success or otherwise of the companies as investment managers, there are two things in their favour. The first is psychological; many people find it hard to save money regularly, and it is a great help to enter into what seems to be a binding contract. You can, of course, escape from a life assurance contract if necessary, but it is difficult and often involves some financial penalty, particularly if you want to surrender the policy completely. The other plus factor is fiscal. Life assurance premiums qualify for a special tax relief by which, subject to certain limits, your taxable income is reduced by two-fifths of the premiums paid, or £10, whichever is the greater. At the other end of the scale, this relief is not permitted by the Inland Revenue to exceed one-sixth of your total income or 7% of the total sum assured. However, assuming your policy falls within these limits, and taking the standard 8s. 3d. rate of tax, the relief is worth two-fifths, or 40%, of 41¼%. This works out at 16½% of each premium payment, which is probably more than enough to meet the deduction for insurance cover and the assurance company's expenses, so it is fair to say that they cost you virtually nothing. Even so, if you are mainly looking for a good way of investing your savings the tax concession is of only marginal importance against the effectiveness of the company's investment policy.

Sad to relate, most life policies measure up poorly on this crucial point. This is not really their fault. In a normal with-profits policy the company contracts to produce a certain minimum result, and to give you some of the benefit if it can do better. Its first objective, therefore, is not to fall below the minimum for which it has contracted. And that leads to a rather defensive, safety-first, investment policy. As a result, assurance companies have been far more cautious than, say, investment trusts about investing in equities. Even now very few show more than half their assets in equities in their balance sheets, although on the basis of market values the number would be greater.

Despite their worries about contractual obligations, it is rather surprising that assurance companies have not tried harder to provide a vehicle for savings better tailored to modern conditions, that is, with greater emphasis on equities. One reason may be that the dual nature of life policies – savings combined with protection – has prevented managements from formulating their objectives with sufficient clarity. Another reason may be that policies are easier to sell when the industry's investment performance is to some extent blurred. After all, if their sales are rising steadily, why should they change their merchandise?

Unfortunately the effects of assurance companies' financial conservatism reach farther than investment policy. Even if the investment management of your savings were highly successful, the chances are that you would not enjoy much of the benefit. Generally speaking, any dividend increases on shares the company invests in would filter through to you in reasonably full measure in the shape of accumulated bonuses. Still, even these would be eaten into by appropriations to reserve and sometimes a small cut for the company's shareholders. As for the benefits of capital appreciation, in many cases they would not be passed on to any great extent. True, some of the more forward-looking companies have recently been including an element of capital appreciation in their bonuses, but you may be sure this is only the tip of the iceberg. In some cases capital appreciation on investments is not even recognized in the assurance company's accounts.

To sum up, the investment attractions of life policies are pretty doubtful. Although the tax concession usually pays for the actual life cover, you are basically investing your savings in a combination of two things: fixed interest and a sort of equity that gives you dividend increases but no capital growth. The proportion between these two varies with individual offices, but is usually weighted towards fixed interest.

What, then, can we say to the equity-minded investor who must have life insurance protection? Well, he can take out a term policy and channel his savings into a unit trust. But what he really needs is some means of securing all the benefits of a life policy – protection, simplicity, the contractual obligation to save, the tax concession – while still reaping the full benefits of investing in equities.

There are in fact two ways this can be done. The most popular (discussed in detail in the chapter on unit trusts) is a scheme by which each premium is split up into its insurance and savings components, and the savings part invested in a unit trust. The policyholder therefore participates fully in the investment risks and rewards. Under this arrangement the final payment is made in units rather than in cash. Not surprisingly, the impetus behind such schemes has come from the unit trust management groups rather than the life offices. The drawbacks are that they are not as flexible as ordinary life assurance; you do not have nearly such a wide choice of terms as, for instance, with an endowment policy, and most schemes do not offer whole life at all. Nevertheless, in our view the investment advantages are so overwhelmingly superior that you should try to adapt your needs to fit a unit-trust-linked policy if at all possible.

As an example, suppose you wish to take out an 'education policy', by which you will make regular payments over, say, fifteen years, and you will then receive the policy proceeds in equal sums over the next three years, to coincide with university education or professional training. A unit trust scheme may not offer exactly this, but it will offer a straight fifteen years endowment. It should not then be beyond you to invest the policy proceeds at the end of fifteen years in some safe short-term security and realize it as needed over the following three years. This will not be called an 'educational' policy, but it will achieve the same result. With a little common sense other policies with special features can often be reproduced in their essentials by a unit trust scheme.

An increasing number of the more adventurous life offices have started offering special equity-linked policies, in an effort to compete with the unit trusts. As we have shown, the investment function of a life office is by far the most important (and the most profitable). If unit trusts were to replace them completely, leaving only the bare function of providing life cover, assurance companies would be only a shadow of their present selves. An equity-linked policy is very much like a unit trust policy, except that the life office in effect provides its own unit trust to cater for the savings part of such policies. Investment-wise, the relative merits of unit trust and equity-linked policies depend on the investment skills of the managers, and this is something on which one cannot generalize. However, as their development proceeds, equity-linked policies should provide the flexibility, in the form of special policy options and so on, that unit trust policies lack.

The Frills of Life Assurance

So far we have discussed life assurance as an investment. But it has several other features which, although they have little to do with the investment aspect, must be taken into account in deciding whether or not to take out a policy.

We have already touched on the great flexibility of life assurance. The varieties in fact are endless. Here are a few examples in addition to those already mentioned:

1. You can increase the insurance element of an endowment policy by paying a little more for extra life cover if you die before the policy matures. You can even double the cover if you like. This is really an endowment policy and a term policy combined. Variations are that the extra may only be payable if death occurs by accident, or that the extra is payable to your dependants as an annual income rather than a lump sum.

2. The option to have the proceeds of the policy payable as an income in this way applies to most policies. In effect, the lump sum that would normally be payable is automatically used to purchase an annuity on pre-arranged terms. As a refinement, you may sometimes opt for part annuity, part cash.

3. A term policy can be adapted to cover some commitment, the amount of which is falling year by year. Called 'reducing term', this is particularly suitable for a mortgage that is gradually being paid off. The insurance simply covers the amount outstanding at any time.

4. If you are young and unsure of your financial position in the future you can take out a convertible policy. This will start off as whole life, but give you an option after, say, five years to convert into a suitable endowment policy. One advantage of this method is that you start the policy when you are medically fit and therefore eligible for best terms.

Annuities

In its simplest form, an annuity is an annual income assured until death, purchased for a lump sum. As with life assurance, there are variations. The annuity can be based on two lives, with the income continuing until the death of the last to die, either at the same or at a reduced rate. The purchase can be made by a series of payments rather than a lump sum, or the start of the income payments can be deferred until some convenient time, like retirement. The payments may be made annually, six-monthly or at shorter intervals.

At first sight, annuities give a very high return on capital. For a man aged sixty-five it could be up to 13%, and higher still if he is older, although less if younger. This is because each income payment is partly your own capital being returned to you, as well as normal interest. Actuarially the capital proportion of each payment increases over the years, but for convenience the Inland Revenue has agreed that the proportion shall remain fixed, based on average expectation of life. Since the average expectation of a man of sixty-five is about fourteen years, the capital return for him would be about 7% of his original purchase cost each year. As such it would be tax free. The extra 6% or so would be interest, and therefore taxable.

If this man knew he was going to live exactly fourteen years he could arrange his own annuity by investing in a building society and withdrawing some capital each year according to a carefully calculated schedule. But this is not something one can know, and an annuity, besides having the advantage of simplicity, is the only way he can run down capital to supplement income, and still be sure his capital will not one day run out. For this assurance he runs the risk of having spent his capital unnecessarily if he should die unexpectedly soon.

There are two points to watch before taking out an annuity. You should see that your dependants will still be properly provided for without the capital you are spending. You should also make sure, as far as you can, that you will not suddenly need the capital for some other purpose and regret having sunk it in an annuity. Provision for dependants can be made, as we have seen, by life assurance, or simply by keeping a healthy proportion of your capital out of the annuity.

From an investment point of view most annuities are effectively fixed-interest investments, but this is appropriate because they are generally purchased by elderly people, whose investment horizon is relatively short. There is, of course, no reason why annuities should not be linked to equities in the same way as life assurance policies can be, and there is now a fair choice of such schemes which have been making their appearance over the last few years.

Property Bonds

One interesting development in the insurance market is the property bond, which offers a direct stake in bricks and mortar, with a little life cover thrown in. In one sense, the insurance element is a frill, because property bonds are effectively the same as units in a property unit trust, but it is a frill which has important tax implications. Whereas property companies have to pay corporation tax at 45% on income and capital gains in their underlying portfolios, the bond funds pay income tax at $37\frac{1}{2}$% and capital gains tax at 30% – a very competitive advantage. When one remembers that the prices of property bonds have mostly followed a pretty smooth upward path, without the disconcerting fluctuations of shares quoted on the Stock Exchange, it is clear that we are dealing with a powerful investment vehicle.

Nevertheless, before going overboard for property bonds, it is as well to remember there are potential snags. For one thing, properties are not as easy to sell as shares, so the bonds cannot be said to be as liquid as unit trusts. It could possibly happen that a period of up to six months could elapse before you could get money out of a property bond. More seriously, the valuation of a fund's property portfolio presents major difficulties. There is, of course, no market place, like the Stock Exchange, for valuing property. Assessments have to be made by valuers, who may or may not be wholly independent of the fund's managers. In any case, the danger is not simply a temptation to keep valuations high in order to boost performance. Conservative undervaluations are equally suspect, because they let new subscribers in on terms which are unfavourable to existing bondholders.

At the root of the problem is the fact that property bonds have no legal or investment status. No doubt official action will soon be taken to rectify this, by bringing bonds under the supervision of the Board of Trade. Until such time, it would be wise to keep cool about property bonds. Even if it means resisting the blandishments of door-to-door salesmen, you should take care that these bonds do not comprise more than a single unit in your total portfolio.

PART IV

TAX

CHAPTER TWENTY-TWO

Tax on Investment Income

ALL INTEREST and dividends, including capital distributions, are liable to tax. Ultimately the rate of tax payable depends on the circumstances of the shareholder receiving the dividend. For administrative convenience, however, tax is deducted at source by the companies making the payment. The rate they take is the standard rate of tax, currently 41·25%. In effect, the companies act as tax collectors for the Inland Revenue.

The position is set out on your dividend warrant, as required by law. These are the points it shows:

(1) the gross amount of the dividend, or the method by which this can be calculated;

(2) the rate of tax deducted, with either the amount or the method for calculating it;

(3) the net amount actually paid.

To illustrate, suppose a company has declared a dividend of 10% and you have 40 of its £1 shares. Your gross dividend of £4 (10% × £40) will be shown on the warrant (Point 1). Sometimes the actual figure is not given, but gross dividends for representative numbers of shares are printed on the back of the warrant. From this you can work out the figure which applies to you.

Tax is deducted at 41·25%, and the amount of tax charged shown separately, i.e. 41·25% × £4 = £1 13s. (Point 2).

The difference between the gross dividend (£4) and the tax charged (£1 13s.) is your net dividend, i.e. £2 7s. (Point 3).

Some companies like to express their dividends in so many shillings and pence per share, but this makes no difference to the form of dividend warrants.

Dividends, in whatever form they are declared, are used to calculate gross yields. Many investors find this irritating, because what they want to know is their actual net return in terms of spending money. The reason for quoting gross yields is that they provide a standard of comparison which everyone can use. You can then make your own allowances for your own tax circumstances.

The procedure for adjusting yields to take account of tax works like this:

Take a gross yield of 4%
Subtract 41·25% to allow for tax (100 − 41·25 = 58·75)
Multiply the gross yield by the amount you actually keep − 58·75%

$$\frac{4 \times 58·75}{100} = 2·35\%$$

This is the calculation taking tax at the standard rate. The same sum can be adapted to take account of reduced tax rates or surtax rates, as follows:

	Tax at 30%	Surtax 68·75%
Gross yield	4%	4%
Net Amount	100 − 30 tax	100 − 68·75
	= 70 net	= 31·25 net
Net yield	$\frac{4 \times 70}{100} = 2·8\%$	$\frac{4 \times 31·25}{100} = 1·25\%$

The fact that the same gross yield − 4% − can end up at such vastly different figures in the net form emphasizes the importance of tax rates.

How can you tell what your tax rate is? It is not possible for us to take account of all the factors, like earned-income relief, children's allowance and so on, which affect individual tax rates. What counts for our present purpose is the amount of tax which people pay on their investment income. This is usually the standard rate − 41·25% − but it can be less, for people with small incomes, or more, for surtax payers. The key thing for you to know is your marginal rate of tax − in other words, the tax you pay on the top slice of your income.

Some indication of the sort of tax rates unearned income attracts can be seen from the following table:

% rate of income tax	Single person, £	Married man, £	Married + 1 child, £
Nil	328	450	490
30%	515	635	750
41·25%	2,000	2,120	2,235
Rates of surtax payable, %	£	£	£
10%	2,500	2,620	2,735
12·5%	3,000	3,120	3,235
17·5%	4,000	4,120	4,235
22·5%	5,000	5,120	5,235
27·5%	6,000	6,120	6,235
32·5%	8,000	8,120	8,235
37·5%	10,000	10,120	10,235
42·5%	12,000	12,120	12,235
47·5%	15,000	15,120	15,235
50%		All extra income	

What the table shows is the upper limit at which unearned income attracts any given rate of income tax and surtax in three different cases, taking account of basic allowances. Thus a man with one child under 11 starts paying tax (at 30%) on £491 and surtax at £2,236. For wage and salary earners, earned income relief and surtax concessions on earned income up to £5,000 would have to be taken into account.

Substandard Taxpayers

There are three main considerations for substandard taxpayers to bear in mind. The first is practical. Tax reclaims take time, and it can be highly inconvenient for people with small incomes to be out of pocket while their claims are being handled. For this reason it is useful to know which forms of investment pay their interest or dividends gross. Then, if there is any tax adjustment later on, at least you will have had the use of the money in the meantime. Here are the principal investments offering this concession:

(1) British Savings Bonds;
(2) War Loan;

(3) Government stocks on the Post Office register;
(4) bank deposits;
(5) hire purchase deposits taken out for periods up to a year.

The second point to remember is that tax-free payments are comparatively unattractive for small taxpayers. With National Savings, for example, the additions to the value of the certificates are at a fairly low rate of interest and free of all tax. From the point of view of someone with a high marginal tax rate this is all very well. But tax concessions are not valuable to people who do not pay much tax.

Thirdly, substandard taxpayers should be wary of building society shares. By arrangement, building societies pay tax on behalf of their investors at a special composite rate agreed each year with the Inland Revenue. This rate, which is supposed to represent an average tax rate for building society shareholders, has in recent years been about 30–35%. Having made this concession, the Inland Revenue is not prepared to grant any further reliefs to substandard taxpayers. In effect, therefore, the tax-paid dividend which building societies distribute is all that substandard taxpayers get. For this reason, building societies are relatively unattractive for them compared with, say, British Savings Bonds.

Surtax payers

For people who pay surtax on their investment income the importance of capital appreciation, even if it is eventually subject to gains tax, is too obvious to need emphasizing here. The main point to discuss is the redemption element in dated fixed-interest stocks. With these stocks you can make allowance for the change in capital value which will take place between the time you buy them and the time when they come up for redemption. To make the most of this you should stick to gilt-edged stocks, because, provided you hold them for more than a year, the gains are free of capital-gains tax.

For example, suppose a gilt-edged stock due for redemption at par in two years' time is now standing at 94. You can expect capital appreciation at the rate of 3 points per annum, near enough, between now and then. As this appreciation is certain, you can take account of it in the overall return on your investment, making appropriate adjustments for your personal rate of tax. For someone paying 68·75% total tax it works like this:

Annual capital appreciation, say	3·0% approx.
Gross up $= \dfrac{3·0 \times 100}{100 - 68·75} =$	9·60%
Add on gross income, say	2·75%
Grossed-up redemption yield	12·35%

This calculation can be adjusted if necessary for capital gains tax by taking off 30% of the capital part of the yield. In fact, the mechanics of the sum are exactly the same for any rate of surtax and for any sort of capital appreciation, provided it is certain and provided the operation falls outside the scope of the short-term gains tax. Otherwise your profit would simply be treated as unearned income for income tax and surtax, and that would cancel out your careful calculations.

Non-residents' Tax

A substantial number of investors making use of the London Stock Exchange are not resident in Britain, and for them there are special rules about their tax liability on interest and dividends.

These rules are based on a series of agreements on double-tax relief, which have been or are being negotiated with other countries. Under these agreements a dividend paid to a non-resident by a British registered company is subject to a withholding tax of 15% instead of tax at the standard rate of 41·25%. Equally a United Kingdom resident receiving a dividend from a foreign company benefits from the same arrangement, and this is allowable as a credit against the 41·25% United Kingdom tax which would otherwise have to be paid. As it is, the paying agent merely deducts further tax at 26·25%. Surtax, if applicable, is charged on the gross amount of the dividend before the withholding tax. Equally anyone entitled to a reduced rate can make a reclaim up to 26·25%, but cannot in any circumstances reclaim any part of the withholding tax.

There are two main exceptions to this rule. First in the case of loan stocks and debentures, interest is paid gross without the deduction of any withholding tax. Non-residents will therefore receive their interest tax free, but United Kingdom residents will still suffer tax at the standard rate. There is also a short list of gilt-edged stocks on which non-residents can receive interest free of tax. They are:

Victory 4% 1976	Exchequer 6% 1970
Exchequer 5% 1976/78	Funding 4% 1960/90
Funding 5¼% 1978/80	Savings 3% 1960/70
Funding 5½% 1982/84	Savings 3% 1965/75
Funding 5¾% 1987/91	
Funding 6% 1993	
Treasury 5½% 2008/12	
Treasury 6½% 1976	
War Loan 3½%	

The stocks in the list on the left, but not those on the right, may be bought with security sterling.

The other main exception concerns the circumstances in which non-residents can claim relief from United Kingdom tax. To qualify, you must come in one of a number of categories, of which the following are the most usual:

British subject
In the service of the British Crown
Citizen of the Irish Republic
Resident in the Channel Islands or the Isle of Man
Resident in a country with an appropriate double-tax-relief agreement.

If you come in one of these categories you are entitled to the same reliefs as you would get if you were a British resident, except that they are scaled down in the proportion that your United Kingdom income bears to your world income. In other words, if your income from all sources, including earned income, is £2,500 and your United Kingdom dividend income is £100, you are only entitled to 4% of the reliefs you could expect if you lived in Britain.

Turning to income which comes from a source outside the United Kingdom, non-residents are not liable to tax. However, with a good many of the securities involved – dominion, colonial and foreign bonds, overseas equities like South African companies, and so on – the agents responsible for paying dividends are in Britain or the sterling area. They would therefore automatically deduct tax at the standard rate unless steps were taken to claim exemption.

The procedure is to submit the appropriate form for claiming exemption (A5). You can do it yourself or ask your bank or broker to help you. If the dividend is to be paid to a British address for the account of a non-resident the claim for exemption has to be cleared with the Inspector of Foreign Dividends, Inland Revenue, New Malden House, Blagden Road, New Malden, Surrey. If for some reason you are unable to claim exemption before your dividend is paid you can claim repayment of tax from the British authorities, on Form A1.

Extra problems arise when it comes to shares held in a nominee account, and to cope with this a special arrangement known as the 'G' arrangement has been devised by the Inland Revenue, who have come to a special agreement with those companies willing to participate in the scheme. A list of these companies is published as a supplement to the Stock Exchange Daily Official List. This is very convenient for the non-resident private investor, since the whole business is handled by the nominee company and the Revenue. What actually happens is that a month or so before a particular dividend is due to be paid the nominee company, which must either be resident or, alternatively, be able to produce a resident guarantor, sends a declaration and claim to the Inland Revenue in respect of all its non-resident holdings, and the Inland Revenue then authorizes the company paying the dividend to grant the appropriate tax relief at source.

As far as investment policy is concerned, non-residents

should not pay too much attention to these tax details at the expense of conventional investment considerations. For example, the advantage of having one's interest on War Loan paid gross has been far outweighed in recent years by the disappointing price performance of the stock itself. The people who should, perhaps, be most aware of the implications of the non-residents' tax rules are income-conscious investors who have retired to a warmer climate overseas. It should be worth their while to keep an eye open for attractive situations among overseas shares, seeing that yields are sometimes high and dividends can be received gross. As we shall see in the next section, non-residents are also exempt from both short- and long-term capital gains tax.

CHAPTER TWENTY-THREE

Capital Gains Tax

IN BRITAIN capital gains accruing after April 6th, 1965, become taxable when they are turned into cash. The principle followed is that gains on sales made within one year of the purchase date are regarded as speculative and taxed as unearned income. Gains taking longer than a year to mature are considered more respectable, and the most you can pay on them is 30%. Both taxes affect other assets as well as shares, including land. In fact, almost anything worth over £1,000 is covered, except your car, your boat and your pet cheetah, which are regarded as wasting assets. In this chapter we shall confine ourselves to Stock Exchange transactions, but the rules for other assets are broadly the same, and it is worth remembering that your loss on that picture that turned out not to be by Rembrandt can be used to offset your gains on shares.

In practice, it is best to think of a two-tier capital gains tax system, the short-term tax and the long-term tax. The short-term tax is a separate compartment for all transactions where the sale takes place within twelve months of the purchase, or where the sale precedes the purchase, regardless of the time between them. If you acquire a share on March 15th, 1969, taking the date on your contract note, or the first day of dealings if you apply for a new issue, and sell it before March 15th, 1970, any profit or loss counts as short term. If you sell on or after March 15th, 1970, it is long term.

In calculating the gain or loss on a particular purchase and sale expenses directly attributable to that holding may be brought into account. In practice this means buying and selling expenses, such as brokerage and stamp duty, and the gain or loss is usually just the difference between the net cost and the net proceeds shown on the two contract notes. At the end of each tax year the losses and gains are totted up for the short-term compartment and again for the long-term compartment, and tax paid in either case if there is a net gain after deducting losses. In no circumstances can a loss in one compartment be offset against a gain in the other. If in either case there is a net loss for the year this can be carried forward and brought into account in the calculations for future years, until it is absorbed.

Your net taxable short-term gains for the year are treated as unearned income and subject to the full rigours of income tax and surtax. On long-term gains you either pay 30% or you can opt for an alternative under which half your net taxable gain up to £5,000 in any one year (plus the whole of any further amount) is treated as unearned income subject to income tax and surtax. For standard-rate taxpayers this alternative can reduce the rate from 6s. in the £ to 4s. 1½d., and for people paying surtax at 2s. in the £ to 5s. 1½d., although, by pushing up your rate of tax, it can be self-defeating if your gains are large. Finally, your tax bill on long-term gains must leave you with £50 over after paying tax. A net gain of up to £50 is therefore completely exempt.

Both taxes apply only to United Kingdom residents. Foreign citizens and British subjects resident overseas escape liability. There are also a number of British institutions, notably pension funds and charities, which are exempt. Private trusts are liable to both taxes, but no transactions of a trust affect the trustees in their personal capacity. On the securities side, gilt-edged are covered by the short-term tax but no longer by the long-term. Increases in value in National Savings Certificates, British Savings Bonds, Defence Bonds and National Development Bonds are free of tax, together with the new Government contractual savings scheme and the prizes on Premium Bonds. Life assurance policies and annuities are also exempt, although life companies pay tax on their own gains at 30%. Remember, too, that gains on most single-premium policies taken out since March 19th, 1968, are liable to surtax.

British registered companies are taxed under the long-term rules for all gains, whether realized within one year or not. This means they can in effect offset short-term gains with

long-term losses, and vice versa. But they pay dearly for this
privilege, because they are charged corporation tax on their
net gains, currently 45%, instead of 30%. Furthermore, if
any of the remaining 55% is distributed to shareholders it is
taxed again as unearned income, while if it is left in the company to increase the value of its shares a second bite of capital
gains tax will eventually be extracted from its shareholders.

Investment trusts, however, are treated much more favour-
ably. They pay only 30% on their net gains, although they
retain the advantage of not being taxed separately on short-
term gains. There is also a provision to prevent their shareholders from being double taxed. Capital gains tax paid by the
trust is credited to shareholders in proportion to their holdings
each year, and can be used to offset any liability when they
eventually sell their shares. Unit trusts are treated in the same
way.

Multiple Transactions

On occasion you may indulge in a series of transactions in
the same share, and there is a strict set of rules for deciding
which sales shall be matched with which purchases. The first
rule is that the short-term tax takes priority over the long-term.
So if you bought 100 shares eighteen months ago and 100
shares six months ago and you now sell half your holding you
are deemed to be selling the 100 shares that you bought most
recently. The operation consisting of your second purchase
and your sale must be put in the short-term compartment.

The first step therefore is to isolate all short-term transactions in this way. Once this has been done the rule within
the short-term compartment is that you are always deemed to
be selling the shares which you have held longest. The only
exception is shares bought and sold for the same Settlement
Day, which in practice means in the same Stock Exchange
Account. These are always matched with each other in priority
to the other rules.

As an example, take the following chain of transactions,
assuming for convenience that the prices are net of dealing
expenses.

May 1st, 1968	Buy 100 shares at 10s.
September 1st, 1968	Buy 100 shares at 20s.
October 1st, 1968	Buy 100 shares at 21s.
October 6th, 1968	Sell 100 shares at 22s.
November 1st, 1968	Buy 100 shares at 25s.
August 1st, 1969	Sell 100 shares at 25s.
December 1st, 1969	Sell 100 shares at 17s. 6d.

In the tax year to April 5th, 1969, this investor is concerned only with the sale of 100 shares on 6th October at 22s. Let us say that this sale was made in the same Stock Exchange Account as the purchase on October 1st. These two transactions are therefore matched, and there is a net gain of 1s. a share or £5 in the short-term compartment. If, however, they had been for different Stock Exchange Accounts the sale would be matched with the purchase on May 1st to produce a short-term gain of 12s. a share or £60.

Try now to work out which purchase should be matched with the sale on August 1st, 1969. It is not May 1st, 1968, because this was more than a year ago and has now moved into the long-term compartment. It would be nice to match it with the purchase on November 1st, as there would then be no taxable gain or loss. However, the rules say that it must be matched with the longest outstanding purchase still within the short-term compartment, and this is the one on September 1st, 1968. The sale therefore produces a taxable short-term gain of 5s. per share, or £25.

Finally, there is the sale on December 1st, 1969. This is more than a year after any purchase, and therefore in the long-term compartment. You first strike out the two purchases that have already been matched. This means the one on October 1st, 1968, matched with the October 6th sale, and the one on September 1st, 1968, deemed to have been sold in August 1969. You are left with the shares bought in May 1968 and in November 1968. Now that we are in the long-term compartment we take an average of all relevant purchases, so these two count as one block of 200 shares bought at an average price of 17s. 6d. There is therefore no gain or loss on this sale, and the residual holding of 100 shares is carried forward at a cost for capital gains tax purposes of 17s. 6d. per share.

This example also brings out the simple rule covering partial sales. Subject to the other matching rules, the cost of the shares being sold is deemed to be the proportion of the total cost which the number of shares you are selling bears to your total holding. In other words, you take average cost. There is, however, a complication if some of the shares were bought before April 6th, 1965.

Shares bought before that date are treated in a separate category in the identification rules, and sales in the long-term compartment are deemed to absorb any shares bought before April 6th, 1965, before they touch any of those bought after. Furthermore, for shares bought before that date you do not take an average. Instead you take the shares you have held longest first and work through them until you come to April 6th, 1965. When you have absorbed all shares bought before April 6th, 1965, you switch to an average basis for the balance.

There are some additional identification rules of particular importance if you are trying to establish a loss. A sale and re-purchase for the same Settlement Day, and therefore in the same Stock Exchange Account, is always treated as a bear operation in the short-term compartment. The sale will not count as a sale of your long-term holding if you have one. If you sell to establish a loss in the short-term compartment you must be careful not to buy back within one month. Again the sale and repurchase would be matched as a bear operation, and your original cost and purchase date would still hold for the shares you repurchased. However, if your sale produced a profit your repurchase, unless in the same Stock Exchange Account, is treated as a fresh acquisition.

April 6th, 1965

Since the long-term tax was introduced on April 6th, 1965, and was not intended to be retrospective, there is a provision to ensure that no tax is paid on appreciation up to that date. Conversely, any fall in value to that date is not allowable as a loss. The rule is simply that in assessing a gain you are allowed to choose between taking your actual cost and the value of your holding on April 6th, 1965, whichever is the higher. However, if you have a loss you must take the lower of your cost or April 6th, 1965, value. This normally produces an area between your cost price and April 6th, 1965, price in which there is no profit or loss, usually called the neutral zone. You should think twice before selling a share standing near the lower end of this zone, because any appreciation to the upper limit would not be subject to tax.

There is an alternative system which you can elect to adopt for sales after March 19th, 1968, under which you simply take April 6th, 1965, value regardless of cost. This method can be chosen for all relevant sales of equities or of fixed interest or of both, but you cannot pick and choose on a share-by-share basis. The election must be made within two years of the end of the tax year in which you make your first sale of the class concerned – equity or fixed interest as the case may be – after March 19th, 1968, and it is irrevocable.

You only gain by adopting this alternative when both your cost and sale proceeds are less than April 6th, 1965, value. If they are both higher you lose, and otherwise it makes no difference. Thus you have to balance the gainers or likely gainers against the losers in each of the equity and fixed-interest categories. This method is useful for people who have not kept complete records of their purchases over the years. Other investors will generally find it may pay to make the election for fixed interest, but probably not for equities.

Capital Changes

Scrip issues, rights issues, takeovers and so on have their own set of rules. With issues to shareholders the basic distinction is between scrip and rights which are issued *pro rata* to existing holdings – as it might be a one-for-one scrip or a two-for-three rights issues – and new issues for which shareholders are simply given exclusive or preferential application forms, without a specific allocation of stock. In the latter case any purchase of the new stock counts as a fresh acquisition, independent of your existing holding. With scrip and rights issues, on the other hand, your acquisition date for tax purposes is the date you bought the parent holding. If this was more than a year ago you can sell the new stock as soon as you like, and any gain or loss will count as long-term.

As to how the gain or loss is calculated, the rules are broadly the same under both the short- and the long-term taxes. The simplest case is a scrip issue in the same class of share. Here you just average the original cost of the parent holding over the number of shares you now hold. For example, if you bought 400 shares at 25s. (cost £500), and you receive an additional 100 shares as a one-for-four scrip, the cost of the 500 shares you now hold is still £500, giving a revised cost per share of 20s. for both the new and the old shares.

The calculation is much the same if you have to pay for the new shares; that is, if it is a rights issue. Your total cost, including the cost of the new shares, is divided evenly over the number of shares held after the issue. If you had had to pay £100 for your 100 new shares in our example above your total cost becomes £600, and your cost per share, old or new, 24s.

If under the long-term tax payment for the new shares is spread over two or more instalments, and you sell after paying the first but before the last one is due, the apportionment of cost is still worked out as if all the calls had been paid. Suppose in our example the £100 for the new shares is in two instalments of £50 each, and you sell the new shares when only the first call has been paid, you work out your cost per share in exactly the same way as if the whole £100 had been paid, and then subtract the unpaid call from the figure you arrive at for the new shares. In this case the unpaid call is 10s. per share, so the cost for tax purposes of the partly paid new shares you sell is 24s. minus 10s., or 14s. per share.

Under the short-term tax this rule about bringing unpaid calls into the calculation applies even if you sell your rights nil paid. With the long-term tax, however, a different method is used if you sell in nil paid form before any call has become due. In that case you apportion your original cost in the ratio of what you get for the rights and the market value of the parent holding on the day you sell. Let us say that in the example we have been following you sell your rights nil paid for £40, and the 400 parent shares are valued at 28s. each, or £560. Your tax cost for the rights is $\frac{40}{560 + 40} \times$ £400, or £27, producing a gain of £13 (rounding off to the nearest £). The tax cost of the parent holding becomes £373 (£400 − £27).

This method of calculation would also apply, both for the long-term and the short-term taxes, if you had received the £40 as a capital distribution not subject to income tax and surtax, and therefore liable to capital gains tax. However, most capital distributions are taxed as income these days, unless they are a return of capital that shareholders have subscribed.

If your sale of nil paid rights had raised not more than 5% of the market value of your holding, including rights, you could have taken advantage of a special concession. The cost of the parent holding could simply have been written down by the net proceeds of the sale of rights, thus postponing payment of tax until the parent holding itself was sold. If you got £15 for the rights, for example, the tax cost of your parent holding becomes £385, not £400. This concession is available only under the rules for the long-term tax.

The rules for sales of nil paid rights, including the special concession we have just described, apply equally to issues of shares of a different class to the parent holding. So does the rule that once you have paid a call you must bring all unpaid calls into the calculation of apportioned cost. This calculation, however, is inevitably a little more complicated when you cannot treat the total combined holding as one. With scrip issues, too, you can no longer just take average cost per share held after the issue.

The method used is an extension of the one for sales of nil paid rights (long-term). Total cost is divided between the old and new shares (or stock), but this time in the ratio of their market values on the day they are first dealt in separately, treating the new shares as fully paid. To go back to our example, let us say that, having bought 400 shares for £500, you are faced with a rights issue of £100 of convertible loan stock at par. On the first day of dealings in the new stock it opens at

10 points premium, nil paid, and the shares are 29s. 6d. ex rights. Your total cost is now £400 plus the £100 you are going to pay for the new stock, the market value of the parent holding is £590 and of the convertible £110 (adding on the £100 call). The tax cost of the convertible, once you have paid the call, is $\dfrac{110}{590 + 110} \times £500$, or £79. The tax cost of the parent holding is therefore £421.

This example incidentally shows how careful you must be about selling shares or stock acquired through a rights or scrip issue made after your original holding has appreciated substantially in value. In effect, some of the appreciation attaches itself to the new stock. If, for instance, you eventually get tired of the convertible and sell it, fully paid, at 105 net of commission, you might think you had made a profit of £5. Your taxable gain, however, would be £26, and your liability at 30% therefore £7 16s. 0d., more than absorbing your £5 profit.

Of course, the position does even out when you eventually sell the parent holding, and much will depend on your personal tax situation – whether you have losses to set against the gain, and whether the rate of tax you pay on capital gains is likely to be higher or lower in the future. Assuming it would pay you to minimize your immediate liability and that we are talking of the long-term tax, you should have sold this convertible in nil paid form before paying the call. Even if you sold it for £10, twice the 'profit', your tax bill would only be 18s. The calculation is, of course, $\dfrac{10}{590 + 10} \times £400$, to give a tax cost of £7 and a taxable gain of £3. Although the position evens out eventually, because the apportioned tax cost of the parent holding always balances that of any shares sold, it pays in the short run to sell in nil paid form when you have a (long-term) gain, but to pay a call first when you have a loss.

The calculation for scrip issues in a different class of share is a simplified version of the one for rights issues. Original cost is apportioned in the ratio of market values on the first day your shares are dealt in ex scrip. In practice, for both scrip and rights issues of this kind it is easier to ask your broker what the officially accepted ratio for apportionment is rather than do the sums yourself.

Before leaving scrip and rights issues, there is one tricky rule that comes into play when the issue is in the same class and you have built up the parent holding by two or more separate purchases, with the last purchase still within the short-term compartment. As long as the new shares are being dealt in separately in allotment-letter form they must be divided up and attributed *pro rata* to their respective parent holding purchases. If you sell them some will therefore be short- and some long-term. As soon as the new shares become indistinguishable from the old, however, the normal matching rules apply, and any sales will first be matched against the shares you have held for less than a year, including the attributable scrip or rights.

As an example, suppose you buy 400 shares in August 1968 and another 100 shares in August 1969. In December 1969 you receive 100 shares through a one-for-five scrip issue, and in January 1970 you sell those 100 shares. If you sell them when the shares are still in allotment-letter form 80 of them will belong to the first purchase and come under the long-term tax, and only 20 will be taxed as short-term. If, on the other hand, they are no longer being quoted separately the sale will be matched with 100 out of the 120 shares which are caught in the short-term tax net. (Remember that you have 100 shares bought in August 1969 plus 20 scrip shares attributable to them.) The advantage or disadvantage of either alternative will naturally depend on your buying and selling prices, but it could be substantial.

With takeovers and mergers, the tax position depends on the terms of the deal. If you are just offered securities, of whatever kind, in exchange for those you already hold you are not liable for gains tax, and the starting date remains unchanged. The new shares simply inherit the gains liability of those they replace. If the offer is in cash it counts as a sale, and if part cash and part shares you must apportion your cost between the two. If you accept a bid that is not aimed at control of your company you are considered to have sold whether you receive cash or shares, but in practice such bids are rare. Redemption of stock counts as a disposal, and therefore attracts tax, the exception being if you convert a convertible stock into shares. Then there is no immediate liability, and the starting date and value for the new shares remain the same as they were with your original holding. Liquidation also counts as a disposal, and if any new securities are offered as part of the scheme of arrangement they are treated as being acquired at that time at market value. Finally, if a security has in practice declined to nothing or some negligible value you can claim loss relief.

Market Value

Some of the calculations we have looked at in this chapter have involved market value; for instance, under the apportionment rules for scrip and rights issues. Market value also crops up with gifts (except those worth less than £100 in total in a single year, which are exempt), at death, on the valuation of trusts and so on.

This raises the question of how market values are assessed. Actually there are two alternatives. One is to take the lower of the two prices in the official quotation and add one-quarter of the spread. If ICI were quoted at 56s. to 57s. the value would be 56s. (the bottom of the quote) + 3d. (one-quarter of the shilling spread between 56s. and 57s.) to make 56s. 3d. The other method is to take the point halfway between the highest and the lowest Stock Exchange marks. If ICI's marks had ranged from 55s. 9d. to 57s. 3d. halfway between would be 56s. 6d. As the lower figure produced by these two methods applies, the answer is 56s. 3d. Incidentally, April 6th, 1965, prices are calculated differently. They are the middle of the quotation or halfway between the highest and the lowest marks, whichever is the *higher*.

Husbands and Wives

The situation for husbands and wives is a little more complicated than it need be. For the purpose of both short- and long-term tax they have to keep separate accounts. This is to their advantage, because it means that if one happens to sell a share which the other has bought within the previous year there is no short-term liability on that account. When it comes to assessment husbands' and wives' gains are added together. Whether or not one's losses can be offset against the other's gains is a matter of choice. With the short-term tax this choice has to be made consciously, but for some reason with the long-term tax it is the other way round. Here losses will be offset against gains automatically unless one partner or the other applies for them not to be, within three months of the beginning of the next financial year. One interesting concession is that shares transferred from one partner to another, whether by way of gift or for cash, do not count as a disposal and acquisition. The new holder inherits the cost and acquisition date of the old. However, if you think you can exploit this to gain a tax advantage you will find there are rules to circumvent you.

Settlements

For settlements the long-term gains tax has some pretty severe repercussions. Not only are they liable to short- and long-terms gains tax on realizations in the ordinary way. In certain circumstances they are also subject to tax by reference to their market value. Broadly speaking, this happens once every fifteen years, though the rules about timing vary from one sort of trust to another. For example, where there are life interests in a trust all its assets are valued the first time a life interest ends after April 6th, 1965, and tax is payable on its accrued gains. With discretionary trusts, where there is no life interest, this shake-out occurs as soon after April 6th, 1965, as they reach the fifteenth anniversary of their creation. With trusts which have been in existence for more than fifteen years the appropriate multiple of fifteen is taken instead.

Death

On death, all a person's assets are deemed to be disposed of at market value, but there are some valuable concessions to mitigate the capital gains tax liability this could give rise to. To start with, the first £5,000 of long-term gains is exempt, and if some tax is still payable it is deducted from the estate before estate duty is calculated.

If executors sell shares while administering the estate any gain or loss from the date of death is subject to the long-term tax regardless of the time interval, but any losses are deductible from the gain on death, and any gains count towards the £5,000 exemption (subject to a three-year time limit). Executors should therefore judge any sales they make with a view to absorbing the £5,000 exemption, and they should be careful not to establish losses which would lead to some of it being wasted.

There is another concession if the notional disposal on the date of death, together with sales in the same tax year up to the date of the death, produces a net loss. The loss can be credited retrospectively against gains for up to the last three years, and tax reclaimed accordingly.

The notional disposal at death does not bring in the short-term tax. Even if a share was bought only a month before, any gain or loss is treated as long term. However, there is an over-riding rule in favour of the short-term tax under which you ignore this notional disposal if a share is actually sold, by the executors or a beneficiary of the estate, within a year of its purchase date. The full gain or loss would then be short term. Apart from this rule, when shares are transferred to beneficiaries the acquisition date continues to be the date of death, and any sales within a year of that date are still treated as long term.

Options

Finally, options. The rule is that the date of acquisition is the day on which the option is exercised, not the date on which it was originally taken out. It follows from this that the cost of the option is not taken into account for gains-tax purposes unless it is exercised. This means that if you exercise a profitable option and then sell the shares at a profit within the twelve-months' period your tax liability will be reduced by the cost of the option. It also means that if you have an option which has gone sour you must exercise it and sell the shares if you want to establish the option cost as an offset-able loss.

Policy

What are the investment implications of capital gains tax? The most obvious point to stress is that very careful records have to be kept. You should keep them up to date on a running basis so you will always know at once whether you can afford to take a profit or whether you need to cut a loss. Shares showing a loss should be looked at carefully about eleven months after purchase, to see if the loss should be established as short term. You should have another look towards the end of each tax year, to see what can be done to minimize your long-term tax liability. If you leave things for your accountant to work out it will probably be too late to take action by the time he comes up with the answer.

To avoid mistakes, keep things simple. It is best, for instance, to avoid entering into a chain of transactions in the same share. You should be wary, too, of averaging – adding to a holding that has fallen to bring down the average purchase price. If recovery comes quickly you will be locked into your earlier purchase as well as the new one if you want to avoid the short-term tax. If you want to average it is a good idea where possible to pick a different but broadly similar share to the one you hold, or perhaps to average in your wife's name. Other practical implications arise from the detailed provisions of the law which we have already discussed, such as the timing of the sale of rights, and taking account of the neutral zone for shares bought before April 6th, 1965.

Your attitude to the short- and long-term taxes should naturally be different. The short-term tax can be avoided and in most cases the rate differential (usually at least double), compared with the long-term tax, makes it important to do so. Still, you may sometimes want to sell a share at a profit within a year, whether because you think the profit will run off or for some other reason. You must then think about keeping your liability as low as possible, by being particularly ruthless about losses. As they can be carried forward, no harm will be done if you come to the end of the year with a back-log on your hands for future use. You could almost say that one of the best arguments for the tax is that it encourages people to cut losses and run profits.

With the long-term tax there is no hope of getting round it altogether, except when you die. For that reason you ought not to let it affect your policy too greatly. Here again, of course, there is scope for matching profits and losses, with the same advantages about losses being available for carrying forward. But once you have built up a big potential tax bill you are in a sense borrowing money from the Government. It will sometimes be worth paying off the debt in the interests of flexibility. In particular, ignore the arguments of some pundits that a share you switch into must make up 143% of the gains tax on the share you sell before you are breaking even – they are quite unsound. On the whole, it is best to give due weight to ordinary investment considerations in your buying and selling decisions, but with a little more emphasis on cutting losses, particularly in a tax year in which you have realized profits to offset.

In market terms we now see tax-loss selling depressing share prices towards the end of each tax year where particular shares have been disappointing. The answer is to make your scrutiny a little earlier than other investors, say in December or January. However, it is worth repeating that tax considerations should not dictate your investment policy. You must make the profits before worrying about paying tax on them. After that it is a matter of accurate accounting and common sense.

CHAPTER TWENTY-FOUR

Company Tax

ALL COMPANIES have to pay corporation tax on their profits, including capital gains. The rate of corporation tax is fixed, usually by the Chancellor of the Exchequer in his Budget speech, by reference to a fiscal year. As a rule, changes in rates are known retrospectively. For example, the increase in corporation tax to 45% introduced in the 1969 Budget, referred to the fiscal year April 1st, 1968, to March 31st, 1969.

Corporation tax is charged in respect of a company's own financial year. If this is different from the fiscal year the tax payable is adjusted accordingly. For example, a company whose financial year ended on December 31st, 1968, paid corporation tax on the first three months' trading at $42\frac{1}{2}$% (the rate ruling for the fiscal year to March 31st, 1968) and 45% on the remaining nine months' trading.

Corporation tax effectively ends the former British system whereby a company and its shareholders were one for tax purposes. However, one relic from that system survives, for the convenience of the Inland Revenue. Companies paying interest on dividends to their own stockholders deduct income tax at the standard rate and remit it, almost immediately, to the Inland Revenue.

Tax and Franked Income

Companies receiving dividends from other British companies do not have to pay corporation tax on them. The technical term for these dividends is franked investment income, which, in other words, is income which has already borne corporation tax. Investment income, franked or unfranked, usually comes to companies after income tax has been deducted at source. They can then claim this tax as a credit against the income tax which they must withhold on their own dividends, and against their own corporation tax liability.

The Tax Effects of Depreciation

Apart from normal business expenses, companies can charge depreciation of certain fixed assets against profits before arriving at a net profit figure on which tax is assessed.

Depreciation is an annual allowance for consumption of capital as plant and equipment wear out. It is, in fact, officially known as writing-down allowances. It continues year by year until the equipment concerned has been written off altogether. With some items these allowances are applied on a straight-line basis; that is, the expenditure is written off at so much per cent a year of the original cost. More usually, though, a higher percentage is written off from a declining total. If, for example, 20% is written off in the first year the basis for calculating the following year's depreciation is only 80% of the original cost (that is 100% minus 20%), so the second year's depreciation is 20% of 80%, or 16% of the original cost.

Traditionally, most Western countries encourage capital investment by generous depreciation provisions. In Britain the main emphasis of investment incentives is currently on investment grants. These are cash grants, and have nothing to do with the tax system. They are selective, in that only certain industries are eligible for them, and they only apply to certain types of equipment. In these cases the grants are treated as capital payments, and deducted from the cost of the relevant assets in calculating depreciation. For plant and machinery not qualifying for investment grants initial allowances of 30% are permitted. Effectively, initial allowances are a device for accelerating depreciation. They have to be balanced by lower depreciation in subsequent years, and so they only postpone tax, rather than save it. There are also initial allowances for new buildings and structures, currently at the rate of 15%.

Tax and Loan Interest

Loan interest, which can be deducted from profits before calculating tax, covers the interest payable on debentures and loan stocks as well as interest on bank borrowings. The investment implications of this are that it is much cheaper for companies to finance themselves with loan capital than with share capital. Suppose a company wanted to raise fresh capital, and could do so with a payment of $8\frac{1}{4}\%$ to the lender. If the $8\frac{1}{4}\%$ were payable as loan interest it could be charged directly against profits. If it were payable as a preference dividend the company would have to earn 15% on its capital to finance that dividend. This is because corporation tax at 45% would absorb $6\frac{3}{4}$ points out of the 15, leaving $8\frac{1}{4}$ points for distribution.

The same argument can be extended to convertible loan capital, the interest on which is also tax deductible. If a company contemplating an ordinary share issue could raise money on a 3·3% yield basis it would be cheaper for it to issue a convertible loan with a 5% coupon, because the gross cost of the ordinary issue, directly comparable with a 5% coupon, would be 6%.

Close Companies

A company's tax status can be affected by its ownership. If it is under the control of its directors, or five or fewer people (counting family members and associates as one for this purpose), it is a so-called close company. It is, of course, possible for quoted companies to be close companies. But if there is a substantial public interest – that is, if 35% of the equity voting control is in the hands of the public – the company is exempt. This provision needs looking at carefully when there are vote-less 'A' shares in issue. It does not matter how big a stake the public has in the 'A' shares; it is the 35% in the vote-carrying equity that counts.

There are a number of disadvantages about close-company status, and many owners of quoted firms have been selling off enough of their holdings to make sure the classification does not apply to them. This is all right by the investing public, because it makes for a better market in shares which had previously been tightly held. Where directors prefer to hang on they are, on paper, obliged to distribute 60% of their net operating profits after corporation tax by way of dividends, plus the whole of any investment income. In practice, they do not have to if they can show that it is necessary, or advisable, to retain the money for the development of the business. It is believed that the Inland Revenue is interpreting this rule leniently. In any case, if a company is forced to pay up this is scarcely likely to bring tears to the eyes of investors at large. On the contrary, at a time of general dividend restraint it can be a positive advantage. The close-company provisions over-ride restraint.

Overseas Tax and British Companies

A company's liability to corporation tax can be affected by its trading overseas. Many British companies – in fact, about half of those quoted on the Stock Exchange – have operations abroad as well as at home. In almost all cases the profits they make from these overseas activities are subject to the taxes in force in the country where they are earned. By the time these profits are received in Britain they have already borne tax. If they were taxed again here they would be taxed twice.

For this reason companies are granted some relief on their British tax. Roughly speaking, it is calculated by assessing the amount of tax which the company would have had to pay at British rates, and then allowing relief equal to the tax it has actually paid abroad. In theory, the relief depends on the existence of a double-taxation-relief (DTR) agreement between Britain and the overseas country where the profits have been taxed. In practice, however, some DTR is allowed by the Inland Revenue, even when there is no agreement, provided the company owns at least 10% (or sometimes 25%) of the overseas firm's capital.

Overspill

These arrangements are broadly the same as those in operation before the switch to corporation tax in 1965. However, relief is now available only in respect of corporation tax, whereas previously it worked its way through to the income tax charged on dividends. The effect of this is that any overseas tax paid in excess of corporation tax is wasted. This change had such severe repercussions for some companies, notably the big oil groups, that special transitional arrangements, known as overspill relief, were made to ease the increased burden of tax.

The detailed terms of these arrangements are extremely complex, and in any case their effect varies markedly from company to company. Briefly, however, it works like this. The company chooses a base year, one of three just before the 1965 Budget. It works out what its overseas tax credit actually was, and what it would have been under corporation tax. For three years the difference between these two is the amount of the relief. After that it declines, year by year, to a smaller proportion of the original amount. In the fourth year it goes down to 80%, then down to 60%, 40% and 20% in the three following years. In the eighth year it vanishes altogether. If during the seven-year period the company raises its dividend above the base-year payment the rate of relief is reduced.

Variations in Tax Ratios

Overseas tax may be the explanation when a company's tax works out to be more or less than the corporation tax rate. This is either because its overseas tax rate is higher than at home or because losses cannot be transferred for tax purposes from one country to another. Suppose a company was in process of establishing itself overseas, and made losses on its operations for the first few years. These losses would be deducted from consolidated group profits, but the consequent tax credits would only be carried forward until profits in the country concerned were big enough to absorb them. Of course, once profits were being earned, and past tax losses were being offset against them, the tax ratio on consolidated group profits might then appear below average.

Variations from the standard corporation tax ratio can also occur because of accounting practices. A company's profit for tax purposes, as agreed with the Inland Revenue, need not necessarily be the same as the profit certified by the auditors in its report and accounts. There is nothing shocking about this. It represents a natural tug-of-war between the tax authorities, who want revenue, and company accountants, who are a conservative breed, brought up not to overstate profitability. In assessing a company's earnings per share it is sensible to calculate them at the standard rate of tax, as well as with the actual tax charge reported by the company.

Selective Employment Tax

In addition to corporation tax, companies also have to pay selective employment tax for each employee. The rates of SET have been substantially increased since its introduction, the current levels, since July 1969, being 48s. a week for men, 24s. for women and boys under 18, and 16s. for girls under 18. In some industries, notably manufacturing and agriculture, companies are entitled to a refund of their contributions. In some regions, designated as development areas, these same industries are entitled to a premium in respect of every employee for whom SET is paid. All SET contributions and premiums are treated as trading items, and form part of the calculation of a company's profit for tax purposes.

SET's main significance, from the investor's point of view, is its effect on the retailing and finance sectors. Stores, banks and to a lesser extent insurance companies are the big employers who have to pay the tax. It is of greatest interest in home-based companies with comparatively stable trading records, because its impact can be calculated closely. The big four banks, for example, appear to have SET bills (at the increased rates) equal to roughly 20–25% of their disclosed profits for 1968. For insurance companies a similar calculation is of doubtful worth, because much of their activities are overseas, and in any case fluctuations in underwriting experience are of much greater importance.

In retailing, the principal effect of SET has been to strengthen the competitive power of the mail-order houses, and the more efficient supermarkets and multiples. For Marks

& Spencer, Tesco and Grattan Warehouses, for example, SET represents about $\frac{1}{2}\%$ on sales and 5–10% on pre-tax profits. These figures rise sharply for labour-intensive groups like department stores, and clothing and footwear chains, where SET can be as much as a quarter or a third of profits. As so often in investment, nothing succeeds like success.

Appendix A

Terms Offered by Institutions Accepting Money on Fixed-interest Deposits

Post Office Savings Bank

Function. The Post Office Savings Bank was set up in 1861 for the safe keeping of savings and the encouragement of thrift. The money is used to buy government stock.

Security. Capital and interest are guaranteed by the Government.

Availability. The following may open accounts at any post office: anyone over 7; another person on behalf of someone under 7; two or more people jointly; trustees; and clubs. Any person or institution with £50 or more in a savings account may have an investment account.

Investment. Minimum 5s. for savings accounts, thereafter not less than 1s. For investment accounts, minimum £1, initially and thereafter. Maximums £5,000, excluding interest and transfers from a deceased estate. Any amount may be deposited in any year.

Withdrawals. Up to £10 a day on demand at any post office. For larger sums, apply for a notice of withdrawal at any post office. For urgent withdrawals, up to £25 by two-way telegram from any post office (cost 6s.) and up to £50 by posting a notice of withdrawal marked 'by telegraph' to Savings Bank Headquarters, which authorizes payment by telegraph (cost 3s.). For investment accounts, one month's notice of withdrawal. Payment is by cash at any post office, or by crossed warrant through a bank.

Interest. Halfpenny per pound per month ($2\frac{1}{2}\%$ per annum). For investment accounts $6\frac{1}{2}\%$ per annum, credited on December 31 each year. Money starts bearing interest from the first day of the month following deposit and stops at the beginning of the month in which it is withdrawn.

Tax. No income tax is payable on the first £15 of any individual's interest (that is, a year's interest on £600, six months' interest on £1,200 and so on). The concession is available to both husbands and wives, that is, a total of £30 between them. All interest should be declared in tax returns. The £15 exemption does not apply to surtax. Interest on investment accounts is taxable, but is credited without deduction of tax.

Other Features. Crossed warrants for sums over £1 are available for transmission of money by post. Regular payments (e.g. for insurance premiums, fuel bills) can be made direct, provided they occur not more than once a month (cost 1s. per payment, yearly in advance). There is a bank book which must be presented for the recording of deposits and withdrawals. It must be sent to Savings Bank Headquarters when crossed warrants are required; annually for the addition of interest; for checking when two pages are full; when two withdrawals of more than £3 have been made within seven days; for renewal when full, and when any withdrawal is required from an investment account.

The Post Office Register. The Post Office Savings Department will buy or sell government securities on behalf of the public, provided the securities in question are on the Post Office Register. In practice, this means most gilt-edged stocks. Up to £5,000 of stock can be bought on any one day, with no limit to the maximum that can be held. Transactions take place at the price ruling at the time, and the Post Office will not undertake to deal at specified prices or times, neither will it give advice. The advantage of the Post Office Register is that interest payments are made without deduction of income tax at source.

The following are the charges for buying or selling:

Nominal amount of stock	Charge
Up to £10	1s.
Over £10 up to £25	1s. 6d.
Over £25 up to £50	2s. 6d.
Over £50 up to £75	3s. 6d.
Over £75 up to £100	5s. 0d.

With a further charge of 1s. for every £50 of stock, or part of £50, above £100.

Trustee Savings Banks

Function. Trustee Savings Banks were set up in the early nineteenth century to encourage thrift. The money is used to buy government stock.

Security. Capital and interest are guaranteed by the Government.

Availability. Anyone can open one or more accounts; in his own name; jointly; on behalf of children of any age; in trust for others. Friendly societies and charitable bodies are eligible. Accounts may be opened in the ordinary department and, in addition, in the special investment department.

Investment. Ordinary department: minimum 1s., maximum £5,000. Special department (subject to a minimum of £50 in the ordinary department): minimum 1s., maximum £5,000.

Withdrawals. Up to £50 on demand and a few days' notice for larger sums. Facilities exist for withdrawing money at other branches when away from home.

Interest. Ordinary department: halfpenny per pound per month ($2\frac{1}{2}\%$ per annum), added to the principal on November 20th each year. Money starts bearing interest from the first day of the month following deposit and stops at the beginning of the month in which it is withdrawn. Special department: around 6%, computed and credited as in the ordinary department.

Tax. No income tax is payable on the first £15 of any individual's interest (that is, a year's interest on £600, six months' interest on £1,200 and so on). The concession is available to both husbands and wives, that is a total of £30 between them. All interest should be declared in tax returns. The £15 exemption does not apply to surtax. The £15 exemption is not available in the special department.

Other Features. Cheques can be issued when depositors wish to make payments. Regular payments (e.g. for rent and other periodic payments) can be made direct. Safe custody of deeds and documents. Stock departments are available for buying government stock and sometimes for advice on investments.

There is a bank book which must be presented for record purposes. A unit trust was formed in 1968.

Building Societies

Function. Building societies, which trace their origins back to the late eighteenth century, use the savings of lenders to help borrowers buy their own homes.

Security. Depositors' and shareholders' security depends on the conduct of each individual society. For minimum standards of investment worthiness see pages 186–8.

Availability. Any individual may open an account (including minors, and parents or guardians on behalf of infants). Loans are accepted from charities, pension funds and other gross funds, but we do not recommend them for tax reasons. Loans are accepted from companies at a lower rate of interest, because the society has to pay tax on corporate funds at the standard rate. For this reason not all societies take money from companies.

Types. 1. Shares (exact designations vary) unlimited in number, and can be cashed with the society.

2. Subscription shares. Offered to encourage regular savings, with interest usually $\frac{1}{4}$–$\frac{1}{2}$% more than on shares. Range of maximum monthly subscriptions: £5–£25.

3. Deposits. Extra security, with a first call on profits and assets. By law, can only be accepted to two-thirds of a society's mortgage assets. Interest usually $\frac{1}{4}$–$\frac{1}{2}$% less than on shares.

4. Term deposits. Only offered by a few societies. Usually higher rate of interest if the set period of time is observed.

5. Investment linked to life assurance available.

Investment. Minimum depends on designation of shares – usually £1, £10 or £25. Maximum £10,000 per society, husband and wife counting separately.

Withdrawals. Usually £50–£100 on demand, more within a matter of days. Societies *can* insist on their minimum period of notice (in the case of deposits at least a month). Check before investing.

Interest. Rates recommended by the Building Societies Association, subject to alteration with perhaps three months' notice. In recent years between 4 and 5%. Societies offering more should be carefully checked for security. Interest is usually payable twice a year, but accrues from time of deposit to time of withdrawal.

Tax. Tax is paid by societies on investors' behalf. No tax refunds can be claimed by investors paying less than the standard rate of tax. Interest is subject to surtax, being grossed up at the standard rate (*not* the composite rate) for the purpose of computing liability.

Other Features. Holdings recorded either by pass books or by certificates.

Hire Purchase Company Deposits

Function. Hire purchase companies, which trace their origins back to the mid-nineteenth century, finance the acquisition of durable goods and equipment by private individuals and companies.

Security. Depositors' security depends on the conduct of each individual firm. For minimum standards of investment worthiness see page 189.

Availability. Firms which accept public deposits at all will usually accept them from companies and other institutions as well as individuals.

Investment. Minimums vary from firm to firm. Among the major companies the following are the minimums at the time of writing:

£10,000 Lloyds & Scottish Finance	£250 Bowmaker
£5,000 Mercantile Credit	£100 Astley Industrial Trust Forward Trust
£500 North Central Finance	£1 United Dominions Trust Lombank (may take less)

These figures should be checked. Some firms refuse to accept deposits when trading conditions do not justify them.

Withdrawals. Depend on the terms of deposit, which are usually for a set period, like a month, three months, six months, a year or occasionally at seven days' notice.

Interest. The large companies pay a little over Bank rate for money at short notice, with small additions as the set periods get longer and the amount higher. Small firms pay more. We recommend investors not to put money on deposit with a hire purchase company offering more than Bank rate plus 1%, without first taking professional advice.

Tax. Interest on deposits for periods up to a year is paid gross. Interest on annual deposits is usually paid net.

National Savings Certificates

Function. National Savings Certificates were introduced in 1916 to help finance the prosecution of the First World War. Nowadays the money is used for government financing.

Security. Capital and interest are guaranteed by the Government.

Availability. Anyone can buy certificates for himself; for others; jointly; in trust for others. Friendly societies and charitable bodies are eligible, but companies and public bodies are not. Certificates are not negotiable and are not recognized as security for a loan.

Investment. Minimum one unit (£1) or less when certificates are being purchased in instalments through National Savings group schemes. Maximum 1,500 units (£1,500) of the current (twelfth) issue. Additional certificates of earlier issues may also be held. Inherited certificates in excess of the maximum need not be cashed.

Withdrawals. Upon written application by the registered holder, the purchase price and accrued interest will be repaid. Forms are obtainable at Post Offices. Repayment is normally in six working days' time, but is not guaranteed in under eighteen days' time.

Interest is not paid, but accrues during the life of the certificate. On the current issue interest is as follows:

At the end of the first year after purchase	6d. is added
During the second year	3d. is added every 4 months
During the third, fourth and fifth years	5d. is added every 4 months
To make	25s. in all.

The terms for extending this issue have not been fixed at the time of writing.

The year-by-year yield is as follows:

Years after purchase	Value at end of year	Yield % for year
1	20s. 6d.	£2 10s. 8d.
2	21s. 3d.	£3 13s. 2d.
3	22s. 6d.	£5 17s. 8d.
4	23s. 9d.	£5 11s. 2d.
5	25s.	£5 5s. 3d.

Tax. Accrued interest is free of income tax, surtax and capital gains tax. The higher your tax, therefore, the more you stand to benefit, compared with other forms of tax-bearing investments. Subnormal taxpayers should avoid Savings Certificates.

Other Features. Holders are issued with a holder's card and a registered number. Marriage or loss of certificates should be notified to the Post Office Savings Department.

British Savings Bonds

Function. British Savings Bonds were introduced by Roy Jenkins in the 1968 Budget as a successor to National Development Bonds and Defence Bonds. The money is used for government financing.

Security. Capital and interest are guaranteed by the Government.

Availability. Any individual, including minors, may buy bonds, either in his own name, jointly or as a trustee. Bonds are available to limited companies, charitable, friendly and provident societies, clubs and corporate bodies generally. Bonds are not transferable.

Investment. Minimum £5, and in units of £5. Maximum £10,000, solely or jointly, apart from bonds inherited from a deceased holder or acquired by the conversion of Defence Bonds or National Development Bonds.

Withdrawals. Holdings may be cashed at par, plus unpaid interest, on one month's notice in writing. Any bond cashed within six months of purchase earns no interest. If any interest has already been paid the amount will be deducted from the repayment. After five years bonds are repaid at £102%.

Interest is paid at the rate of 7% a year, on March 15th and September 15th.

Tax. Tax is not deducted at source, but interest is subject to income tax and surtax, and must be declared on tax returns. There is no capital gains tax on repayment premiums.

Other Features. Holdings are recorded in bond books.

Premium Bonds

Function. Premium bonds were introduced by Harold Macmillan in the 1956 Budget as an extra arm of the National Savings Movement. The money is used for government financing.

Security. Capital is guaranteed by the Government.

Availability. Anyone over 16 may buy bonds, and parents or guardians may buy on behalf of persons under that age. Bonds may not be held jointly, nor in the name of clubs, societies or companies. Bonds are not transferable.

Investment. Minimum 1 unit (£1), maximum 1,250 units (£1,250).

Withdrawals. All or part of the holding may be cashed on six days' notice (more may be necessary in the case of newly bought bonds).

Interest. Bonds do not bear interest to individual owners. An amount equal to one month's interest at the rate of $4\frac{5}{8}$% a year on eligible bonds is paid into a prize fund for a weekly draw. Bonds are eligible for the draw after they have been held for three clear months; in other words, bonds bought in April are eligible for the draw at the beginning of August. They remain eligible, even if they have won a prize, till repaid or till twelve months after the death of the holder. For scale of prizes and odds see the discussion on pages 197–9. This scale, and the rate of interest, are liable to alteration at three months' notice.

Tax. Prizes are free of income tax, surtax and capital gains tax.

Other Features. Winners are notified by post, and asked to complete a claim form. There is no time limit for claiming. Winning numbers are published in the *London Gazette* (but names are not disclosed). Marriage, change of address and loss of bonds should be notified to the Premium Savings Bond Office.

Appendix B

Stockbrokers' Commission Rates

Security	Rate
1. Gilt-edged stocks Dominion and colonial stocks Corporation stocks	$\frac{3}{8}$% up to £10,000 of stock $\frac{1}{4}$% on balance above £10,000 of stock
2. Debentures and loan stocks	$\frac{3}{4}$% of the money
3. Preference shares and ordinary shares	$1\frac{1}{4}$% of the money

4. Small bargains:

Up to £10	At discretion
£10 to £100	Not less than £1
£100 to £160	Not less than £2

5. Large bargains:

For gilts, Dominion and colonial stocks and Corporation stocks:

(a) *£2,500 rule.* Full commission is charged up to £2,500 of money and half commission on the excess. Continuation of this concession is granted over a period of three months.

(b) *£50,000 rule.* On a bargain which exceeds £50,000 of stock $\frac{1}{8}$% is charged on the entire amount.

For other securities:

(a) *£5,000 rule.* Full commission is charged up to £5,000 of money and half commission on the excess. Continuation of this concession is granted over a period of three months.

(b) *£25,000 rule.* On a single order which exceeds £25,000 of money half commission may be charged on the entire amount.

6. *Closing.* For bargains in the same security opened and closed within the same account, no commission is charged on the second transaction.

7. There is a special scale for dollar stocks.

INDEX

Harry Hyams, Charles Clore, Jack Cotton, Maxwell Joseph, Harold Samuel...

They built success on bricks and brains...

The boardroom battles of the property kings...

THE PROPERTY BOOM 7/6

Oliver Marriott

The astonishing story of the men and the companies who emerged £700 million richer from the post-war world of property development.

'A stupefying display of other men's riches ... it has great sweep and pace'.
The Times

'Detailed information concerning the main personalities, their thoughts, methods and differences make it an interesting and at times exciting commentary'—
The Financial Times

Illustrated   Pan Piper

One of the PAN MANAGEMENT AND MARKETING SERIES.